PENGUIN CLASSICS

THE LADDER OF PERFECTION

Although Walter Hilton is considered one of the greatest English mystics of the fourteenth century very little is known about his life. Born in 1340, it is thought that he became a hermit before joining the Augustinians at the Priory of St Peter in Thurgarton, Nottinghamshire. It was here that he composed his great work *The Ladder of Perfection*, which was first printed in 1494 and became a popular devotional classic. There are also several other works attributed to him. Walter Hilton died in 1396.

Leo Sherley-Price served in the Royal Navy for twenty-seven years, his last appointment being with the Royal Naval College, Greenwich. Subsequently he has been Rural Dean and parish priest in Devon. He has translated *Bede's History of the English Church and People*, Thomas à Kempis' *Imitation of Christ*, *The Little Flowers of Saint Francis* and a number of other historical and theological books.

Clifton Wolters was born in London and trained for the priesthood at Durham University and the London College of Divinity. He was Vicar of Wimbledon Park, Rector of Sanderstead and Canon of Newcastle. In 1962 he was appointed Vicar of Newcastle and Provost of the Cathedral. Upon retirement he became Provost Emeritus and Chaplain to the Society of St Margaret. Now fully retired, he lives in Eastbourne. He has translated *The Cloud of Unknowing*, Richard Rolle's *Fire of Love* and Julian of Norwich's *Revelations of Divine Love* for Penguin Classics.

WALTER HILTON

THE LADDER OF
PERFECTION

TRANSLATED BY
LEO SHERLEY–PRICE
WITH AN INTRODUCTION BY
CLIFTON WOLTERS

PENGUIN BOOKS

PENGUIN BOOKS

Published by the Penguin Group
27 Wrights Lane, London w8 5tz, England
Viking Penguin Inc., 40 West 23rd Street, New York, New York 10010, USA
Penguin Books Australia Ltd, Ringwood, Victoria, Australia
Penguin Books Canada Ltd, 2801 John Street, Markham, Ontario, Canada l3r 1b4
Penguin Books (NZ) Ltd, 182–190 Wairau Road, Auckland 10, New Zealand

Penguin Books Ltd, Registered Offices: Harmondsworth, Middlesex, England

This translation first published by Penguin Books 1957
Reissued with an Introduction 1988

Translation copyright © Leo Sherley-Price, 1957
Introduction copyright © Clifton Wolters, 1988
All rights reserved

Printed and bound in Great Britain by
Cox & Wyman Ltd, Reading
Set in Monotype Bembo

Lord Jesus Christ, I pray that the fiery and honey-sweet power of Thy love may detach my soul from everything under heaven, so that I may die from love of Thy love, who out of love for Thy people didst die upon the tree of the Cross. Amen.

S. FRANCIS OF ASSISI

CONTENTS

INTRODUCTION   xvii

Book One

1 How the inward and outward lives of a Christian should correspond   1

2 The active life and its duties   2

3 The contemplative life and its duties   3

4 The first degree of contemplation   3

5 The second degree of contemplation   5

6 The lower stages of the second degree   6

7 The higher stage in the second degree   6

8 The third degree of contemplation   7

9 The difference between the third and second degrees   8

10 How things seen and felt in the bodily senses may be good or evil   10

11 How to know whether sensible experiences are good or evil   11

12 What unites Jesus to the soul, and what separates Him from it   13

13 The occupation of a contemplative   14

14 How virtue begins in the reason and will, and is perfected in love   14

15 On three means to attain contemplation   15

16 How humility fosters discernment   16

17 Who may reprove the faults of others, and who may not   18

18 Why humble people should respect others, and regard themselves as inferior to all   20

CONTENTS

19 Advice to those who lack any love for humility ... 21

20 How for lack of humility hypocrites and heretics consider themselves better than all others ... 21

21 Articles of faith to be firmly held ... 23

22 On a firm and whole-hearted intention ... 25

23 A summary of the previous argument, and its application ... 27

24 On prayer as an aid to purity of heart and other virtues ... 28

25 How we should pray, and the matter of our thoughts in prayer ... 28

26 On the fire of love ... 29

27 How the vocal prayers ordained by God or approved by Holy Church are best for those who are under obligation to use them ... 30

28 The danger of abandoning the appointed prayers of the Church for meditation too early in the spiritual life ... 31

29 The second degree of prayer, which follows the impulses of devotion without any set form ... 32

30 How this kind of prayer is very pleasing to God, and wounds the soul with the sword of love ... 33

31 How the fire of love consumes all physical desires ... 33

32 On the third degree of prayer, which is in the heart alone, and is without words ... 34

33 How to deal with distractions in prayer ... 35

34 On meditation for sinners after they have turned wholly to God ... 37

35 That meditation on the humanity and passion of Christ is given by God, and how one may recognize it when given ... 39

36 That for various reasons meditation on Christ's passion is often withdrawn from those to whom it has been given ... 40

37 On the various temptations of the devil ... 41

CONTENTS

38 On various remedies against temptations of the devil   42

39 How God allows His chosen to be tried and tempted, and afterwards comforts and establishes them in grace   44

40 That a man should not yield to idleness, or neglect the grace given him by God   45

41 That everyone should know the measure of his own gift, and always desire a better, so that he can accept it when God wills to give it   46

42 That a man should study to know his own soul and its powers, and to destroy the roots of sin in it   48

43 How a man should know the high estate and dignity first given to his soul by God, and the wretched misfortune into which it has fallen by sin   50

44 How every person, however sinful, may be saved by the passion of Christ if he ask it   51

45 That we should strive to recover our nobility, and restore the likeness of the Trinity within us   55

46 How Jesus is to be sought, desired, and found   56

47 How profitable it is to have the desire for Jesus   58

48 Where and how Jesus is to be sought and found   59

49 Where Jesus is lost, and through His mercy found again   61

50 The things that prevent our hearing and seeing Jesus within us   62

51 That humility and charity are the especial livery of Jesus, through which man's soul is reformed to His likeness   62

52 How a man may recognize the origins of sin in himself   63

53 The real nature of this image of sin   64

54 Whoever wishes to find Jesus must be ready to fight in spiritual darkness against this image of sin   65

55 The image of sin, and what flows from it   67

56 What pride is, and when it is sin   68

ix

CONTENTS

57 When pride is mortal sin : its effect in worldly people   69

58 How pride in heretics is mortal sin   70

59 How pride in hypocrites is mortal sin   71

60 How impulses of pride and vainglory in good people are only
    venial sins   72

61 How different states in the Church have different rewards in
    heaven : of two rewards, supreme and secondary   74

62 A short address on humility and charity   76

63 How one may learn the extent of one's pride   77

64 On anger and envy, and their branches   78

65 That it is a great achievement to love men sincerely while
    hating their sin   78

66 That men will have different rewards for the same actions   79

67 That all seemingly good actions should be regarded as such,
    excepting those of heretics and excommunicates   80

68 That no good deed can assure a man's salvation without char-
    ity, and that God only grants His gift of charity to the humble   81

69 How we may know how much anger and envy is hidden in
    our hearts   83

70 How to ascertain whether you love your fellow-Christian, and
    how to follow Christ's example in this matter   84

71 How to discover the extent of your inward covetousness   86

72 On gluttony, sloth, and lust   89

73 How the roots of lust must be destroyed by spiritual means
    rather than physical   92

74 How a man must exert himself to overcome all sinful impulses,
    especially those to spiritual sins   92

75 How hunger and physical distress greatly hinder spiritual pro-
    gress   93

CONTENTS

76 Remedies against indiscreet eating and drinking 94

77 How the ardent desire and pursuit of humility and charity enable a man the sooner to acquire all other virtues 95

78 On the five bodily senses 96

79 How lack of knowledge causes the soul to seek outward pleasures through the five senses 97

80 How the soul should seek its needs inwardly from Jesus, and not from outward things 97

81 How the windows of the imagination need to be closed, as well as those of the senses 98

82 When the use of the senses or imagination is mortal sin, and when venial 99

83 How a man or woman vowed to the life of religion should conduct themselves towards visitors 100

84 How the limbs of this image in the soul, defiled by the seven deadly sins, can be destroyed 102

85 The limbs of this image of sin 103

86 Of what the image of Jesus and the image of sin consist 104

87 How we must crucify this image of sin, and quicken the image of Jesus 104

88 The advantage of guarding the heart, and the close attachment of the soul to what it loves 105

89 How the image of sin is to be destroyed 106

90 How to control impulses of pride and other vices 107

91 What best helps a man to know and obtain what he needs, and destroys sin in him 108

92 How a man is to be conformed to the likeness of Christ, and Jesus formed in him 110

93 Why this book is written, and how the person for whom it was written should use it 110

CONTENTS

Book Two

1 How the soul of every good man reflects the image of God 113

2 How God's justice requires that sin cannot be forgiven unless amends are made 114

3 How there are two kinds of people who are not reformed by the merits of the precious passion of our Lord Jesus Christ 117

4 How man's soul, which is God's image, may be restored to His likeness in this life 119

5 How the soul may be restored to the likeness of Christ in two ways, by faith or by experience 121

6 How a soul may lose its likeness to God and its chance of reformation through two kinds of sin, original and actual 122

7 How a soul that has lost the likeness of Christ through mortal sin can be fully restored by recourse to the sacrament of penance 123

8 How a soul reformed through the sacrament of penance must hold firmly to the Church's faith 125

9 How we should believe that we have received this gift of reformation if our conscience witnesses to our renunciation of sin and our resolve to live a good life 127

10 How one whose soul is completely restored to the image of God makes every effort to avoid sin and keep himself in perfect charity with God and his neighbour 128

11 How reformed souls need to fight constantly against temptations to sin: and how a soul may know whether it yields to temptation or not 131

12 Although the soul is reformed, this image remains both lovely and ugly during this life: and how reformed and unreformed souls differ in their secret reactions 135

CONTENTS

13 On three types of people: those who have been reformed, those who are unreformed, and those who are reformed both in faith and feeling   138

14 How sinners come to resemble the animals, and are known to be lovers of this world   139

15 How those who love this world hinder the reformation of their souls in various ways   141

16 Those who love this world are advised what to do if their souls are to be reformed before they die   143

17 How reform of feeling and faith cannot be achieved all at once; it is effected by grace after a long time and with much bodily and spiritual effort   145

18 One reason why comparatively few souls achieve reformation in faith and feeling   147

19 Another reason for this failure, and how an unwise reliance on outward forms of devotion sometimes hinders souls from receiving greater grace   149

20 How perfection can only be attained by constant effort and by purification of the desires   151

21 How one who wishes to reach Jerusalem, City of Peace, which represents contemplation, must have faith, be very humble, and endure troubles of body and soul   154

22 How anyone on this road will have to fight enemies, and how he must conquer them by the knowledge of our Lord Jesus, by sacramental confession, sincere contrition, and satisfaction   159

23 A general remedy against the evil influences of the world, the flesh and the devil   161

24 How a soul conformed to the likeness of Jesus desires nothing but Him: and how He puts this desire into the soul, and Himself desires your soul   163

25 How the desire for Jesus, felt in this glowing darkness, conquers every evil inclination and enables the soul to see the spiritual light of the heavenly Jerusalem, that is, of Jesus   168

CONTENTS

26 How one may recognize the false lights caused by the trickery of the devil from the true light of knowledge which comes from Jesus   170

27 How a soul led by grace into this glowing darkness receives great benefits, and how one should prepare oneself to enter it   174

28 How our Lord Jesus leads a soul to be reformed by four different stages: He calls, justifies, honours, and glorifies it   180

29 How beginners and those who are growing in grace sometimes show greater outward signs of love than those who are perfect; but outward appearances are misleading   183

30 How to attain self-knowledge   186

31 The means by which a soul is reformed in feeling, and the spiritual gifts that it receives   193

32 How God opens the eyes of the soul to perceive Him, not all at once, but gradually. An example showing the three stages in a soul's reformation   195

33 How Jesus is heaven to the soul, and why He is called Fire   198

34 How we are to realize that it is not created love which brings the soul to the spiritual vision of God, but Love uncreated, that is, God Himself, who bestows this knowledge   201

35 How some souls, moved by grace and reason, love Jesus with fervent devotion and natural affection. And how some, inspired by the special grace of the Holy Spirit, love Him more quietly with a spiritual love alone   206

36 How the gift of His love is the most valuable and desirable of all God's gifts: how God, out of love alone, is the source of all good in those who love Him: and how divine Love makes the practice of all virtues and good works light and easy   209

37 How, when the soul is granted the grace of contemplation, divine Love overcomes all inclinations to pride, and renders the soul perfectly humble by removing all desire for worldly honours   212

CONTENTS

38 How divine Love quietly destroys all stirrings of anger and envy in the soul, and restores the virtues of peace, patience, and perfect charity to its fellow-men, as it did in the Apostles 216

39 How divine Love destroys covetousness, impurity, and gluttony, together with all enjoyment of sensual pleasures, doing so quietly and easily through the grace of contemplation 219

40 On the virtues and graces which a soul receives when its spiritual eyes are opened and it is given the grace of contemplation. How these cannot be won by its own unaided efforts, but only with the assistance of especial grace 223

41 How the special grace of the contemplation of God is sometimes withdrawn from a soul: how the soul should act in the absence or presence of God: and how a soul should constantly desire the gracious presence of God 229

42 A commendation of the prayer offered to God by a contemplative soul: how stability in prayer is a sure foundation: how every experience of grace in a chosen soul may be said to be of God: and the purer the soul the higher the grace received 235

43 How a soul, by the opening of its spiritual eyes, receives the grace of love, which enables it to understand Holy Scripture: and how God, hidden in the Scriptures, reveals Himself to those who love Him 240

44 How the secret voice of God sounds within the soul, and how the illuminations brought to the soul by grace may be called God's voice 245

45 How when grace opens the eyes of the soul, it is given wisdom which enables it humbly and surely to recognize the various degrees in the Church Militant, and the nature of the angels 247

46 How by the same light the soul may perceive the nature of the blessed angels, and recognize how Jesus is both God and man, transcending all things 250

INTRODUCTION

BEFORE printing was invented, and books became more widely available, authors tended to write for the instruction and benefit of particular individuals, even when they were confident that their work would reach a larger circle. Richard Rolle might have offered his *Fire of Love* 'for the attention of the simple and unlearned who were seeking to love God', but he was unusual in this frank acknowledgement of an accepted fact. Most writers dedicated their works to particular people.

In *The Ladder of Perfection* the recipient addressed was a 'ghostly sister in Jesus Christ'. Anonymous in name, status and situation, she does not seem to have been a fictional character invented by Walter Hilton to give verisimilitude to his teaching, but a real person prepared to accept whatever he had to say. We would like to know who she was, but it is of no importance; she serves her purpose by drawing out from him some of his best writing. In this sense she is marginal, for our concern is with the diffuse and warm exposition of spirituality set before us in *The Ladder*.

THE SOLITARY LIFE

This 'ghostly sister' was an anchoress; that is, she was a solitary nun, living alone in a cell, seeking to pray, to contemplate God and to live solely for his glory. The religious life has always provided opportunity for such a purpose and, though the practitioners may be fewer today, many branches of the Church have and sustain their own hermits. From the first the intention of such solitude has been to increase the time for prayer and contemplation, and thereby to love God more. But the motives leading to this most praiseworthy and desirable end vary from individual to individual. For some, even the monastic life has been found to be unbearable for the practice of such prayer, and they have retired, alone, into their hermitages; others have gone temporarily into isolation to tone up their spiritual life, and to return in due course to the outside world; some have withdrawn in order to study or to write. There has always been much variety in vocation and attitude, and the danger of escapism has always been recognized, and measures taken to guard against it.

This state is not peculiar to Christianity; most of the great religions provide for it, which suggests that there is something basic to human nature in the desire to 'get away from it all' and to be with God. Sometimes the exile is thrust upon one by outside forces, sometimes it is voluntary; it can be temporary, but often it is for ever. The Church has accepted the need for some sort of solitude since its inception. The first steps may have been taken by St Paul, for immediately after his conversion he spent three years in Arabia (Galatians 17–18). He went of his own volition, and it is probable that during that time he worked out his theology. Even when isolation is not voluntary but enforced, it may turn to spiritual benefit, for St John's apocalyptic vision was received when he was an exile on the Island of Patmos (Revelation 1:9). In the post-apostolic age when Christianity was a proscribed religion, the number of religious solitaries increased considerably. It would be a mistake, however, to conclude from this that only renegades practised this form of religion: the contrary is the case. The deserts into which the first hermits went were regarded as the abodes of Satan, and to go there was the act of a soldier of Christ battling for the Faith in the stronghold of the enemy. It was a vocation followed by many, and it persists to this day.

The eremitic (or desert) life expresses itself in one of two ways, though the underlying premise is common to both. 'Anchorites' are solitaries who seek to remain all their life in the place of their enclosure. In the early days they had regarded themselves free to leave their cells at will and return to normal life, but since the Middle Ages tradition has denied them such liberty, and they live 'according to rule' under the immediate or delegated authority of their director. Hermits on the other hand, though as solitary as anchorites, can, and sometimes do, move their abode when the will takes them or the situation demands. Normally they too are licensed by a bishop but subscribe to no uniform rule or pattern. In the past hermits occasionally joined together and when this happened there was the nucleus of a monastic community.

The medieval solitary was probably more active physically than his modern counterpart, for some of the work now done by local and district authorities was then done by him. Admittedly the scale would be very different, but in essence it was similar, and we are told that such roads and bridges as existed were sometimes serviced by local hermits who would also act as guides through unfamiliar territory, or perform other good and useful works. This social work was not thought to break the spirit of prayer, and it gave to the solitary the human contacts necessary to preserve his sanity. But this would be possible only for comparatively few recluses, and many would find their outlet as confessors, counsellors and directors in person or in writing.

HERMIT WRITINGS

Many anchorites have written about the spiritual life, and some of their works have lasted to this day. This is true of the four great masters of medieval English devotion known to us, Richard Rolle, Walter Hilton, Dame Julian and the anonymous author of *The Cloud of Unknowing*. Certainly the first three had experiences as solitaries, and it is a reasonable assumption that *The Cloud* author had too.

Though their works were close together in time there is no evidence that they were dependent upon each other for their mystical exposition. The most that can be said is that there are one or two passages which might indicate a common source, but they are still sufficiently dissimilar to prevent us confidently asserting that they spring from the same stock. What they have in common, of course, is their faith, and the conviction that even in this life God can be experienced, loved and known. Today we call them 'mystics' and their teaching 'mysticism'; words intended to convey to the reader their principles and practice. They would not have themselves used such expressions, for the words only came into vogue centuries later. They regarded themselves as teachers of the

INTRODUCTION

higher reaches of prayer, helping towards 'contemplation . . . in which the soul is oned with God'.

'Mysticism' as a word has almost as many facets as exponents, and those who attempt to write of it will generally define the limits within which they understand the term. Yet with all this variety most Christians would accept as a basis the definition given by Evelyn Underhill in *Practical Mysticism*: 'Mysticism is the art of union with Reality. The mystic is a person who has attained that union in a greater or lesser degree; or who aims at and believes in such attainment.' We can expand it to give it a more specific Christian reference by adding that the union can only be achieved by man's responding in love to God's love, and that this has been made possible by the self-revelation of God in Jesus Christ. With this fuller understanding the four medieval mystics would agree, for each of them is saying in his own distinctive way that readers should seek to fulfil the purpose for which they have been created, namely to be united with the source, sustainer and secret of all life, God himself.

It is almost impossible to describe spiritual development without recourse to spatial metaphor. Thus we speak of *Pilgrim's Progress*, or *The Ascent of Mount Carmel*, with no fear of being misunderstood. *The Ladder of Perfection* is another example of this practice, albeit a less obvious one. The title of Walter Hilton's great work indicates its purpose: it is concerned with the growing life of the soul, in the words of M. del Mastro, 'the upward progress of a spiral staircase'.

To judge by the surviving manuscripts Hilton was the most widely read, and possibly the most popular, of the medieval English masters, for he is credited with at least eight works of which *The Ladder of Perfection* is best known.* Of the man himself, however, we have very little information. He is thought to have been a graduate of Cambridge, a priest who had at some time in his

* Besides *The Ladder*, we have *The Epistle to a Devout Man in Temporal Estate*, the *Song of Angels*, *Expositions* of three Biblical passages (Psalm 90 (91 A.V.), 91 (92 A.V.) and the *Benedictus*), a tract (*Stimulus Amoris*), and a translation of the meditations of *James of Milan*. There are also four epistles in Latin, and an academic *Quaestio* on the veneration of images.

life lived as a hermit. He became a canon of the Augustinian Priory at Thurgarton in Nottinghamshire, and it was here he died in 1396. The Priory was an important one, owning and administering estates in Nottinghamshire, Derbyshire and Lincolnshire, and its Prior was an influential figure in public life. But none of this is even hinted at in *The Ladder*, which in fact gives little away of local interest, and virtually nothing about its author. We are left to surmise on the basis of subjective reactions to such of his writings as have survived.

Hilton does not fit easily into any particular mystical 'slot', for he was writing at a time before any consensus of terms descriptive of spiritual experience had emerged, when writers of the spiritual life wrote independently of each other. A common doctrine had not so far produced its own vocabulary, and the unity of teaching is the more striking for this variety of expression.

But a definite development may be detected in these early writings. What Rolle seems sometimes to be feeling his way towards has been crystallized and corrected by the time of *The Cloud of Unknowing* (1370), and the similarity of its teaching to that of *The Ladder* is close enough for some scholars to suggest that both works come from the same pen. Not all experts share this view, and in the absence of hard evidence it is wiser to suspend judgment.

For many, Hilton is regarded as the first of the English mystics, both historically and theologically, and is, for that reason, to be valued. It may be doubted if he saw himself in this light, for, as we have noted, his great work was written not so much as a text-book, but to be of immediate help to a nun in her spiritual growth. He was not unaware that his words would benefit other readers as well, though it is unlikely that he foresaw that he would still be regarded as a master of the spiritual life six centuries later.

HILTON AND CONTEMPLATION

Hilton wants his nun to realize her vocation as a contemplative, and to know something of that life which 'consists of perfect love and charity inwardly experienced through the spiritual virtues, and in a true knowledge and perception of God and spiritual things'. Whereas many writers on spirituality tend to stress the mystery and remoteness of the Godhead, Hilton is emphatic that he has fully revealed himself in Jesus Christ, and that the nun must 'direct her whole intention and purpose' to him, 'desiring to seek, feel or find nothing except the grace and presence of Jesus'. In him she will find 'the light of understanding, love and delight'.

But not necessarily all at once. He spends little time on the 'warm-up' preliminaries customary in treatises on such matters, but from his third chapter onwards expounds the meaning of contemplation* and its requirements. Fundamentally it is love for God, and an awareness of him and spiritual things.

There are, says Hilton, three grades of contemplation. The first, an intellectual knowledge of God and spiritual matters, is available to all. It is not true contemplation, and may be known by 'heretics, hypocrites, and men of worldly life' as well as by disciples. Because of this wide availability it is open to abuse, and its practitioners can be tempted to misuse it to increase their 'reputation, worldly rank, honour and riches'. But not so the believer:

* Contemplation is a word rich in theological significance. It can be used to describe a variety of experiences from our reaction to the starry heavens to the wordless transport of the ecstatic rapt 'in wonder, love and praise'. In religious terms it means the awareness of the presence of God, which awes, stills and entrances the soul before such wonder. Such knowledge will vary in depth according to the sensitivity and dedication of the beholder, as well as to the will and generosity of God, who permits such blessing. There is a strong element of trust in this, for the worshipper has no right as such to claim this privilege, and indeed, in some cases, he has to say with Job, 'though he slay me, yet will I trust in him' (Job 13:15). This ravishing experience normally seems to last a comparatively short time, but there is no common factor governing the length of such moments. The rapture can last much longer. St Teresa of Avila, who was fairly frequently granted such visions, suggested that half an hour was the norm for their duration, but clearly no time limit may be set for what is always held to be a divine visitation. But long or short, percipients know themselves to be held in a loving embrace beyond their power to describe and, when the immediacy of the rapture fades, as in due course it will, its effects will still be felt, and the soul will go on with lighter tread and greater confidence.

given the right attitude it can, for him, become 'burning love'. The next grade is in loving God, and it is quite independent of intellectual ability. It has two stages, the first being open to every Christian who wishes for it; the second reserved for those who, like his nun, have withdrawn from the world, and who 'live in great peace of body and soul in fellowship with God'. Hilton calls it 'love on fire with devotion'. The third grade unites the two previous ones, and knows and loves God perfectly; the soul experiences an ecstatic union with God, and is conformed to the likeness of the Trinity. It is 'love on fire with contemplation', much more wonderful than anything known earlier. Only a contemplative or a solitary can know this in its fullness.

But Hilton does not expect his nun to have reached this stage yet. She is not wholly re-formed and, before Jesus is found, has to acquire proper humility and to go through a period of darkness and temptation. This desolating experience – not to be confused with the 'dark nights' of St John of the Cross – is described in terms of the seven deadly sins,* and Hilton expounds these causes of spiritual failure, and gives his remedies for them, protesting at the same time that he does not practise what he is preaching. His analysis demonstrates his commonsense and his humility. If we are to cope successfully with these sins we must fix our minds on Jesus Christ. Humility and charity will not only fashion us to the likeness of his humanity, but 'at length transform us to the true likeness of Jesus in his Godhead'.

Once he has proclaimed his purpose, Hilton proceeds to tell his reader how she may attain to this union with God. Fundamentally this is a matter of prayer and meditation, but these must be infused with humility, orthodoxy, unswerving purpose and the utmost energy if she is to realize it. But it is not enough to tell her what to do: like the wise director that he is, Hilton shows her how to do it.

First he deals with prayer, for that will help her to be ready and able to receive God's grace. He then goes on to meditation. Next he warns of the difficulties that she will encounter, stressing especially the various temptations of the devil, and the remedies

---

* They are pride, envy, anger, gluttony, covetousness, lust and sloth.

against them. Honest self-appraisal will restore the likeness of the Trinity within herself, and this will be achieved if she seeks with unceasing longing her Lord Jesus Christ. The search is not 'the work of an hour or a day . . . and it demands both bodily toil and spiritual effort'.

The last section of the book is given to a thorough-going look at the fact of sin and the spiritual struggle that engages the Christian's every power. Many matters arise in the course of this discussion: the deadly sins, true charity, the need for humility and love, victory over sin, the effect of unbridled pleasure in creature comforts, the dangers of excessive asceticism – and the availability of Our Lord's help. The very last chapter of Book I tells us why Hilton has written as he has: it is to spur himself to do better, and to help others to greater devotion in contemplation. And if what he has written is not found helpful, the nun (and by extension every reader) should put it aside and only use such parts as do help.

The second book develops this teaching. The nun is not wholly satisfied, so Hilton seeks to oblige her. She wants to know how the soul can be restored to the likeness of Christ in this present life. After a simple statement on the Fall of Man, and the Redemption wrought by Christ, Hilton describes the Christian life in terms of re-formation. It is not unimportant to remember the hyphen whether literally present or not, for by it we are reminded of the change that the Passion of Our Lord achieves in the human soul. On earth such re-form can only be partial, but in heaven it will be complete. Partial re-form is twofold and known by faith alone, or by faith and experience; this latter way demands considerable spiritual effort, for sin has to be dealt with: baptism cleanses us from original sin, and penance all subsequent sin. Hilton calls this 're-formation in faith', and recognizes that its maintenance is not easy. In fact, in this life it is impossible to live free from temptation, for consciousness of God is not permanent. This unawareness of him is not in itself a sinful condition, but if it causes tension one should seek the help of one's confessor, and go ahead in faith.

Meanwhile the soul is mounting the spiritual ladder rung by rung until it reaches perfection. It is the highest state attainable in this life, but it can only be reached by the grace of God. Two fundamental virtues enable the seeker to realize this beatitude: humility and love. A quiet beauty pervades these concluding chapters as Hilton describes the divine action which reveals deep truths in contemplation, and brings indescribable light and love to the attentive soul. The last sentence of the book sums up all that Hilton has been seeking to convey to his readers: 'a soul that is clean, stirred by grace to use of this working, may see more in an hour of such ghostly matter, than might be written in a great book'.

BOOK ONE

CHAPTER 1: *How the inner and outer lives of a Christian should correspond*

DEAR SISTER IN JESUS CHRIST, I BEG YOU to be content and remain steadfast in the vocation through which God has called you to His service. Strive by the grace of Jesus Christ and with all the powers of your soul to live a life of true holiness, befitting the calling that you have embraced. Since you have forsaken the world and turned wholly to God, you are symbolically dead in the eyes of men; therefore, let your heart be dead to all earthly affections and concerns, and wholly devoted to our Lord Jesus Christ. For you must be well aware that if we make an outward show of conversion to God without giving Him our hearts, it is only a shadow and pretence of virtue, and no true conversion. Any man or woman who neglects to maintain inward vigilance, and only makes an outward show of holiness in dress, speech, and behaviour is a wretched creature. For they watch the doings of other people and criticize their faults, imagining themselves to be something when in reality they are nothing. In this way they deceive themselves. Be careful to avoid this, and devote yourself soul and body to God alone, conforming yourself inwardly to His likeness by humility, charity, and other spiritual virtues. In this way you will be truly converted to God. I do not say that you can be converted immediately, and possess all virtues in the same way as you can enclose yourself in a cell; but you should bear in mind that the purpose of your present bodily enclosure is to enable you more readily to attain spiritual enclosure.* You are

I

shut away from dealings with other folk in order that your heart may be withdrawn from all worldly affections and fears. And in this little book I propose to tell you as well as I can how you may best achieve this purpose.

CHAPTER 2: *The active life and its duties*

YOU must understand that, as Saint Gregory says, there are two ways of life in Holy Church through which Christians may reach salvation; one is called active and the other contemplative. One or other of these is necessary to salvation.

The active life consists in love and charity shown outwardly in good works, in obedience to God's Commandments, and in performing the seven corporal and spiritual works of mercy* for the benefit of our fellow-Christians. This is the life suited to all who live in the world, and who enjoy wealth and ample goods. It is also suited to all who hold positions of rank, authority, and responsibility over others, and who have means at their disposal, whether they are learned or unlettered, laymen or churchmen: in short, all men of the world. These are bound to execute their duties with zeal and wisdom as common sense and discretion require. If a person is wealthy, let him be generous; if he has little, let him give less. Even if he has nothing, let him show goodwill. These are the spiritual and material duties of the active life.

Another requirement of the active life is the disciplining of our bodies by fasting, vigils, and other severe forms of penance. For the body must be chastised with discretion to atone for our past misdoings, to restrain its desires and inclinations to sin, and to render it obedient and ready to obey the spirit. Provided that they are used with discretion, these practices, although active in form, greatly assist and dispose a person in the early stages of the spiritual life to approach the contemplative life.

CHAPTER 3 : *The contemplative life and its duties*

THE contemplative life consists in perfect love and charity inwardly experienced through the spiritual virtues, and in a true knowledge and perception of God and spiritual things. This life belongs especially to those who for love of God forsake all worldly riches, honours, and outward affairs, and devote themselves body and soul to the service of God in spiritual occupations. Now since your state requires you to be a contemplative – for the purpose of your enclosure is that you may give yourself more freely and completely to spiritual things – you must toil night and day both in body and soul in order to attain this state of life as best you may, employing whatever means seem best to you.

But before I tell you of the means, I will first tell you a little more about the life of contemplation itself, so that you may understand something of what it is. You can then set it before you as the goal towards which you can direct all your energies.

CHAPTER 4 : *The first degree of contemplation*

IN the contemplative life there are three degrees. The first degree consists in knowledge of God and of spiritual matters. It is reached through the use of reason, through the teachings of others, and by study of the Holy Scriptures; it is not accompanied by feelings of devotion infused by a special gift of the Holy Spirit. Learned men and great scholars who have devoted great effort and prolonged study to the Holy Scriptures reach it to a greater or less extent as a result of natural intelligence and regular study, employing the gifts which God gives to every person who has the use of reason. This knowledge is good and may be termed a part of contemplation inasmuch as it implies perception of truth and a knowledge of spiritual things. But it is only a figure and shadow of true contemplation, because it does not bring with it any spiritual experience or inward savour of God, for these graces are granted only to those who have a great love for Him. This fountain of love issues from our Lord alone, and no stranger may approach it. But knowledge of this kind is common to good and bad alike, since it can be acquired without love. Therefore it is not true contemplation, since heretics, hypocrites, and men of a worldly life are sometimes more knowledgeable than many true Christians although they do not possess this love. Saint Paul describes this kind of knowledge: *Si habuero omnem scientiam et noverim mysteria omnia, caritatem autem non habuero, nihil sum* (1 Cor. xiii, 2). If I had full knowledge of all things and knew all secrets, but had no love, I should be nothing. Nevertheless, if those who have knowledge of this kind keep themselves in humility and charity, shunning worldliness and sins of the flesh with all their might, they are following a good way which will prepare them for true contemplation if they sincerely and devoutly ask this grace from the Holy Spirit.

Some people who possess this knowledge become proud and misuse it in order to increase their personal reputation, worldly rank, honours and riches, when they should use it humbly to the praise of God and for the benefit of their fellow-Christians in true charity. Some fall into heresies, errors, and other public sins, through which they become a scandal both to themselves and to the whole Church. Saint Paul says of this kind of knowledge: *Scientia inflat, caritas autem aedificat.* Knowledge by itself stirs the heart to pride, but united to love it turns to edification. By itself this knowledge is like water, tasteless and cold. But if those who have it will offer it humbly to our Lord and ask for His grace, He will turn the water into wine with His blessing as He did at the request of His Mother at the marriage-feast.

4

In other words, He will turn this savourless knowledge into wisdom, and cold naked reason into spiritual light and burning love by the gift of the Holy Spirit.

CHAPTER 5: *The second degree of contemplation*

THE second degree of contemplation consists principally in loving God, and does not depend upon intellectual light in spiritual matters. This degree is commonly attained by simple, unlearned folk who give themselves completely to devotion, and it is felt in these ways. When a person is meditating upon God, the grace of the Holy Spirit may move him to feelings of love and spiritual fervour at the thought of Christ's Passion or some other event in His earthly life. Or he may feel great trust in the goodness and mercy of God, His forgiveness of our sins, and His gifts of grace. Or there may come to him a heartfelt fear and awe of the hidden and unsearchable judgements of God and His justice. Or again, while at prayer he may feel his heart detach itself from all earthly things, all its powers uniting to reach up to our Lord in fervent desire and spiritual ecstasy. At such times there is no particular intellectual illumination in spiritual matters, or in the mysteries of Holy Scripture: the person simply knows that he desires nothing more than to pray and feel as he is doing, so great is the joy, delight, and comfort that he experiences. He cannot describe it, but knows that this feeling is real, for from it spring sweet tears, burning desires, and inexpressible grief. These scour and cleanse the soul from all stains of sin, and cause it to melt with wonderful love for Jesus Christ, so that it becomes obedient, responsible, and ready to do God's will. So profound is this experience that he does not care what becomes of him, provided that God's will be done. And there are many other feelings which I am unable to describe, and which cannot be experienced without great grace;

but whoever has them is in charity. And although this fervour passes away, charity cannot be lost or lessened except by mortal sin. This affords great comfort. This may be called the second degree of contemplation.

CHAPTER 6: *The lower stages of the second degree of contemplation*

THIS degree has two stages. When God visits the soul with His grace, this stage may be experienced as strongly and fervently by those living the active life as by those who are wholly devoted to the life of contemplation and have received this gift. But this feeling of fervour does not come at the soul's desire, nor does it often last long, but comes and goes at the will of Him who gives it. Therefore whoever enjoys it should be humble and thank God, keeping it hidden – unless he reveals it to his confessor – and preserving it with discretion as long as he may. And when it is withdrawn he should not be too anxious, but firmly persevere in faith and humble hope, waiting patiently until it returns. This fervour is a small foretaste of the sweetness of God's love, of which David speaks in the psalms: *Gustate et videte quam suavis est Dominus* (Ps. xxxiv, 8). Taste and see the sweetness of our Lord.

CHAPTER 7: *The higher stage in the second degree of contemplation*

THE higher stage in this degree can only be reached and retained by those who live in great peace of body and soul, and who by the grace of Jesus Christ and through prolonged bodily and spiritual discipline have found peace of heart and purity of conscience, so that they desire nothing more than to live quietly in constant prayer to God, and in meditation on our Lord. The thought of the blessed Name of Jesus brings them comfort and joy, and meditation on it feeds their love for Him. And not only the Name of Jesus, but all other prayers, such as the *Our Father*, the *Hail Mary*, hymns, psalms, and other devotions used by Holy Church become sources of spiritual joy and melody that comfort and strengthen them against all sin, and relieve them in bodily distress.

Saint Paul says of this degree of contemplation: *Nolite inebriari vino sed implemini Spiritu Sancto, loquentes vobismetipsis in hymnis et psalmis, et canticis spiritualibus, cantantes et psallentes in cordibus vestris Domino* (Eph. v, 18). Do not be drunk with wine, but be filled with the Holy Spirit, speaking to yourselves in hymns and psalms and spiritual songs, singing and making melody in your hearts to the Lord. Whoever enjoys this grace must be humble, and ensure that his constant desire is to attain to greater knowledge and awareness of God in the third degree of contemplation.

CHAPTER 8: *The third degree of contemplation*

THE third degree of contemplation, which is the highest attainable in this life, consists of both knowledge and love; that is, in knowing God and loving Him perfectly. This is achieved when the soul is restored to the likeness of Jesus and filled with all virtues. It is then endowed with grace, detached from all earthly and carnal affections, and from all unprofitable thoughts and considerations of created things, and is caught up out of its bodily senses. The grace of God then illumines the mind to see all truth – that is, God – and spiritual things in Him with a soft, sweet, burning love. So perfectly is this effected that for a while the soul becomes united to God in an ecstasy of love, and is conformed to the likeness of the Trinity. The beginnings of this contemplation may be experienced in this life, but its consummation is reserved for the bliss of heaven. Saint Paul says of this union and conformation to our Lord: *Qui adhaeret Deo, unus spiritus est cum illo* (1 Cor. vi, 17). That is, whenever a soul is united to God in this ecstasy of love, then God and the soul are no longer two, but one: not, indeed, in nature, but in spirit. In this union a true marriage is made between God and the soul which shall never be broken.

CHAPTER 9:. *The difference between the third and second degrees of contemplation, and the excellence of the third degree*

THE second degree of contemplation may be called love on fire with devotion; the third is love on fire with contemplation. The former is a lower state, and the latter a higher. The former is more satisfying to the natural senses, and the latter to the spiritual faculties, for it is more interior, more spiritual, more noble, and more wonderful. Although imperfect, it is a true foretaste and promise of the joys of heaven, now perceived not clearly but dimly, which will be revealed and fulfilled in the bliss of heaven. As Saint Paul says: *Videmus nunc per speculum in aenigmate; tunc autem videbimus facie ad faciem* (1 Cor. xiii, 12). Now we see God in a mirror, as it were dimly; but in heaven we shall see Him clearly, face to face. This is the illumination of the understanding coupled with the joys of His love to which David refers in the Psalter: *Et nox mea illuminatio mea in deliciis meis* (Ps. cxxxix, 11). Night is as light to me in my joy. The other degree of contemplation is as milk for children; this is solid meat for perfect souls of experienced judgement, who can discern good and evil. As Saint Paul says: *Perfectorum est solidus cibus qui habent sensus exercitatos ad discretionem boni et mali* (Heb. v, 14).

No one can have the full exercise of this gift unless he is first reformed in the likeness of Jesus by bringing virtue to perfection. And no one living in this mortal body can retain it constantly in all its fullness and excellence, but only when he is visited by grace. And we learn from the writings of holy men that this is only for short periods, for we soon return to our normal level of perception. This gift springs wholly from love. As I understand him, Saint Paul is speaking of his own experience when he says: *Sive excedimus, Deo, sive sobrii sumus, vobis; caritas Christi urget nos* (II Cor. v, 13). Whether we transcend our bodily senses in contemplation of God, or whether we remain at our normal level of perception, it is the love of Christ that moves us. Saint Paul also expressly describes this stage of contemplation and of being conformed to God: *Nos autem revelata facie gloriam Domini speculantes, transformamur in eamdem imaginem, a claritate in claritatem tamquam a Domini Spiritu* (II Cor. iii, 18). In other words, Saint Paul says of himself and of others made perfect: Being first reformed in virtue, with our inward vision clarified, we see the joy of heaven as in a mirror; we are transformed and united to His likeness, passing from clarity of faith to clarity of knowledge, and from clarity of desire to the clarity of true love. All this is brought about in a soul by the Spirit of God, as Saint Paul says. God gives this degree of contemplation where He will, both to learned and to simple, to men and women in spiritual authority, and to solitaries; but it is an especial favour, and not common. And although a person living the active life may receive this gift as an especial favour, none but a contemplative or solitary can possess it in all its fullness.

CHAPTER 10: *How things seen and felt in the bodily senses may be good or evil*

FROM what I have said you may understand that visions or revelations by spirits, whether seen in bodily form or in the imagination, and whether in sleeping or waking, do not constitute true contemplation. This applies equally to any other sensible experiences of seemingly spiritual origin, whether of sound, taste, smell, or of warmth felt like a glowing fire in the breast or in other parts of the body; anything, indeed, that can be experienced by the physical senses. None of these things, however comforting and pleasing, constitute true contemplation. Although good, they are unimportant, and are secondary to the spiritual virtues and to the pursuit of virtue and the knowledge and love of God; for in the knowledge and love of God there can be no deception. Feelings of this kind may be good, and caused by a good angel, or they may be deceptions caused by a wicked angel posing as an angel of light. And since they may be good or evil, it is clear that they are not of great significance. Remember that, when God permits it, the Devil has power to affect the bodily senses in the same way as a good angel. For as a good angel can appear in light, so can the Devil; and the same thing applies to the other senses. A person who has experienced both is able to tell which are good and which are evil, but one who has experienced neither, or only one, can easily be deceived; for although they are similar as regards the outward senses, their inward effect is very different. For this reason the soul should not have a great desire for them, nor should it experience them without caution, but use its discretion to distinguish good from evil, and so avoid deception. As Saint John says: *Nolite credere omni spiritui, sed probate si ex Deo sint* (1 John iv, 1). Saint John warns us not to believe every spirit, but first to test it to see whether it comes from God or not. So I will tell you of one method by which I think you can distinguish the good from the evil in such instances.

CHAPTER 11: *How to know whether sensible experiences are good or evil*

SHOULD you see any light or brightness, whether outwardly or in your imagination, which is not visible to other people, treat it with caution. And should you hear any sweet melody or suddenly taste a sweet but unaccountable savour in your mouth, or a fiery heat in your breast, or any other kind of pleasurable sensation elsewhere in your body, be on your guard. Even if a spirit such as an angel appears to you in bodily form to comfort and guide you, or if you have some experience that is not attributable to any bodily creature, treat it with reserve both then and afterwards, and test the reactions of your soul. If the pleasure that you feel leads you to abandon the thought and contemplation of Jesus Christ, and your spiritual exercises and prayer, so that you neglect self-examination and cease to long for virtue and the spiritual knowledge and love of God, then beware. And take care lest you allow the inmost desire of your heart, your pleasure and your peace of mind to depend principally on these experiences, regarding them as part of the joy of Heaven and the happiness of the angels, so that you do not wish to pray or think of anything else. For if your sole desire is to preserve and enjoy such experiences, beware of these feelings, for they come from the devil. Therefore, however pleasing and attractive they may appear, reject them and do not yield to them. When the devil sees a soul devote itself wholly to spiritual things he is greatly angered, for he hates nothing more than to see a soul in this sinful body enjoying the savour of the knowledge and love of God, which he as a spirit wilfully lost. So that if he cannot injure it by open sins, he tries to hinder and beguile it into spiritual pride and false security by means of sensible enjoyments and intellectual pleasures. In this way he tricks it into thinking that it is experiencing the joys of Heaven or is half-way to Paradise when in reality it is nearing the gates of Hell. Thus through pride and presumption such a person may fall into errors and delusions, and may suffer other bodily and spiritual harm.

However, an experience of this kind may not discourage you from spiritual exercises, and may enable you to pray more fervently and devoutly, and to think more readily of spiritual things. If this be so, although it may be disturbing at first, it will later transform and quicken your heart to a deeper desire for virtue, increase your love towards God and your fellow-Christians, and make you more humble in your own eyes. By these indications you may know that it comes from God, and is brought about by the presence and action of a good angel. Such an experience is granted by God in His goodness to comfort simple devout souls, to increase their trust and desire for Him, and to make them seek to know and love Him more perfectly. In the case of souls made perfect, it is granted to afford them such joy as will give them a promise and foretaste of the glory that awaits them in Heaven. I do not know whether there is any such person living on earth, but it seems that Mary Magdalene had this privilege, when she lived alone in a cave for thirty years, and was daily borne up by angels and fed in body and soul by their presence. We read this in the legend about her.*

Saint John speaks of this way of testing the spirits in his epistle, and teaches us: *Omnis spiritus qui solvit Jesum hic non est ex Deo* (1 John iv, 3). Every spirit that denies Jesus is not of God. These words may be understood in many ways, but in one sense they apply to what I have been saying.

CHAPTER 12: *What unites Jesus to a man's soul, and what separates Him from it*

JESUS is united to a man's soul by goodwill and by a deep desire to possess Him alone, and see Him spiritually in His glory. The stronger this desire, the closer the union between Jesus and the soul: the weaker this desire, the looser the union. Any spirit or experience that weakens this desire and distracts the soul from constant thought of Jesus Christ and its proper aspiration for Him will damage and disrupt this union between Jesus and the soul. It is therefore not of God, but the work of the devil. But if some spiritual experience or revelation fires the desire, draws the knot of love and devotion to Jesus more tightly, clarifies the soul's spiritual vision and knowledge, and makes the soul more humble, then it comes from God. From this you will understand that you may not deliberately allow your heart to depend on or derive all its pleasure from any sensible consolations of this kind even if they are good. Regard them as of little significance compared with the spiritual desire and constant thought of Jesus Christ, and do not allow your thoughts to become too engrossed in them.

Devote all your energies to prayer, so that your soul may come to a real perception of God; that is, that you may come to know the wisdom of God, the infinite might of Our Lord Jesus Christ, His great goodness in Himself and towards His creatures. For true contemplation consists in this, and not in these other matters. Thus Saint Paul says: *In caritate radicati et fundati, ut possitis comprehendere cum omnibus sanctis, quae sit longitudo, et latitudo, sublimitas, et profundum* (Eph. iii, 17). Be rooted and grounded in love – not in order to experience sound or sweet savours or other physical sensations – but that with all the saints you may know and experience something of the greatness of the infinite Being of God, the wideness of His wonderful love and goodness, the height of His almighty majesty, and the boundless depths of His wisdom.

CHAPTER 13 : *The occupation of a contemplative*

THE occupation of a contemplative consists in acquiring the knowledge and experience of these four things, upon which depend the whole science of the spiritual life. This is the one thing that Saint Paul desired, when he said: *Unum vero, quae retro sunt obliviscens, in anteriora me extendam, sequor si quo modo comprehendam supernum bravium* (Phil. iii, 13). In other words, one thing I earnestly desire, and that is to forget all that is behind me, and to reach forward with all my heart to grasp and enjoy the supreme reward of endless bliss. All material things are behind us, before us are the spiritual; therefore Saint Paul desires to forget all material things, even his own body, so that he may see those that are spiritual.

CHAPTER 14 : *How virtue begins in the reason and the will, and is perfected in love*

I HAVE told you a little about contemplation and what it means, so that you may keep it before you as your goal, and make it your lifelong desire by the grace of our Lord Jesus Christ to reach some degree of it. Contemplation conforms the soul to God, but this cannot take place until the soul is reformed by the practice of all virtues, and comes to love virtue for its own sake.

Many a man practises such virtues as humility, patience, and charity towards his fellow-Christians prompted only by his reason and will, and without any spiritual delight in them. He

often performs them grudgingly, reluctantly, and coldly, prac-
tising them only because his reason moves him to the fear of
God. Such a man is virtuous in his reason and will, but has no
real love of virtue. But when, by the grace of Jesus and as a result of spiritual exercises and bodily discipline, acts prompted
by reason alone become prompted by enlightenment, and acts
of will become acts of charity, then this man has a love of virtue.
He has gnawed through and broken the bitter shell of the nut,
and feeds on its kernel. In other words, virtues which were formerly burdensome have become pleasant and desirable, so that
he takes as much delight in humility, patience, purity, temperance, and love as in any worldly pleasures. Indeed, until virtue
turns into love, he may reach the second degree of contemplation, but he certainly will not attain the third. Now since virtues
predispose us to contemplation, it is essential for us to employ
the right means to acquire them.

CHAPTER 15: *On three means to attain contemplation*

THERE are three means most commonly employed by those
who devote themselves to contemplation; these are reading the Holy Scriptures and books of spiritual guidance, meditation, and constant prayer. Since you are not able to read the
Holy Scriptures, you should spend more time in prayer and
meditation. By means of meditation you will see how deficient
you are in virtues, and by prayer you will obtain them. By
meditation you will realize your own wretched state, your
wickedness, and your sins of pride, greed, gluttony, and impurity, evil impulses to envy, wrath, hatred, melancholy, anger,
bitterness, sloth, and senseless despair. You will see that your
heart is full of foolish shame, concern for your bodily needs, and
fear of the world's opinion. All these emotions will constantly
bubble up in your heart like foul water from a contaminated

spring. They will obscure your spiritual vision, so that you can neither realize nor feel the love of Jesus Christ. For remember that until your heart is thoroughly cleansed from such sins by knowledge of the truth and by constant remembrance of Christ's humanity, you cannot reach a true and spiritual knowledge of God. Christ Himself witnesses to this in the Gospel: *Beati mundo corde, quoniam ipsi Deum videbunt* (Matt. v, 8). Blessed are the pure in heart, for they shall see God. In meditation you will also recognize the virtues that you ought to possess: humility, gentleness, patience, righteousness, strength of spirit, temperance, purity, peace, self-control, faith, hope, and love. In meditation you will see the goodness, beauty, and value of these virtues. In prayer you will learn both to love and to acquire them, for without them you cannot become a contemplative. For Job says: *In abundantia ingredieris sepulchrum* (Job v, 26). In the fullness of good works and spiritual virtues you shall enter the tranquillity of contemplation.

CHAPTER 16: *How humility fosters discernment*

Now if you wish to use these spiritual exercises wisely and persevere in them safely, you must begin at the beginning, and there are three things which you need as a secure foundation on which to build; these are humility, firm faith, and a whole-hearted intention towards God. First of all you must acquire humility in this way. Discipline your will and, if possible, your feelings to recognize that you are unfit to live among other folk, unworthy to serve God in the fellowship of His servants, unprofitable to your fellow-Christians, and lacking both knowledge and strength to perform the good works of the active life for the benefit of your fellows as other men and women do. Consequently you are a wretched outcast, rejected by everyone, and confined to a cell alone, so that, since you cannot help anyone by good works, you may not harm anyone by your evil example. Consider further that since you are unable to serve our Lord in active works, you are even more unworthy and incapable of serving Him in spiritual activities. For our Lord is a spirit, as the prophet says: *Spiritus ante faciem nostram Christus Dominus* (Lam. iv, 20). The Lord Christ is a spirit before our face. The service which we owe to Him is spiritual, as He Himself says: *Veri adoratores adorabunt Patrem in spiritu et veritate* (S. John iv, 23). His true servants will worship the Father in spirit and in truth. But since you are so undisciplined, so sensual, so worldly, so blind to spiritual things, and to the state of your soul in particular – which ought to be your first consideration if you wish to come to the knowledge of God – how can you feel yourself worthy or capable of entering the contemplative life which, as I have said, consists above all else in the spiritual knowledge and experience of God? I do not say this to discourage you from your intention or to make you regret your enclosure, but in order that if possible you should really feel this humility in your heart. For what I say is true, and no exaggeration. So you must long and labour constantly to come as near to perfection as you may in the vocation which you have embraced, firmly trusting that by the mercy of God this way is the best for you. And although you may not reach perfection in this life, yet make a good beginning in it, with a sure trust that by God's mercy you will attain it in the joys of heaven. Indeed, my own life is like this; I feel myself so wretched, so weak, so worldly, and so far from the full experience of what I have been saying that I can do nothing but beg for mercy and long for this state of perfection, trusting that our Lord of His grace will bring me to it in the joy of heaven. Do the same, and do better if God gives you grace. This realization of your own unworthiness will drive out of your heart all unreasonable interest in other people's affairs and criticism of their actions, and will compel you to look at yourself alone, as though there were no one in existence but God and yourself. You should consider yourself more vile and wretched than any living creature, so that you can hardly endure yourself, so great will be your consciousness of inward sin and corruption. For I assure you in all sincerity that if you wish to become truly humble you should come to have this feeling, and regard venial sin in yourself as more serious and painful than mortal sin in others. For whatever defiles your soul or hinders its knowledge and experience of God must be very grievous and painful to you. But a venial sin of your own is a greater obstacle to your experiencing the perfect love of Jesus Christ than the sin of anyone else, however great it may be. It is clear, then, that you must harden your heart against yourself, humbling and detesting yourself more strongly for all the sins that hold you back from the vision of God than you detest the sins of others. For if your own heart is free from sin, the sins of others will not hurt you. Therefore, if you wish to find peace, both in this life and in heaven, follow the advice of one of the holy fathers, and say each day: 'What am I?', and do not judge others.

CHAPTER 17: *Who may reprove the faults of others, and who may not*

BUT you may object: 'How can this be so? It is an act of charity to reprove people for their faults, and an act of mercy to rebuke them to obtain their amendment.' My reply is that it is not fitting for you or for any contemplative to neglect your own soul in order to note and rebuke others for their faults, unless the need is so urgent that a person may lose his soul unless you correct him. But those who lead the active life and exercise authority and responsibility over others, such as prelates, clergy, and such men, are bound both by their office and in charity to notice and correct other men's faults. They should not do so out of any desire or pleasure to punish them, but only when need arises; then they must act in the fear of God and His Name, and with a desire to save souls. Others who lead the active life, but have no authority over their fellows, are in charity bound to reprove the faults of others only when the sin is mortal and no one else can correct them, and when they think that the sinner may be won back by their rebuke. For unless this is so, it is better to refrain. The truth of this is evident in Saint John, who was a contemplative, and Saint Peter who was a man of action. During the Last Supper with His disciples, our Lord told Saint John – who had been secretly prompted by Saint Peter – how Judas would betray Him. But Saint John did not inform Saint Peter as he had asked, but turned and laid his head on Christ's breast, and was transported by love into the contemplation of God's secrets. So great was his reward that he forgot both Judas and Saint Peter. This is a lesson to all who aspire to contemplation that they should be ready to do the same.

You will now understand that you should not judge other people, or deliberately cherish evil suspicions about them. Indeed you should love and honour those who lead an active life in the world and undergo many trials and temptations of which you in your cell have no experience. They endure hardship and toil for their own and others' living; and many of them would choose to serve God in tranquillity as you do if they had the opportunity. Nevertheless, despite their worldly business, they avoid many sins which you, in their place, would fall into, and they do many good deeds which you could not do. There is no question that many live in this way, but you cannot know who they are.

CHAPTER 18: *Why humble people should respect others, and regard themselves as inferior to all*

HONOUR all men and regard them as your betters, behaving humbly in their company, and seeing yourself as the most worthless and insignificant of men. It will do you no harm however much you humble yourself, even though in God's sight you have more grace than another. But it is dangerous for you to consider yourself superior to anyone else, even though he may be the most depraved and wicked scoundrel alive. For our Lord says: *Qui se humiliat exaltabitur, et qui se exaltat humiliabitur* (S. Luke xiv, 11). Whoever exalts himself shall be humbled, and whoever humbles himself will be exalted. It is necessary for you to acquire this degree of humility as a start, for by this and by God's grace you will at length attain perfect humility and all other virtues. Whoever possesses this one virtue possesses all others, for whatever your degree of humility, the same your degree of charity, patience, and other virtues, although they may not show outwardly. Therefore try to learn humility and keep it, for it is the first and last of all virtues. It is the first because it is the foundation of all virtues; as Saint Augustine says, if you plan to build a high house of virtues, first lay deep foundations of humility. It is also the last because it preserves and guards all other virtues: as Saint Gregory says: Whoever acquires any virtues without humility is like a man who carries powdered spices in the wind. And however numerous your good deeds – fasts, vigils, or anything else – they are valueless without humility.

CHAPTER 19: *Advice to those who lack any love for humility, and how they should not be too anxious on this matter*

NEVERTHELESS, if you are unable to feel any real love for humility in your heart as you would wish, do whatever you can and humble yourself by reason, knowing that you ought to be humble, as I say, even though you do not feel it. Regard yourself all the more as a sinner because you cannot feel yourself to be what you are. And, although your inclinations rebel and refuse to submit to your will, do not be over-anxious, but endure the misguided feelings of your nature as a penance. Despise and reprove these feelings and subdue your rebellious heart, knowing that you would well deserve to be trodden and spurned under the feet of all men as an outcast. And so by the grace of Jesus Christ and by constant meditation on the humbleness of His precious humanity, you will greatly abate the impulses of pride, while the virtue of humility, formerly dependent on your will alone, will become the object of your love. Without this virtue, either truly desired or loved, whosoever tries to serve God in the contemplative life will stumble like a blind man, and will never attain his purpose. The higher he seeks to climb by bodily penance and other virtues without humility, the lower he falls. For as Saint Gregory says: One who cannot utterly despise himself never yet found the humble wisdom of our Lord Jesus.

CHAPTER 20: *How the lack of humility causes hypocrites and heretics to consider themselves superior to all others*

HYPOCRITES and heretics do not possess this humility either in will or feeling. For lack of this gentle virtue their hearts and instincts are dry and cold, and they are all the further from it because they think they have it. They gnaw at the dry shell of the nut, but cannot reach the kernel with its sweet savour. They make an outward show of humility in dress, pious speech, and modest bearing, and seem to possess many virtues of mind and body. But in their will and affection, where humility should be especially evident, it is only pretended. For they condemn, despise, and belittle those who will not do as they do or accept their teachings. They regard them either as ignorant fools or as blinded by sensual living. So they exalt themselves in their own opinion above all others, thinking that they alone possess the secret of a good life, and are favoured by God with the grace of knowledge and devotion beyond all other men. From this complacency springs a delight in self-admiration and praise, as though there were none like them. They praise and thank God with their lips, but in their thievish hearts they steal the worship and thanks due to God alone and bestow it on themselves; consequently they neither desire nor feel humility. A sinner who falls daily and is sorry for it is humble in will, even though he may not feel humble. But a heretic or hypocrite is neither. He is in the same condition as the Pharisee described by our Lord in the Gospel (S. Luke xviii, 9), who came into the temple with the publican to pray. When he came, he did not offer prayer, and asked nothing of God, for he thought that he had no need, but he began to thank God saying: 'Lord, I thank you for giving me grace above all others, so that I am not as other men are, robbers, fornicators, and sinners of that sort.' And he looked around him and saw the publican, whom he knew for a sinner, beating his breast and crying for mercy. Then he thanked God that he was not such a man as he was, saying, 'Lord, I fast twice a week, and pay my tithes honestly.' And when he had ended, says our Lord, he returned home without grace as he had come, and gained nothing. But you may say, 'How did this Pharisee do wrong, since he thanked God, and what he said was true?' I answer that the Pharisee did wrong because he judged and condemned the publican, who was justified by God. He also did wrong in thanking God only with words, meanwhile taking a secret pride in himself because of God's gifts, stealing the honour and praise due to God, and bestowing it upon himself. Heretics and hypocrites are in just the same state as the Pharisee. They do not pray willingly, and when they do pray, they do not humble themselves and acknowledge their sins honestly, but make a pretence of thanking and praising God, giving Him lip-service only. Their satisfaction is shallow and false, for their delight is not in God at all, although they imagine otherwise. They cannot praise God, for as the wise man says: *Non est speciosa laus in ore peccatoris* (Ecclus. xv, 9). The praise of God in the mouth of a sinner is neither fair nor seemly. Therefore sinners like you and me must take care to avoid the condition of this Pharisee with his pretended praise of God, and imitate the publican in humility, asking mercy and forgiveness for our sins, and the gift of spiritual virtues. We can then thank and praise Him sincerely with a pure heart, and offer Him our worship without pretence. For our Lord asks through His prophet: *Super quem requiescit spiritus meus, nisi super humilem et contritum spiritum et trementem sermones meos?* (Isaiah lxvi, 2). Upon who shall My spirit rest? and He answers Himself; and says: Upon none but the humble, the poor, the contrite in heart, and those who fear My words. Therefore if you desire to have the spirit of God to rule your heart, be humble and fear God.

CHAPTER 21: *Articles of faith to be firmly held*

THE second thing necessary to you is a firm belief in all the articles of faith, and in the sacraments of the Church, holding them steadfastly with all your heart and will. And although the suggestions of the devil may stir up qualms of doubt and uncertainty in your mind about any of them, be steadfast, and do not pay too much attention to such feelings. Set aside your personal opinions without examining and revolving them in your mind, and conform your own faith wholly to the Faith of Holy Church. Do not harass your mind with any doubts that seem contrary to it, for these doubts are not what you believe; the Faith of Holy Church is what you believe, though you neither see it nor feel it. So endure these difficulties patiently, as a trial sent by God to purify your heart and strengthen your faith.

It is also your duty to cherish and respect all the laws and regulations made by prelates and others who rule Holy Church, whether issued to define the Faith and sacraments, or for the direction of Christians in general. Accept them humbly and sincerely, and although you may not understand the reason for them and think some of them unreasonable, do not criticize or condemn them. Observe them all, although they may not greatly concern you. Do not accept any other opinions or fancies which appear more holy, as some foolish folk do, whether they spring from your own mind or from the teaching of others, if they run contrary to the ordinances or general teaching of Holy Church. You should also firmly believe that by God's mercy you are called by our Lord to be saved as one of His chosen. Never abandon this hope. Whatever you may hear or see, whatever temptations assail you, and even though you consider yourself so great a sinner that you desire to be cast into Hell because of your failure to do good and to serve God as you ought, yet hold firmly to this faith and hope, and all shall be well. Even though all the devils in hell were to appear to you in bodily form, and tell you that you cannot be saved, do not believe them. And were all the people of the world and all the angels of heaven to tell you the same thing, do not believe them or abandon this hope of salvation. I tell you this because some who have devoted themselves wholly to the service of God are so weak and simple that if the devil stirs up evil inclinations in them, or if his prophets – whom people call fortune-tellers – inform them that they cannot be saved or that their way of life is displeasing to God, they become distressed and despondent. So in their ignorance they sometimes fall into great depression and almost despair of salvation. Therefore I am sure that everyone who is fully resolved by the grace of our Lord Jesus to forsake sin should have a firm trust in salvation. For so long as his conscience assures him clearly that any mortal sin that he has committed has been promptly confessed and absolved, and if he humbly approaches the sacraments of Holy Church, he may rightly hope for salvation. This applies even more strongly to those who give themselves entirely to God, and do their utmost to avoid even venial sin. In contrast, anyone who deliberately remains in a state of mortal sin and yet hopes for salvation is in a perilous state, for he relies on this hope, but neither forsakes his sin nor submits himself humbly to God and Holy Church.

CHAPTER 22: *On a firm and whole-hearted intention*

THE third thing that is essential at the outset is a firm and wholehearted intention; that is, a sincere resolve and desire to please God. For this is love, without which all your efforts are valueless. Make it your intention always to learn and labour to please Him, and never willingly to abandon good works, whether corporal or spiritual. Do not set any limits to them, telling yourself that you will serve God for a certain time, and then deliberately allow yourself to relapse into trivial thoughts and unprofitable occupations in order to obtain rest and comfort by indulging the senses and enjoying worldly pleasures. You may do this under the impression that such recreation will enable you to resume your spiritual exercises with renewed fervour, but I am sure that this is a mistake. I do

not say that you can always fulfil your intention in practice, because your bodily needs – such as food, sleep, conversation, and
natural frailty – will often intrude themselves and hinder you,
however active you may be. Resolve never to be idle, and
always be engaged in some spiritual or bodily activity, constantly, raising your heart's desire to God and the joys of
heaven, whether you are eating, drinking, or performing any
other outward action. Hold to this resolve as closely as you can,
for with it you will always be ready and eager for your work.
And if through frailty or negligence you lapse into any useless
occupation or unprofitable conversation, it will prick your
heart as sharply as a needle, and make all such foolishness so
irksome that you will quickly return to meditation on Jesus
Christ or to some good occupation. With regard to your
bodily needs, it is good to use discretion in food, drink, sleep,
and in all kinds of bodily penance, as well as in the matter of
long vocal prayers or feelings of fervent devotion accompanied
by tears and heightened imagination. If you lack the grace for
these things it is wise to observe discretion, for restraint is best.
But in fighting to destroy sin by a guard over the heart, in constant desire for virtue and the joys of heaven, and in fostering
the interior knowledge and love of Jesus Christ, cast aside restraint; the more you aspire to these the better. For you must
hate sin, together with all the worldly loves and fears in your
heart without ceasing, and if possible have a boundless desire
and love for virtue and purity. I do not say that this is essential
to salvation, but I am sure that it is valuable. And if you persevere in this resolution you will make greater progress in virtue
in a single year than you would in seven years without it.

CHAPTER 23 : *A summary of the previous argument, and its application*

Now I have already told you of the goal that you must bear in mind : exert all your energy to attain it. I have also told you how to begin and what factors are necessary, namely humility, a firm faith, and an intention directed wholly towards God. On this foundation you must build a spiritual temple by prayer and meditation, and other spiritual virtues. I now add this : whether you pray or meditate, or whatever else you do – whether it is rendered good by grace or spoiled by your own frailty – whatever you feel, see, hear, smell, or taste, whether physically or mentally ; and whatever you learn or perceive by reason, submit it all to the truth and judgement of Holy Church. Cast it all into the mortar of humility, grind it small with the pestle of the fear of God, throw its powder into the fire of desire, and offer it to God. I assure you that this offering will be pleasing to the Lord Jesus, and the smoke of its burning will be acceptable before Him. My meaning is this : test all your feelings by the truth of Holy Church, and submit yourself humbly to it. Offer the desires of your heart to the Lord Jesus alone, longing to possess Him and nothing but Him. If you do this, the grace of Jesus Christ will enable you to overcome every assault of the devil. Saint Paul teaches us this when he says : *Sive manducatis, sive bibitis, sive quid aliud facitis, omnia in nomine Domini facite* (I Cor. x, 31). Whether you eat, or drink, or whatever you do, do all in the name of our Lord Jesus Christ. Forsake self, and offer it up to Him. The principal means that you must use, as I have already said, are prayer and meditation. I shall begin by showing you something of prayer, and then of meditation.

THE LADDER OF PERFECTION

CHAPTER 24: *On prayer, as an aid towards purity of heart and other virtues*

PRAYER is helpful, and enables us to acquire purity of heart by the destruction of sin and the winning of virtues. The purpose of prayer is not to inform our Lord what you desire, for He knows all your needs. It is to render you able and ready to receive the grace which our Lord will freely give you. This grace cannot be experienced until you have been refined and purified by the fire of desire in devout prayer. For although prayer is not the cause for which our Lord gives grace, it is nevertheless the means by which grace, freely given, comes to the soul.

You may now perhaps desire to learn how to pray, to what you should direct your thoughts during prayer, and what form of prayer is best for you to use. As to the first, my answer is that when you first wake and are ready to pray, you may feel sluggish and heavy, obsessed by unprofitable thoughts and fancies, or preoccupied by thoughts of a worldly or personal nature. It is essential to rouse your heart by prayer, and stir it to devotion as strongly as you can.

CHAPTER 25: *How we should pray, and the matter of our thoughts in prayer*

WHEN you pray, detach your heart from all earthly things, and use all your efforts to withdraw your mind from them, so that it may be stripped and freed of these things and rise continually to Jesus Christ. You will never be able to see Him as He is in His divinity, nor can your imagination conceive of Him as He is; but devout and constant recollection of the humility of His precious humanity will enable you to experience His goodness and the grace of His divinity. If, when you pray, your heart is lightened, helped, and freed from the burden of all worldly thoughts and affections, and rises up in the power of the spirit to a spiritual delight in His presence so that you are scarcely conscious of earthly things or are little distracted by them, then you are praying well. For prayer is nothing other than the ascent of the heart to God, and its withdrawal from all earthly thoughts. Therefore prayer is compared to fire, which of its own nature always leaves the earth and leaps into the air. Similarly, prayerful desire, when touched and kindled by the spiritual fire of God, constantly leaps upwards to Him from whom it comes.

CHAPTER 26: *On the fire of love*

THOSE who speak of the fire of love do not always fully understand what it is. Indeed, I cannot myself tell you what it is, but I can tell you that it is not physical, nor is is a bodily sensation. A soul may experience it during prayer and devotion, but although the soul dwells within the body, it does not feel it through its bodily senses. For although it may happen that the working of this fire in the soul may cause a sensation of bodily heat, as though the body warmed in response to the exertions of the spirit, nevertheless the fire of love is not a bodily sensation, for it is caused by the spiritual desire of the soul. Nobody who experiences this devotion has any doubt on the matter, but simple people sometimes imagine that because it is called fire it must be hot like natural fire. And that is why I have mentioned this.

CHAPTER 27: *How the vocal prayers ordained by God or approved by Holy Church are best for those who are under obligation to use them, as well as for those who are beginners in prayer*

I WILL now give you my opinion on the second point: namely, how to know what kind of prayer is best. You should understand that there are three degrees of prayer. The first is vocal prayer, whether enjoined by God, as is the *Our Father*, or more generally by Holy Church, such as Matins, Vespers, and the other Hours. There are also prayers written by devout persons and addressed to our Lord, our Lady, or the Saints. As to this kind of prayer, known as vocal, I am certain that, since you are a religious and are bound by custom and rule to recite Matins and the Hours, it is proper for you to say these as devoutly as you are able. In reciting Matins, you say in particular the *Our Father*, and in order to stir you to greater devotion it has been ordained that you should also say psalms, hymns, and such like which, like the *Our Father*, have been inspired by the Holy Spirit. So it is not right to say the Divine Office hurriedly and carelessly as though the obligation were a heavy burden. So stir your affections and collect your thoughts, that you may recite it with greater care and devotion than any other prayers, in the sure knowledge that since it is the prayer of Holy Church, there is no vocal prayer so profitable to your regular use as the Divine Office. Therefore put away all heaviness, and by God's grace you will transform a duty into a delight, and an obligation into great freedom. If you do not, it will be an obstacle to your spiritual life. As well as the Divine Office you may, if you wish, use the *Our Father* and other such prayers, and I think it will be best for you to use those in which you find most joy and spiritual comfort.

This form of prayer is usually more helpful than any other
spiritual exercise to a person in the beginning of his spiritual
life. For unless he is granted especial grace, a person is at first
undisciplined and worldly, and he cannot meditate on spiritual
things because his soul is not yet cleansed of his former sin. And
so I think it best for such to use the *Our Father*, the *Hail Mary*,
and to recite the Psalms. For one who cannot readily pray with
the spirit, because the feet of his knowledge are lamed by sin,
needs to have a firm staff to support him. This staff is the particular forms of vocal prayer ordained by God and Holy Church
to help men's souls. By this prayer the soul of a wordly man,
who is always relapsing into worldly thoughts and carnal desires, is raised up and supported as if by a staff. He is nourished
by the sweet words of the prayer as a child is nourished with
milk. And he is guided by it so that his mind does not fall into
errors and foolish fancies. There is no possibility of a mistake in
this form of prayer for anyone who will patiently and humbly
persevere in it.

CHAPTER 28 : *The danger of abandoning the appointed prayers
of the Church for meditation too early in the spiritual life*

CONSEQUENTLY, you will realize that it is a mistake for
any who have felt some fervour at the beginning of their
conversion, and before their spiritual life is established, to abandon vocal prayer and outward forms of devotion and give
themselves exclusively to meditation. For they often rely on
their own ideas and feelings in spiritual matters for which they
have not as yet received the necessary grace. By such indiscre-
tion they frequently overstrain their minds and injure their
health, so that they fall into strange fancies and misconceptions
or into obvious errors, and by their foolish ideas they obstruct
the grace that God gives them. The cause of all this is secret
pride and presumption ; for having experienced a little grace,

they consider it so great and exceptional that they fall into vain-glory, and by so doing they lose it. If they realized how little they feel compared with what God gives or may give, they would be ashamed to speak about it unless it was absolutely necessary. In the psalms David says of vocal prayer: *Voce mea ad Dominum clamavi: voce mea ad Dominum deprecatus sum* (Psalm cxlii, 1). In order to stir others to pray both with heart and voice, this prophet said: 'I cried to the Lord with my voice, and prayed to Him with my lips.'

CHAPTER 29: *The second degree of prayer, which follows the impulses of devotion without any set form*

THE second degree of prayer is vocal, but employs no particular set form. This is when anyone by the grace of God experiences the grace of devotion, and out of this devotion speaks to God as though he were bodily in His presence, using such words as best express his feelings and come to his mind at the time. He may recall his sins and wretchedness, the malice and deceits of the devil, or the goodness and mercy of God. Out of the desire of his heart he calls on our Lord as a man will do when in peril among his enemies or in sickness, showing his hurts to God as he would to a physician, and saying as David said: *Eripe me de inimicis meis, Deus meus* (Psalm lix, 1). 'Deliver me from my enemies, O God.' Or else, *Sana animam meam, quia peccavi tibi* (Psalm xli, 4). 'Heal my soul, for I have sinned against Thee.' Or such other petition as comes to his mind. He knows the greatness of God's goodness, grace, and mercy, and wishes to love Him with all his heart, and to thank Him with such words and psalms as will fittingly express his love and praise of God. As David said: *Confitemini Domino quoniam bonus, quoniam in saeculum misericordia ejus* (Psalm cxxxvi, 1). 'Love and praise the Lord, for He is good and merciful.' And he will use any other prayers that he is moved to say.

CHAPTER 30: *How this kind of prayer is very pleasing to God, and wounds a man's soul with the sword of love*

THIS kind of prayer is very pleasing to God because it springs directly from the heart, and is therefore never offered without some reward of grace. It belongs to the second degree of contemplation, as I have already said. Whoever receives this gift of fervour from God should withdraw from the company of other people and be alone, so that it may not be interrupted. Let whoever has it retain it while he can, for its fervour will not remain long. For whenever grace comes powerfully it imposes a great strain on the spirit, even while it brings joy. It is also a great strain on the body if experienced often, for at the mighty surge of grace the body stirs and moves about like that of a madman or drunkard who can find no ease. This is one effect of passionate love, which in its violence utterly destroys all love of earthly things and wounds the soul with the sword of joyful love, so that the body collapses, unable to bear it. So potent is God's touch on the soul that were the most wicked sinner on earth to be touched only once by this sharp sword, he would thenceforward be a graver and better man. He would loathe all sinful lusts and desires, and cease to be attracted by the worldly things that had once been his chief delight.

CHAPTER 31: *How the fire of love consumes all physical desires, just as natural fire consumes material objects*

THE prophet Jeremiah describes this type of experience: *Et factus est in corde meo quasi ignis exaestuans, claususque in ossibus meis, et defeci, ferre non sustinens* (Jer. xx, 9). That is to say, the love and experience of God became not merely a fire, but a

33

glowing fire in my heart. For as natural fire burns and consumes every material object that it touches, so supernatural fire – that is, the love of God – burns away and consumes all worldly loves and pleasures in the soul. This is the fire which the prophet describes as 'hidden in his bones'. That is to say, this love fills all the powers of my soul – mind, reason, and will – with grace and sweetness as marrow fills a bone; but its influence is internal, and is not perceptible externally. Nevertheless, this love works so powerfully within the soul that it affects the body, and makes it quake and tremble. This experience is so unlike any normal experience, and is so unfamiliar that the soul cannot understand or endure it, and the body fails, as the prophet describes. Our Lord therefore tempers it, withdraws the fervour, and allows the soul to return to a state of greater calm and repose. Whoever can pray often in this way makes swift progress in the spiritual life. He will acquire greater virtue in a short while than another person of equal merit without this grace will acquire after a long period of penance. And whoever enjoys this grace from time to time has no need to task his body with greater penance than it reasonably requires.

CHAPTER 32: *On the third degree of prayer, which is in the heart alone and is without words*

THE third degree of prayer is in the heart alone; it is without words, and is accompanied by great peace and tranquillity of body and soul. One who wishes to pray in this way must have a pure heart, for the gift comes only to those who, either through long bodily and spiritual effort, or through such sudden visitations of love as I have described, have attained quietness of soul. As a result, their affections become wholly spiritual, their hearts are continually at prayer, and they can love and praise God without serious hindrance from temptations or worldly thoughts, as I said earlier when describing the second degree of contemplation. Of this kind of prayer Saint Paul says: *Nam si orem lingua, spiritus meus orat, mens autem mea sine fructu est. Quid ergo? orabo et spiritu, orabo et mente: psallam spiritu, psallam et mente* (1 Cor. xiv, 14). Meaning, that if I pray with my tongue only, by an effort of will, the prayer is commendable but my soul is not satisfied, because it cannot taste the fruit of spiritual joy through the understanding. 'What shall I do then?' saks Saint Paul. And he answers: I will pray with spiritual effort and desire. I will also pray more inwardly in my spirit without effort, and will taste the sweetness of the love and sight of God. It is this perception and experience of the love of God that will satisfy my soul. This – as I understand – was how Saint Paul prayed. In Holy Scripture God speaks of this way under a symbol: *Ignis in altari meo semper ardebit, et cotidie sacerdos surgens subjicit ligna, ut ignis non extinguatur* (Lev. vi, 12). That is to say: the fire of love shall always be alight in the soul of the devout and pure man or woman; for the soul is the altar of God, and every morning the priest shall lay on sticks and feed the fire. In other words, a man shall feed the fire of love in his heart with holy psalms, pure thoughts, and fervent desires, so that it shall never be extinguished. Our Lord gives this peace to some of His servants as a reward for their labours and a foretaste of the love which they will have in the joys of heaven.

CHAPTER 33: *How to deal with distraction in prayer*

BUT you may now complain that I am speaking in over-exalted terms about this kind of prayer, since it is easy enough to talk about it, but by no means easy to practise. You state that you are unable to pray in the devout and whole-hearted way that I have described. For when you wish to raise your heart to God in prayer, many useless thoughts fill your mind, of what you have done, of what you are going to do, of what others are doing, and such like. These thoughts hinder and distract you so much that you feel no joy, peace, or devotion in your prayer. And often the more you struggle to collect your thoughts, the more obstinate and wandering they become. Sometimes this lasts from the beginning to the end of your prayer, and you think all your efforts are lost.

When you say that I spoke in over-exalted terms about prayer, I frankly admit that I am describing something that I cannot practise. Nevertheless, I do so because we ought to understand how to pray well. And since we cannot pray well, we should humbly acknowledge our weakness and cry to God for mercy. Our Lord Himself told us this when He said: *Diliges Dominum Deum tuum ex toto corde tuo, ex tota anima tua, et ex omnibus viribus tuis* (S. Luke x, 27). You shall love God with all your heart, and all your soul, and all your strength. It is impossible for anyone to fulfil this command perfectly in this life, but our Lord nevertheless bids us love in this way. And its purpose, as Saint Bernard says, is that we should recognize our weakness and humbly cry for mercy, and we shall receive it. However, I will give you my advice on this question.

When you pray, begin by directing your will and intention to God as briefly, fully, and purely as possible; then continue as well as you can. And although your original purpose may seem largely frustrated, do not be distressed and angry with yourself or impatient with God because He does not give you feelings of devotion and spiritual joy that you imagine He gives to others. Recognize in this your own weakness, accept it readily, and humbly hold to your prayer, poor as it is, firmly trusting that our Lord in His mercy will make it good and profitable, more than you know or feel. For remember that your good intention is accepted in discharge of your duty, and will be rewarded like any other good deed done in charity, even though your mind was distracted when you did it. Therefore do your duty, and allow our Lord to do what He will; do not try to teach Him his part. And although you know yourself to be thoughtless and negligent, yet for this, as well as for all venial sins that cannot be avoided in this wretched life, lift up your heart to God, acknowledge your sinfulness, and plead for mercy with firm trust in His forgiveness. Give up struggling against yourself, and do not worry about it any longer, as though you could force yourself not to have these feelings. Leave your prayer and turn to some other good occupation, either spiritual or physical, and resolve to do better another time. Although you fail another time in the same way – even a hundred or a thousand times – yet do as I have said, and all will be well. Furthermore, a soul who never finds peace of heart in prayer but has to struggle against distracting and troublesome thoughts all her life, provided that she keeps herself in humility and charity in other ways, shall receive full reward in heaven for all her trouble.

CHAPTER 34: *On meditation for sinners after they have turned wholly to God*

I WILL now tell you a little about meditation. You must understand that in meditation no fixed rule can be laid down for everybody to keep. It is the free gift of God, and depends upon the varying dispositions and states of chosen souls. And as they grow in virtue and reach a higher state, God increases their spiritual knowledge and love of Himself through their meditation. For it is apparent that one who makes little advance in the knowledge of God and spiritual things makes little advance in the love of God. This is clearly seen in the case of the Apostles; for, when they were filled with burning love by the Holy Spirit on the Day of Pentecost, they were not made foolish, but were endowed with wisdom as great as man may have in this life, which enabled them both to know and to speak of God and spiritual things. Holy Scripture says of them: *Repleti sunt omnes Spiritu sancto, et coeperunt loqui magnalia Dei* (Acts ii, 4). 'They were all filled with the Holy Spirit, and began to proclaim the great wonders of God.' And all this knowledge was granted them in an ecstasy of love by the Holy Spirit.

There are various meditations that God puts into a man's heart. Some of these I shall describe to you, so that if you experience any of them you may take better advantage of them. At the beginning of his conversion, a man who has been tainted by worldly and bodily sins usually thinks mostly on his sins. He feels great compunction and heartfelt sorrow for them, with grief and tears, humbly and urgently asking God's mercy and forgiveness for them. If he is deeply touched by contrition because God desires to cleanse him swiftly, his sins will always remain before him, so that he can hardly endure the burden of them. And however full a confession he makes, he will still feel his conscience pricking and tormenting him, so that he thinks that he has not received full absolution for them. He can hardly rest, and could not endure such agony of mind did not God of His mercy grant him comfort at times by giving him feelings of great devotion to the Passion or some such thing. In this way God works in some men's hearts in greater or less degree as He wills it. And God's great mercy consists in this; that He will not only forgive the guilt of sin, but will remit its punishment in purgatory for a little pain and remorse of conscience here. Also, if God wishes to dispose a person to receive any special gift of the love of God, he must first be purged and cleansed by experiencing the fire of compunction for all the great sins that he has committed. David speaks of this trial of purification in many places in the psalms, and especially in the psalm *Miserere mei Deus, secundum magnam misericordiam tuam* (Ps. l, 1).

CHAPTER 35: *That meditation on the humanity and passion of Christ is given by God, and how one may recognize it when given*

AFTER this trial, and sometimes during it, our Lord gives to such a person – or to one who by the grace of God has preserved his innocence – a meditation on His humanity; this may be on His birth or passion, or on the compassion of our Lady Saint Mary. When this meditation is inspired by the Holy Spirit it is most valuable and consoling, and you may recognize it by this sign : when you are moved to meditate on God, your mind is suddenly withdrawn from all worldly and material things, and you seem to see our Lord Jesus in your soul in bodily form as He lived upon earth. You see Him taken by the Jews and bound as a thief, beaten and despised, scourged and condemned to death. You see with what humility He bore the cross on His back, and with what cruelty He was nailed to it. You see the crown of thorns on His head, and the sharp spear that pierced Him to the heart. At this sight you feel your heart stirred to such compassion and pity towards your Lord Jesus that you mourn, weep, and cry out with every power of body and soul, marvelling at the goodness and love, patience and humility of your Lord Jesus, who was willing to suffer such pain for so sinful and wretched a creature as yourself. At the same time you feel the goodness and mercy of our Lord so strongly that your heart leaps for joy and love of Him, and you shed many sweet tears, having a sure trust in the forgiveness of your sins and the salvation of your soul through the merits of His precious passion. Therefore, when the remembrance of Christ's Passion or of any other event in His earthly life comes to your mind in a spiritual vision of this kind, accompanied by devout love, you may feel certain that it is not the result of your own imagination or the deception of a wicked spirit, but comes by the grace of the Holy Spirit, and is sent to open your spiritual perception to the humanity of Christ. Saint Bernard calls it the natural love of God, inasmuch as it is directed towards the human nature of Christ. It is an excellent gift, for it helps to destroy grave sins and implant virtues, and leads in time to the contemplation of the Godhead. For a person cannot come to have spiritual delight in the contemplation of Christ's divinity until he first constantly considers His manhood with sorrow and compassion. Saint Paul did this, saying first: *Nihil judicavi me scire inter vos, nisi Jesum Christum, et hunc crucifixum* (1 Cor. ii, 2). I showed you nothing at all save Jesus Christ and Him crucified. Which is as though he had said: My knowledge and my trust is in the Passion of Christ alone. Therefore he said also: *Mihi autem absit gloriari, nisi in cruce Domini nostri Jesu Christi* (Gal. vi, 14). Far be from me all manner of joy and delight save in the cross and Passion of our Lord Jesus Christ. Nevertheless he said afterwards: *Praedicamus vobis Christum, Dei virtutem et Dei sapientiam* (1 Cor. i, 23): meaning, First I preached the humanity and Passion of Christ; now I preach to you His divinity. That is, Christ the power of God and the endless wisdom of God.

CHAPTER 36: *That for various reasons, meditation on Christ's passion is often withdrawn from those to whom it has been given*

ONE cannot always have this kind of meditation at will, but only when our Lord wills to give it. To some men and women He gives it throughout their lives whenever He visits them, for some are so tender in their affections that when they hear others speak of Christ's precious Passion, or when they think on it themselves, their hearts melt with devotion, and they are refreshed and strengthened against all temptations of the devil. This is a great gift of God. To others He at first gives it freely, and afterwards withdraws it for various reasons; if, for instance, a man falls into pride because of it, or commits some other sin which makes him unable to receive this grace. Or else our Lord may withdraw it and all other devout feelings from a person to allow him to be tried by the temptations of the devil. By this means He will lead him towards a more spiritual knowledge and perception of Himself. For He himself said to His disciples : *Expedit vobis ut ego vadam; si autem non abiero, Paracletus non veniet ad vos* (S. John xvi, 7). It is expedient for you that I withdraw My bodily presence from you, for if I do not, the Holy Spirit cannot come to you. For so long as He was with them they loved Him deeply, but it was with a natural love for His humanity. It was therefore desirable that He should withdraw His bodily form from their sight, so that the Holy Spirit might come and teach them to love and know Him in a more spiritual way, as He did on the Day of Pentecost. In the same way, it is for the good of some that our Lord should withdraw his bodily likeness somewhat from the eyes of the soul, so that the heart may devote itself with greater zeal to desire and seek Him in His divinity.

CHAPTER 37 : *On the various temptations of the devil*

NEVERTHELESS a man must first suffer many temptations, and through the malice of the devil these temptations often assail men and women in various ways whenever consolation has been withdrawn. For instance, when the devil perceives that devotion has been withdrawn from a soul, leaving it as it were exposed for a while, he sometimes sends such violent and consuming temptations to impurity or greed that those so afflicted think that they have never experienced such grievous temptations in their lives, even when they gave themselves most to sin. So strong are these temptations that they think it impossible to endure and resist them for long, and they are certain to yield unless they have help. Consequently they are greatly distressed both by the lack of comfort and devotion that they once enjoyed, and also by the fear of falling away from God by such open sins. And by God's permission the devil does this to them to make them abandon their good intention and return to their former sin. But if a person will stand firm awhile, endure a little trouble, and utterly refuse to return to sin under any circumstances, our Lord is very near him and will soon bring him help. For God will keep him in safety, although he knows not how. As the prophet David said in the person of our Lord: *Cum ipso sum in tribulatione, eripiam eum et glorificabo eum* (Ps. xci, 15). I am with him in trouble, and in temptation I will deliver him, and will make him glorious in My joy. The devil maliciously tempts some people with spiritual sins, such as doubts about the Faith, or about the Sacrament of the Lord's Body: also with despair, or blasphemy against our Lord or His Saints, or loathing of life, or bitterness and unreasonable depression, or with undue concern about themselves and their bodily needs if they devote themselves wholly to God's service. He tempts others – especially men and women who lead the solitary life – with fears and horrible fancies, either in bodily shape or in the imagination, both in sleeping and waking, and he so vexes them that they can hardly obtain rest. He also tempts them in many other ways too numerous for me to mention.

CHAPTER 38: *On various remedies against temptations of the devil*

THE first remedy for those who are troubled in these or other ways is to put their whole trust in our Lord Jesus Christ, and often to recall His Passion and the pains that He suffered for us. Then they should understand that all the trouble and sorrow that they endure in such temptations – when it seems to an uninstructed person that God has forsaken him – is not a sign that He is reproving or forsaking them, but is a trial sent for their amendment. Its purpose may be to purge their former sins, to increase their merit, or to prepare them to receive great grace if they will only endure and stand firm awhile, and never of their own choice return to their sin. Another remedy is that they must not fear, nor regard as sin, or take to heart any evil impulses to sin or blasphemy, or doubts about the Sacrament, or any other such ugly temptations; for to experience these temptations defiles the soul no more than the bark of a dog or the bite of a flea. They trouble the soul but do not harm it provided a man puts them aside and ignores them. It does no good to struggle against them, or to try and master them by force, for the more a person struggles against them, the more persistent they become. Therefore turn your mind away from them as best you can, and direct it to some other occupation. Should they still persist, it is best not to get impatient or discouraged, but to bear them with a sure trust in God, just as you would bear a physical pain or chastisement sent by God to purge your sins. Bear them as long as He wills for love of Him who was scourged and bore the cross for love of you. In addition, it is good to open your heart to some wise man before they take firm root; abandon your own judgement, and follow his advice. But do not be in a hurry to discuss these matters with an inexperienced or worldly person who has never felt such temptation, for he might easily reduce a simple soul to despair through his ignorance. For the consolation of those who are tempted in these ways, and who think themselves forsaken and forgotten by God, our Lord says through His prophet: *In modico dereliqui te, et in momento indignationis meae percussi te, et in miserationibus meis multis congregabo te* (Isa. liv, 7). For a little while I forsook you – that is to say, I allowed you to be troubled a little – and in a moment of wrath I smote you; that is, all the penance and pain that you suffer here is but a moment of My wrath compared to the pain of hell or purgatory. Yet in My manifold mercies I will gather you to Me; that is, when you think yourself forsaken, then in My great mercy I will gather you to Me again. For when you think that you are lost, our Lord will come to your help, as Job says: *Cum te consumptum putaveris, orieris ut lucifer et habebis fiduciam* (Job xi, 17). That is to say, When you are brought so low by the assault of temptation that you think there is no help or comfort to be had, and that you are utterly defeated, still stand firm in hope and pray to God. You shall suddenly rise up in gladness like the morning star, and as Job said, have a sure trust in God.

CHAPTER 39: *How God allows His chosen to be tried and tempted, and afterwards comforts them and establishes them in grace*

To comfort such people so that they may not despair, the wise man says of our Lord: *In tentatione ambulet cum eo. In primis elegit eum. Timorem, et metum, et approbationem inducet super illum; et cruciabit illum in tribulatione doctrinae suae, donec tentet illum in cogitationibus suis, et credat animae illius. Et iter directum adducet ad illum, et firmabit illum, et laetificabit illum; et denudabit abscondita sua illi, et thesaurizabit super illum scientiam et intellectum justitiae* (Ecclus. iv, 18–21). In other words, the wise man wishes no one to despair in temptation, and says to comfort him: our Lord does not forsake a man in temptation, but walks with him from the beginning to the end. For he says that He first chooses him – this is when He draws a man to Him by the comfort of devotion – and afterwards brings on him sorrow, fear and testing – this is when He withdraws devotion and allows him to be tempted. He also says that He tries him with tribulation until He has thoroughly tested him in his thoughts, and until a man will place his whole trust in Him. After this our Lord leads him out into the right way, holds him fast to Himself, and gives him joy. Then He reveals His secrets to him, and gives him His treasure of knowledge and right understanding.

Through these words of Holy Scripture you may see that these and any other temptations, however troublesome, are necessary and profitable to anyone who is firmly resolved by God's grace to forsake sin. But he must endure them as best he may and abide God's will, refusing to return to the sins he has forsaken whatever the sorrow, pain, or fear of temptation. He must always stand firm in the struggle, and pray with trust and hope. Our Lord of His infinite goodness, who has pity and mercy on all His creatures, will in His own time lay to His hand and strike down the devil and all his power. He eases them of their trouble, and puts away the fear, sorrow, and darkness out of their hearts. He brings into their souls the light of grace, and opens their inward vision to see that all their trials were profitable. He also gives them new spiritual strength to withstand with ease all the efforts of the devil and all deadly sins, and leads them into the ways of good and holy living. If they are humble, He preserves them in these ways to the end, and then receives them wholly to Himself. So I repeat: if you are troubled and beset by any of these temptations do not be afraid. Do as I have said, and better if you can, and I trust that by the grace of Jesus Christ you will never be overcome by your enemy.

CHAPTER 40: *That a man should not yield to idleness, or neglect the grace given him by God*

AFTER you have escaped from such temptations, or if God has kept you from being overmuch distressed by them — as in His mercy He has kept many — then it is good that you should not allow your peace to degenerate into inactivity, for there are many who allow themselves to relax too soon. If you are willing, you can begin a new exercise and endeavour, which is to examine your own soul by means of meditation in order to learn its true nature, and by this means come to the spiritual knowledge of God. For Saint Augustine says: By knowing myself I shall come to the knowledge of God. I do not say that it is essential or obligatory for you or anyone else to attempt this, unless he feels moved and and called to it by grace. For our Lord gives various gifts as He wills, not all to one person or one to all, with the exception of charity, which is common to all. Therefore if a man or woman has received some particular gift from God, such as devotion in prayer or to the Passion of Christ, or any other gift however small, let him not leave it too soon for any other unless he feels sure that the other is better; but let him hold to what he has and labour steadfastly in it, desiring always a better when God will give it. Nevertheless, if after a while this gift is withdrawn and he sees a better to which his heart feels drawn, then it would seem that God is calling him to the better. Let him then set himself to acquire and develop it as fully as he can.

CHAPTER 41: *That everyone should know the extent of his own gift, and always desire a better, so that he can accept it when God wills to give it*

THE holy fathers in years gone by have taught us that we should know the extent of our gift and labour to perfect it, without pretending to have more than we know ourselves to possess. We may always desire the best gifts, but we may not always obtain them, because we have not yet received the grace necessary for them. A hound that only runs after the hare because he sees other hounds run rests when he is tired or returns home. But if he runs because he sees the hare, he will not stop until he has caught it, tired though he may be. Our spiritual progress is very similar. Whoever has some grace, however small, and wilfully neglects to develop it, but sets himself to obtain some other grace that he has not yet been granted merely because he sees or hears that other people possess it, may indeed run for a while until he is weary, but will then return home again. And unless he is careful, he may in consequence injure his powers before he gets home. But whoever uses such grace as he has, and aspires after greater grace with humble and constant prayer, provided he remains humble, may safely pursue his quest once he feels moved to follow after the grace which he desired. Therefore desire from God as strongly as you may, without measure or discretion, all that belongs to His love and to the joy of heaven; for whoever desires most of God will receive most from Him. Do your utmost, and ask God's mercy for whatever you cannot do. Saint Paul seems to refer to this when he says: *Unusquisque habet donum suum ex Deo, alius autem sic, alius vero sic* (I Cor. vii, 7). *Item unicuique nostrum data est gratia secundum mensuram donationis Christi* (Eph. iv, 7). *Divisiones gratiarum sunt, alii datur sermo sapientiae; alii sermo scientiae* (I Cor. xii, 4–8). *Item ut sciamus quae a Deo donata sunt nobis* (I Cor. ii, 12). Saint Paul says that each man has his gift from God, one man this, another that. For to each man who will be saved is given grace according to the measure of Christ's gift. We therefore need to know the gifts given us by God, so that we may use them, for by these we shall be saved. For some by corporal works and acts of mercy, some by severe bodily penance, some by lifelong sorrow and penitence, some by preaching and teaching, and some by different graces and gifts of devotion will be saved and come to the bliss of heaven.

CHAPTER 42: *That a man should study to know his own soul and its powers, and to destroy the roots of sin in it*

Nevertheless, there is one work in which it is both very necessary and helpful to engage, and which – so far as human efforts are concerned – is a highway leading to contemplation. This is for a person to enter into himself, and to understand his own soul with all its powers, virtues, and sins. In this interior examination you will come to recognize the honour and dignity proper to the soul at its creation, and the wretchedness and error into which you have fallen through sin. This realization will bring with it a heartfelt desire to recover the dignity and honour which you have lost. You will be filled with disgust and contempt for yourself, and with a firm resolve to humble yourself and to destroy everything that stands between you and that dignity and joy. Those who wish to make rapid progress in this task will at first find it hard and painful, for it is a conflict in the soul against the root of all sins great and small, and this is nothing other than a false and misplaced love of self. From this love, as Saint Augustine says, springs every kind of sin, both mortal and venial. Indeed, until this root is completely dug up and exposed, and as it were almost dried up by the casting out of all loves and fears of the world and the flesh, the soul can never experience the burning love of Jesus Christ. It cannot enjoy the closeness of His gracious presence, nor can its understanding be opened to a clear insight into spiritual things. This task, however, is necessary if a person is to detach his heart and mind from the love of all earthly things, from vain thoughts, and from material considerations, and from misplaced love of self, so that his soul may find no satisfaction in them. Then, in so far as the soul cannot find its satisfaction in the love and sight of Jesus Christ, it is bound to

48

suffer pain. This task is difficult and arduous to a degree; nevertheless, I am sure that it is the way which Christ teaches in the Gospel to those who wish to love Him perfectly, saying: *Contendite intrare per angustam portam; quia arcta est via quae ducit ad vitam, et pauci inveniunt eam* (Matt. vii, 14). Strive to enter by the narrow gate, for the way that leads to heaven is narrow, and few men find it. And how narrow this way is our Lord tells us in another place: *Si quis vult veniere post me, abneget semetipsum, et tollat crucem suam, et sequatur me* (Matt. xvi, 24). *Item qui odit animam suam in hoc mundo, in vitam aeternam custodit eam* (John xii, 25). That is to say: Whoever wishes to follow Me, let him forsake himself and hate his own soul. In other words, forsake all worldly love and hate his own bodily life and the vain desires of his bodily senses for love of Me. And let him take the cross – that is, suffer the pain of this world awhile – and then follow Me in the contemplation of My humanity and My divinity. This way is so strait and narrow that no earthly thing may pass through it, for it demands the slaying of all sin. As Saint Paul says: *Mortificate membra vestra quae sunt super terram, immunditiam, libidinem, concupiscientiam malam* (Col. iii, 5). Slay your earthly members – not the bodily members, but those of the soul – such as impurity, lust, and immoderate love of self and earthly things. Therefore, as your efforts hitherto have been to withstand grave material sins and open temptations of the devil, which originate outside yourself, you must now undertake this spiritual task within yourself, and, so far as you are able, destroy and break up the roots of sin in yourself. I will now give you what advice I can, so that you may more readily bring this about.

CHAPTER 43 : *How a man should know the high estate and dignity first given to his soul by God, and the wretched misfortune into which it has fallen by sin*

THE soul of man is a life consisting of three powers, memory, understanding, and will. It is made in the image and likeness of the blessed Trinity, whole, perfect, and righteous. For the mind was created strong and steadfast by the virtue of the Father, so that it might hold fast to Him, neither forgetting Him nor being distracted and hindered by created things; and so it has the likeness of the Father. The understanding was made clear and bright, without error or obscurity, and as perfect as might be in a body not glorified; and so it has the likeness of the Son, Who is eternal Wisdom. The will and its affections was made pure, rising like a flame towards God without love of the flesh or of any creatures, by the sovereign goodness of God the Holy Spirit; and so it has the likeness of the Holy Spirit, Who is holy Love. So man's soul, which may be called a created trinity, was made complete in the mind, sight, and love of the uncreated and blessed Trinity, Who is God. This is the dignity and honourable state natural to man's soul at its creation. This state was yours in Adam before man's first sin; but when Adam sinned, choosing to love and delight in himself and in creatures, he lost all his honour and dignity, and you also in him, and he fell from that blessed Trinity into a vile, dark, and wretched trinity : that is, into forgetfulness and ignorance of God, and into a debasing and deliberate love of himself. For as David says in the psalms : *Homo, cum in honore esset, non intellexit; comparatus est jumentis insipientibus, et similis factus est illis* (Ps. xlix, 20). When man had honour he did not know it; therefore he lost it and became like a beast. See, then, the present wretched plight of your soul. Your mind, once firmly fixed on God, has now forgotten Him and tries to find satisfaction in creatures, first in one and then another; but it can never find true peace, because it has lost Him in whom alone true peace may be found. Your will also, once pure, taking a joy and delight in spiritual things, has now turned to a degraded love of self, of creatures, and of material pleasures. As a result your senses are corrupted by greed and impurity, and your mind by pride, vainglory, and covet-ousness. So deep is this corruption that you can hardly do any-thing good without being tainted by vainglory; and you can scarcely direct any of your senses to some desirable object with-out your heart becoming obsessed and inflamed by a vain desire to possess it. This drives from your heart and makes impossible all spiritual experience of, and desire for, the love of God. Everyone who lives by the spirit knows this well. It is the spiritual misery and mischief caused by man's first sin, to say nothing of all the other wickedness and sin that you have deliberately added to it. And remember, that even though you had never committed a venial or mortal sin, but had only inherited the guilt of original sin – so called because it is the first sin, and is nothing other than the loss of the righteous state in which you were created – you would never have been saved unless our Lord Jesus Christ had delivered and restored you again by His precious Passion.

CHAPTER 44: *How every person, however sinful, may be saved by the Passion of Christ if he ask it*

IF you think that I have been proposing too high a standard, and that you cannot undertake or carry it out, I will now come down to as simple a level as you wish, both for your profit and my own. But I say this, that however vile a wretch you may be, and however great the sins that you have com-mitted, forget yourself and all that you have done, both good and bad. Ask for mercy with humility and trust, and seek salvation through the virtue of Christ's precious Passion : you will undoubtedly receive it, and will be saved both from original sin and from all other. This applies not only to you, an enclosed anchoress, but to all other Christian souls who trust in the Passion and humbly acknowledge their wretchedness, asking mercy and forgiveness through the merits of Christ's Passion alone, and humbly approaching the Sacraments of Holy Church. Even though they have borne the burden of their sins all their lives, and never tasted the sweetness of supernatural joy or had any spiritual knowledge of God, yet if they have faith and goodwill, they will be saved through the merits of the most precious Passion of our Lord Jesus Christ, and come to the joys of heaven.

All this you know well, but it delights me to speak of it, that you may see the endless mercy of our Lord, and how low He stoops to you, and to me, and to all poor sinners. Ask his mercy, then, and you will receive it. For as the prophet said in the person of our Lord : *Omnis enim qui invocaverit nomen Domini salvus erit.* Let everyone, whoever he may be, call on the Name of God – that is, ask salvation through Jesus and His Passion – and he shall be saved. Some people understand the charity of our Lord and are saved by it ; others, relying on this mercy and kindness, continue in their sins, thinking that it may be theirs whenever they wish. But this is not so, for then they are too late and are taken in their sins before they expect it, and so damn themselves.

But you may say : 'If this is true, then I am very surprised at what I find written in the books of some holy men. For I understand some to say that one who cannot love the blessed Name of Jesus in this life, or find great spiritual joy and delight in it, will be excluded from the supreme joy and happiness of heaven, and will never attain it. When I read such words they astonish and alarm me, for I hope that, as you say, by the mercy of God many will be saved by keeping God's commandments and by true repentance for their past sinfulness, although they may never have felt any spiritual sweetness or inward delight in the Name of Jesus or in His love. I am therefore the more surprised that these books seem to state the contrary.' My answer to this is that, rightly understood, what they say is true, and is not contrary to what I have said. For in English the Name of Jesus means nothing other than *health* or *healer*. Now in this life of sorrow every man is spiritually sick, for no man lives without sin, which is spiritual sickness. As Saint John says of himself and others made perfect: *Si dixerimus quia peccatum non habemus, ipsi nos seducimus, et veritas in nobis non est* (1 John i, 8). If we say that we have no sin, we deceive ourselves, and the truth is not in us. Therefore no one can come to the joys of heaven until he is first healed of this spiritual sickness. But no one with the use of reason can have this spiritual health until he desires it, loves it, delights in it, and hopes to have it. Now the Name of Jesus is none other than this spiritual health; therefore they speak the truth when they say that no one can be saved who does not love and delight in the Name of Jesus, since no one can have health of soul unless he loves and desires it. If a man were sick in body, nothing on earth would be so necessary and desirable to him as bodily health; for although you were to give him all the riches and honours in the world without health – were this in your power – you would not give him any pleasure. It is just the same with a man who is sick in soul and suffers the pain of spiritual sickness. Nothing is so dear to him, or so necessary and desirable to him, as spiritual health. And this is Jesus, for without Him all the joys of heaven cannot satisfy him.

I think this is why our Lord, when He became man for our salvation, did not wish to be called by any name that signified His eternal Being, His power, His wisdom, or His holiness, but only by one that signified the purpose of His coming, which was the salvation of man's soul; for this salvation was most dear and most necessary to man. And the Name of Jesus signifies this salvation. Hence it seems true that no one will be saved unless he loves salvation and hopes to have it through the mercy of our Lord Jesus and by the merits of His Passion.

One who lives and dies in the lowest degree of charity may have this love. On the other hand, one who cannot love this blessed Name of Jesus with spiritual delight or enjoy its heavenly melody in this life will never have or experience the fulness of supreme joy possessed in heaven by one who in this life delighted in Jesus in the abundance of perfect charity. So the statement of these writers may be understood. Nevertheless, one who in this life possesses only the lowest degree of charity and keeps God's commandments shall be saved and have his full reward in the sight of God; for our Lord Himself says: *In domo Patris Mei multae mansiones sunt* (S. John xiv, 2). In My Father's house there are many different dwellings. Some are for perfect souls who in this life were filled with charity and the grace of the Holy Spirit, and sang the praises of God in contemplation with wonderful sweetness and heavenly delight. These souls will have the highest reward in the joys of heaven because their charity was greatest, and they may be called the intimate friends of God. Other souls, who are not called to the contemplation of God, and do not have the fulness of charity possessed by the Apostles and martyrs in the early years of the Church, will have a lesser reward in the joys of heaven, and may be called the friends of God. In Holy Scripture God calls them chosen souls, saying: *Comedite, amici, et inebriamini, carissimi* (Cant. v, 1). Eat, my friends, and drink deep, my best-beloved. As though our Lord had said: You who are My friends, because you kept My commandments and placed love of Me before love of the world, and loved Me above all earthly things, shall be fed with the spiritual food of the bread of life. But you who are My beloved, who not only kept My commandments, but also of your own free choice carried out My will, and furthermore loved Me solely and entirely with all the strength of your souls, burning with My love – in the same way as the Apostles, martyrs, and all other souls who by My grace received the grace of perfection – shall drink deep of the richest and best wine in My cellar, which is the supreme joy of love in the bliss of heaven.

CHAPTER 45: *That we should strive to recover our nobility, and restore the likeness of the Trinity within ourselves*

NEVERTHELESS, although this is the truth concerning God's infinite mercy towards you and me and all mankind, we should not therefore presume upon it and be wilfully reckless in our way of living. For now that we may hope to be restored by the Passion of our Lord to the dignity and happiness which we lost through Adam's sin, we should be all the more eager to please Him. And although we may never attain it in this life, we should desire to recover some degree and likeness of that dignity, so that the soul may be re-formed by grace to a shadow of the image of the Trinity which it once had by nature, and which it will have fully in heaven. This is the true life of contemplation, which has its beginning here in this feeling of love and in the spiritual knowledge of God, which comes when the eyes of the soul are opened. This life will never be lost or taken away from us, but will be perfected on another plane in the joys of heaven. Our Lord promised this to Mary Magdalene, who was a contemplative, when He said to her: *Maria optimam partem elegit, quae non auferetur ab ea* (Luke x, 42). Mary has chosen the best part – that is, the love of God in contemplation – for it shall never be taken away from her. I do not say that you may in this life recover such entire and perfect purity and innocence, knowledge and love of God, as you had at first or shall have in the life to come. Nor do I say that you can escape all the sorrows and penalties of sin, nor that in this life you can wholly destroy and overcome false, vain self-love, or avoid all venial sins. For these will always well up in your heart like water from an impure spring, unless they are stopped by great and fervent charity. But if you may not entirely overcome them, strive to reduce them somewhat, and come as near to purity of soul as you can. For God assured the children of Israel when He led them into the land of promise, and figuratively all Christians, saying: *Omnis locus, quem calcaverit pes tuus, tuus erit* (Deut. xi, 24). That is to say, as much land as you may tread upon with the foot of true desire shall be yours in the land of promise – that is, in the joy of heaven – when you enter it.

CHAPTER 46: *How Jesus is to be sought, desired, and found*

SEEK then what you have lost, so that you may find it. I am convinced that anyone who could once have a little insight into the spiritual dignity and beauty which belong to the soul by nature, and which it may regain by grace, would loathe and despise all the joy, love, and beauty of the world as he would the stench of corruption. But for the frailty and essential needs of bodily nature, his sole desire night and day would be to long, lament, pray, and seek how he might regain it once more. Nevertheless, since you have not yet seen fully what it is, because the eyes of your soul are not opened, I know well one word in which is found all that you can seek, desire, and find, for in that word is all that you have lost. This word is JESUS. I do not mean this word Jesus as it might be painted on a wall, or written in a book, or spoken by the lips, or pictured inwardly by the workings of your mind, for in these ways a man without charity may find Him. I mean Jesus Christ the blessed One, God and Man, son of the Virgin Mary, whom this name expresses, and Who is all goodness, endless wisdom, love, and sweetness; your joy and your worship, your everlasting happiness, your God, your Lord, and your salvation.

If, then, you feel a great longing in your heart for Jesus – either by the remembrance of His Name Jesus, or of any other word, prayer, or deed – and if this longing is so strong that its force drives out of your heart all other thoughts and desires of the world and the flesh, then you are indeed seeking your Lord Jesus. And if, when you feel this desire for God, for Jesus – for it is all one – you are helped and strengthened by a supernatural might so strong that it is changed into love and affection, spiritual savour and sweetness and knowledge of truth, so that for the time your mind is set on no created thing, nor on any feeling or stirring of vainglory nor self-love nor any other evil affections (for these cannot appear at such a time) so that you are enclosed in Jesus alone, resting in Him with the warmth of tender love, then you have found something of Jesus. Not Jesus as He is, but an inward sight of Him; and the more fully you find Him, the more you will desire Him. So whatever form of prayer, meditation, or activity leads you to the highest and purest desire for Him, and to the deepest experience of Him, will be the means by which you may best seek and find Him. Therefore, if you will consider what you have lost and what you seek, life up your mind and heartfelt desire to Jesus Christ, even though you are blind and can see nothing of His Godhead. Say to yourself that it is He whom you have lost, and He alone whom you desire to have, that you may be with Him where He is, since there is no other joy, no other bliss in heaven or in earth except in Him. And even though you feel His nearness through the gift of devotion or knowledge or in any other way, do not rest content with this feeling as though you had fully found Jesus. Forget what you have found, and always desire Jesus more and more, so that you may find Him more fully, as though you had so far found nothing. For consider this, that however great your experience of Him may be – even though you were carried up in spirit to the third heaven like Saint Paul* – you have not yet known Jesus as He is in His glory. However deep your knowledge and experience of Him, He utterly transcends it. Therefore, if you wish to find Him as He is in the realms of love and joy, let your soul never cease to long for Him in this present life.

CHAPTER 47 : *How profitable it is to have the desire for Jesus*

I WOULD rather feel in my heart a true and pure desire for my Lord Jesus Christ, although I had very little spiritual knowledge of Him, than perform all the bodily penances of all men living, or enjoy visions and revelations of angels, hear sweet sounds, or experience any other pleasurable outward sensations were they unaccompanied by this desire. In short, all the joys of heaven and earth would have no attraction for me unless I might also have this desire for Jesus. I think that the prophet David felt this when he wrote : *Quid enim mihi est in caelo? et a te quid volui super terram?* (Ps. lxxiii, 23). Lord, what have I in heaven but Thee? And what can I desire on earth but Thee? As though he had said : Lord Jesus, what heavenly joy can satisfy me, unless I desire Thee while I am on earth, and love Thee when I come to heaven? Meaning, none indeed! Therefore, if you wish to have any inward knowledge of Him, whether in body or soul, seek nothing but an earnest desire for His grace and His merciful presence, and recognize that your heart can find no satisfaction in anything outside Him. This was David's desire, when he said : *Concupivit anima mea desiderare justificationes tuas in omni tempore* (Ps. cxix, 20). Lord, my soul longed for the desire of Thy righteousness. Therefore seek desire by desire, as David did. And if in your prayers and meditations

* II Cor. xii, 2.

your desire leads you to feel the inward presence of Jesus Christ in your soul, hold firmly to it in your heart so that you do not lose it: then if you should fall, you may soon find Him again.

Therefore seek Jesus whom you have lost. He wishes to be sought, and longs to be found, for He Himself says: *Omnis qui quaerit, invenit* (Matt. vii, 8). Every one who seeks shall find. The search is arduous, but the finding is full of joy. Therefore if you wish to find Him, follow the counsel of the wise man, who said: *Si quaesieris quasi pecuniam sapientiam, et sicut thesauros effodieris illum: tunc intelliges timorem Domini, et scientiam Dei invenies* (Prov. ii, 4). If you seek wisdom – which is Jesus – like silver and gold, and dig deep for it, you shall find it. You must dig deep in your heart, for He is hidden there, and you must cast out utterly all love and desire of earthly things, and all sorrows and fears with regard to them. In this way you shall find Jesus the true Wisdom.

CHAPTER 48: *Where and how Jesus is to be sought and found*

Be like the woman in the Gospel, of whom our Lord said: *Quae mulier habens drachmas decem, si perdiderit unam, nonne accendit lucernam, et everrit domum suam, et quaerit diligenter donec inveniat eam? Et cum invenerit, convocat amicos suos, dicens: Congratulamini mihi, quia inveni drachmam quam perdideram* (Luke xv, 8). What woman is there who will not light a lamp, and turn her house upside down, and search until she finds it? Implying: none. And when she has found it, she calls her friends to her and says: Rejoice with me, for I have found the coin that I had lost. This coin is Jesus, whom you have lost: if you wish to find Him, light the lamp of God's word. As David says: *Lucerna pedibus meis verbum tuum* (Ps. cxix, 105). Lord, Thy word is a lamp to my feet. By this lamp you will see where He is, and how you may find Him. You may light another lamp if you wish, which is your reason, for our Lord says: *Lucerna corporis tui oculus tuus* (Matt. vi, 22). The light of your body is the eye. Similarly it may be said that the lamp of the soul is the reason, by which the soul may come to see all spiritual things. With this lamp you will certainly find Jesus if you hold it up from underneath the measure. As our Lord says: *Nemo accendit lucernam et ponit eam sub modio, sed super candelabrum* (Matt. v, 15). No one lights a lamp in order to set it under a measure, but on a lampstand: that is to say, your mind must not be engrossed in worldly activities, useless thoughts, and earthly desires, but must always aspire above all earthly things to the inward vision of Jesus Christ. If you do this, you will see all the dust, dirt, and small blemishes in your house, that is, all the worldly loves and fears within your soul. Yet not all, for as David says: *Delicta quis intelligit?* (Ps. xix, 12). Who may know all his sin? Meaning, no one. Cast out all these sins from your heart, sweep your soul clean with the broom of the fear of God, wash it with your tears, and you shall find your coin, Jesus. He is the coin, He is the penny, and He is your heritage. It is easier to describe this coin than to find it, for the search is not the work of an hour or a day, but of many days and years, and it demands both bodily toil and spiritual effort. But if you do not give up, but search diligently, sorrow deeply, grieve silently, and humble yourself until tears of pain and anguish flow because you have lost Jesus your treasure: then at length and when He wills it you shall find Him. And if you find Him as I have said – that is, if you are able with a pure conscience to feel the close and peaceful presence of our blessed Lord Jesus Christ, given as a fore-shadowing and glimpse of Him as He is – then you may if you wish call your friends to sing and make merry with you because you have found your coin, Jesus.

CHAPTER 49 : *Where Jesus is lost, and through His mercy found again*

SEE now the courtesy and mercy of Jesus. You have lost Him. But where? In your own house; that is, in your soul. If you had lost Him outside your own house – that is, if you had lost the power of reason through original sin – you would never have found Him again. But He left you your reason, and so He is within your soul, and will never be lost outside it. Nevertheless you are no nearer to Him until you have found Him. He is within you, although He is lost to you; but you are not in Him until you have found Him. In this, too, is His mercy, that He would suffer Himself to be lost only where He may be found. There is no need to travel to Rome or Jerusalem to search for Him: but turn your thoughts into your own soul where He is hidden, and seek Him there. For as the prophet says: *Vere tu es deus absconditus* (Isa. xlv, 15). Truly, Lord, Thou art a hidden God. And Christ himself says in the Gospel: *Simile est regnum caelorum thesauro abscondito in agro; quem qui invenit homo, prae gaudio illius vadit, et vendit universa quae habet, et emit agrum illum* (Matt. xiii, 44). The kingdom of heaven is like a treasure hidden in a field, which when a man finds, for joy of it he goes and sells all that he has and buys that field. Jesus is the treasure hidden in your soul. If you could find Him in your soul, and your soul in Him, I am sure that you would gladly give up the love of all earthly things in order to have Him. Jesus sleeps spiritually in your heart as he once slept bodily in the ship with His disciples. But they, fearing to perish, awoke Him, and He quickly saved them from the tempest. Therefore rouse Him as they did by prayer, and wake Him with the loud cry of your desire, and He will quickly rise and help you.

CHAPTER 50: *The things that prevent our hearing and seeing Jesus within us*

NEVERTHELESS I expect that you are more often asleep when you should be calling on Him than He when you call, for He often calls you with His sweet secret voice, silently stirring your heart to leave all the clamour of worldly vanities in your soul that you may listen to Him alone. For David said of our Lord: *Audi, filia, et vide, et inclina aurem tuam, et obliviscere populum tuum et domum patris tui* (Ps. xlv, 10). Listen, daughter, and see; turn your ear to me, and forget the folk of your worldly thoughts, and the house of your natural affections. Here you may see how our Lord calls you and all others who will listen to Him. What hinders you, then, that you can neither see Him nor hear Him? Indeed, there is so much din and disturbance in your heart arising from foolish thoughts and bodily desires that you can neither hear Him nor see Him. Therefore put away all this restless noise, and break your love of sin and vanity; bring into your heart the love of virtues and true charity, and you will hear our Lord speak to you. For as long as He does not find His likeness re-formed in you, He remains a stranger and far distant from you.

CHAPTER 51: *That humility and charity are the especial livery of Jesus, through which man's soul is reformed to His likeness*

PREPARE yourself, therefore, to be clothed with His likeness – that is, in humility and charity which are His livery – and then He will admit you to His friendship and show you His secrets. He Himself said to His disciples: *Qui diligit me diligetur a Patre meo, et manifestabo ei meipsum* (John xiv, 21). Whoever

loves Me shall be loved by My Father, and I will show Myself
to him. There is no virtue that you can acquire or work that
you can do that will make you like our Lord without humility
and charity, for these two are God's especial livery. This is
clearly seen in the Gospel, where our Lord speaks of humility:
Discite a me, quia mitis sum et humilis corde. Learn of Me, He says,
not to go barefoot, or fast in the desert for forty days, or choose
disciples, but learn from Me humility, for I am gentle and humble of heart. And of charity He says: *Hoc est praeceptum meum;
ut diligatis invicem sicut dilexi vos. Item in hoc cognoscent homines
quia discipuli mei estis, si dilectionem habueritis ad invicem* (John xiii,
34). This is My commandment, that you love one another as I
have loved you; for in this shall men know you for My disciples.
Not because you work miracles, or cast out devils, or preach
and teach, but because each of you loves the other in charity.
If you will be like Him, be humble and loving. And charity
means that you must have a true love for your fellow-Christian.

CHAPTER 52: *How a man may recognize the origins of sin in
himself*

Now you have heard a little of what your soul is, its original
dignity, and how it lost it. I have also told you that this
dignity may in part be recovered and enjoyed again by grace
and by diligent effort. I shall now try to explain, however inadequately, how you may enter into yourself to recognize the
origin of sin and destroy it as completely as you can. By this
means you may recover some part of your dignity. For a time
you must abandon all physical activity and outward affairs as
far as possible. Then withdraw your thoughts from your bodily
senses, so that you pay no attention to what you hear, see, or
feel; for your heart must not be fixed on these things. After
this exclude from your mind all material images, and all thought

of your former activities and those of other people. This requires little interior discipline when you enjoy the grace of devotion; but you must also do this when you feel no devotion,
and this is very much harder. Direct your whole intention and
purpose to the Lord Jesus, desiring to seek, feel, or find nothing
except the grace and presence of Jesus. This requires great effort,
for vain thoughts throng into your mind to divert your attention to them. But if you keep Jesus Christ constantly in mind
you can withstand them, and if you do so, you will find something – not Jesus the object of your search, but the simple recollection of His Name. What else? Indeed, you will find nothing
but a dark and painful image of your own soul, which has
neither the light of the knowledge of God nor any love and
devotion to Him. This image, if you examine it carefully, is
entirely enveloped in the black cloak of sin – pride, anger,
spiritual indolence, covetousness, gluttony, and lust.

CHAPTER 53 : *The real nature of this image of sin*

THIS is not the image of Jesus, but the image of sin, which
Saint Paul calls the body of sin and the body of death
(Rom. vi, 6). You carry about this image and black shadow
with you wherever you go, and from it spring many streams
of sin, both great and small. In the same way, if the image of
Jesus were re-formed within you in beams of spiritual light,
there would rise heavenwards from it burning desires, pure
affections, wise thoughts, and all the noble virtues. So out of
this image spring movements of pride, envy, and other sins
which debase man's true nature to the level of the beasts.

But perhaps you are now beginning to wonder what this
image is like; and lest you should remain long in doubt, let me
tell you that it is nothing material. What is it then? you ask. In
reality it is nothing, and you may ascertain this if you will test

it as I have told you. Withdraw your thoughts from all material things, and you will find nothing in which your soul may rest. This 'nothing' is none else than darkness of mind, and lack of love and light, just as sin is nothing other than lack of God.

Were the roots of sin greatly reduced and dried up in you, and your soul rightly re-formed in the image of Jesus, then if you looked into your heart you would not find nothing. You would find Jesus, not the bare recollection of His Name, but Jesus Christ himself waiting to teach you. Through Him you would find the light of understanding, and not the darkness of ignorance. In Him you would find love and delight, and not the pangs of bitterness and sorrow. But because you are not yet re-formed, when your soul withdraws from all material things and finds nothing but darkness and depression, it seems a hundred years before it emerges again through some bodily pleasure or vain thought. This is not surprising, for if a man came home to his house and found nothing but a smoking fire and a nagging wife, he would quickly run out again. Similarly, when your soul finds no comfort within itself, but only the black smoke of spiritual blindness and a constant nagging by carnal thoughts which rob it of all peace, it is soon anxious to escape again. This is the darkness of mind and the dark image about which I have spoken.

CHAPTER 54: *Whoever wishes to find Jesus must be ready to fight in spiritual darkness against this image of sin*

NEVERTHELESS you must struggle and strive in this darkness of mind; that is, you must withdraw your thoughts from all material things as completely as you can. And then, when you find nothing but sorrow, pain, and blindness in this darkness, you must be patient and endure it awhile if you wish to find Jesus. And here you must take pains to keep Jesus Christ in your thoughts, constantly considering His Passion and His humility, and by His power your mind will surmount this darkness with fervent desire for God. Do not permit your thoughts to dwell on this 'nothing', but on Jesus Christ whom you desire: resolve to break down this 'nothing' and pass through it. You must dread and detest this darkness as you would the devil out of hell, for it hides Jesus and His joy from you. But all your seeking will not find Him unless you pass through this darkness of mind. This is the spiritual conflict that I spoke of, and the purpose of all my writing is to stir you to enter upon it if you feel the grace to do so.

This darkness of understanding and this 'nothing' of which I speak is the image of the first Adam. Saint Paul knew this well, for he said of it: *Sicut portavimus imaginem terreni hominis, ita portemus imaginem iam et caelestis* (1 Cor. xv, 49). As we have formerly borne the image of an earthly man, that is, the first Adam, so we may now bear the image of the heavenly man, who is Jesus, the second Adam. Saint Paul often found this image very heavy, for it was so burdensome to him that he cried out: *O quis me liberabit de corpore mortis?* (Rom. vii, 24). Oh, who will deliver me from this body and from the image of death? And then he comforted himself as well as others, saying: *Gratia Dei per Jesum Christum* (Rom. vii, 25). The grace of God through Jesus Christ.

Now I have told you a little about this image, and how it is nothing. However, if you cannot understand how I can rightly say that nothing can be an image – since nothing always remains nothing – I will try to elucidate my meaning. This image is a false and misguided love of self. From this love spring all kinds of sin in seven rivers. These are pride, envy, anger, spiritual indolence, covetousness, gluttony, and lust. This is something that you can experience for yourself, for every kind of sin flows out in one or other of these rivers. If the sin is mortal it destroys charity in you, and if venial it diminishes its fervour.

CHAPTER 55 : *The image of sin, and what flows from it*

Y O U can now see that this image is not nothing, for it is a great evil, it is a strong spring of self-love, from which flow these seven rivers as I have said. But you may say : 'How can this be true? I have forsaken the world, I am enclosed in a cell, and I have no dealings with others. I do not compete against them, I do not buy or sell, nor do I have any worldly business. By the mercy of God I keep myself pure, and have renounced worldly pleasures. Furthermore, I pray, keep vigils, and labour in body and in spirit as well as I can. How then can this image be so great in me as you say?' In reply I grant that you may do all these things and more, and I hope this is true. You make every effort to block the outflow of these rivers, but perhaps you are leaving their real source intact. You are like a man who had in his garden a contaminated well with many channels running from it. He went and blocked these channels but left the spring untouched, thinking that all was now safe. But the water sprung up at the bottom of the well and stood stagnant for so long that it ruined all the beauty of the garden, although no water flowed out. It may be the same with you, if by grace you have blocked the rivers of this spring from escaping. So far so good, but beware of the spring within. Unless you block it and cleanse it as thoroughly as you can, it will poison all the flowers in the garden of your soul, however lovely they may outwardly appear to those who see them.

But you may now ask: 'If I undertake this task, how shall I know when the spring is completely blocked?' I will therefore tell you how to determine whether this image exists within you and its extent, so that you may know how effectively or ineffectively its source has been stopped. And since pride is the principal river, I will deal with this first.

CHAPTER 56: *What pride is, and when it is sin*

ACCORDING to scholars, pride is nothing other than love of your own excellence; that is, of your own reputation. Therefore the more you love and delight in your own reputation, the greater is your pride, and the greater is this wicked image within you. If pride stirs in your heart, leading you to imagine yourself holier, wiser, better, and more virtuous than others, or that God has given you grace to serve Him better than others; or if you regard other men and women as inferior to yourself, and hold exaggerated opinions of your own excellence in comparison with others; or if as a result you feel complacent and self-satisfied, it is a sure sign that you bear this black image within you. And although it may be hidden from the eyes of other men, it appears clearly in the sight of God.

But you say that you cannot escape these stirrings of pride, for you often feel them against your will; therefore you do not hold them to be sin, or if sin, only venial. My reply to this is that merely to feel these stirrings of pride and such like is no sin, whether they spring from the corrupt influence of this evil image within you, or from the instigation of the devil. This is a grace and privilege granted by virtue of the Passion of Jesus Christ to all Christians baptized by water and the Holy Spirit: but for Jews and Moslems who do not believe in Christ all such stirrings are mortal sin.* For Saint Paul says: *Omne quod non est ex fide peccatum* est (Rom. xiv, 23). All that is done without faith in Christ is mortal sin. But through His mercy we Christians have this privilege that such feelings are not sin, but are the penalty of original sin. Nevertheless, when through negligence or ignorance of our true nature we entertain these feelings and come to cherish them, then there is sin, which is great or less in proportion to your pleasure in them; sometimes it is venial and sometimes mortal. When it is venial and when mortal I cannot define in detail; however it seems right that I should say a little.

CHAPTER 57: *When pride is mortal sin: its effect in worldly people*

WHEN the stirrings of pride are welcomed and enjoyed, so that the heart chooses to rest content in it with pleasure and seeks nothing better than to revel in it, then this pride is mortal sin. For he who chooses this pleasure as his god, not resisting it with reason and will, makes it a mortal sin. But you may say: 'Who is so foolish as to choose pride as his god? No man living would do so.' I answer that I cannot and will not define in particular who sins through mortal pride, but I say in general that there are two forms of pride, one bodily and the other spiritual.

Bodily pride affects men of worldly life, while spiritual pride affects hypocrites and heretics. These three sin mortally through pride. I allude to worldly living men such as Saint Paul speaks of: *Si secundum carnem vixeritis, moriemini* (Rom. viii, 13). If you live according to the flesh, you shall die. And I say that a worldly man who loves and seeks his own reputation above all else, and chooses it as his supreme aim and joy, commits mortal sin. But you may say: 'Who would choose to love and honour himself instead of God?' My answer is that anyone who loves his reputation so much that he wishes to appear better or greater, richer or of higher rank than others, and who devotes all his energies to this, commits mortal sin if in order to win and keep it, he breaks the commandments of God, sets aside love and charity to his fellow-Christians, or is ready and willing to do so rather than imperil his own reputation, position, or personal ambitions. One who committed this mortal sin would deny that he chose pride as his god: but he is deceiving himself, for he chooses it by his own behaviour. But another type of worldly man, who loves and seeks to enhance his own reputation – but not to the extent that he would commit mortal sin or neglect charity to his neighbours in order to win or maintain it – sins venially but not mortally; his guilt is proportionate to his self-love and depends on circumstances.

CHAPTER 58: *How pride in heretics is mortal sin*

A HERETIC sins mortally through pride, because he takes a delight in clinging to his own opinion, maintaining it to be true although it is contrary to God and Holy Church.* He will not retract his opinion, but holds to it as truth, and so makes it his god. But he deceives himself, for God and Holy Church are in such unity and accord that whoever opposes one opposes both. Therefore anyone who says that he loves God, and keeps His commandments, but despises Holy Church and disregards the laws and ordinances made by its supreme head for the direction of all Christians, is a liar. He does not choose God, but chooses the love of himself, which is the opposite to the love of God, and in so doing he commits mortal sin. And in the very matter in which he thinks to please God most, he displeases Him most, for he is blind and will not see. Of this blindness and false confidence in one's own opinions the wise man says: *Est via quae videtur homini recta; et novissima ejus deducunt ad mortem* (Prov. xiv, 12). There is a way which seems right to a man, but which leads him at length to eternal death. This is especially true of heresy, for other worldly sinners who commit mortal sin and continue in it usually come to recognize their errors and are smitten in conscience that they are not in the right way. But the heretic always supposes that his doings and opinions are good, and that no one is better than he. So he thinks that his own way is right, and therefore feels no qualms of conscience or humility of heart. Indeed, unless God in His mercy sends him humility while he lives, he will in the end go to hell. Yet he thinks that he has done well, and that he will win the joys of heaven by his teachings.

CHAPTER 59: *How pride in hypocrites is mortal sin*

THE hypocrite also commits mortal sin through pride. A hypocrite is one who makes self-esteem his sole satisfaction and chief delight. It comes about in this manner. When a man does many good deeds, both corporal and spiritual, the devil later suggests to him how good and holy he is, how he deserves other people's esteem, and how high he is in the sight of God above other men. He considers this suggestion and fully accepts it, for he thinks of it as coming from God, inasmuch as it is true that he does all these good deeds better than other men. But once he accepts this suggestion as true, self-love and self-satisfaction spring up in his heart, and he thinks himself so good, so holy and so full of grace that for a time his mind becomes so intoxicated that it excludes all other thoughts, both spiritual and material, and his heart becomes absorbed in this vain self-esteem. This intoxication of spiritual pride is enjoyable, so that he clings to it and fosters it as much as he can. For the sake of this self-love and vain delight he will pray, keep vigils, fast, wear a hair shirt, and afflict himself in various ways, and will suffer these things lightly. Sometimes he will offer verbal thanks and praise to God, and even squeeze a tear from his eye, and think himself assured of salvation. But in reality he does all these things for love of his own praise, which he chooses and enjoys in place of love and joy in God. And that is the root of all his sin. He does not deliberately choose sin as sin, but chooses this

71

pleasure and joy in which he delights as good and as his spiritual objective, making no effort of will against it, and mistaking it for joy in God. But this is not so, and he therefore commits mortal sin. Job says of a hypocrite: *Gaudium hypocritae ad instar puncti. Si ascendit in caelum superbia ejus et caput ejus ad nubes tetigerit, quasi sterquilinium in fine perdetur* (Job xx, 5, 6). The joy of a hypocrite is no more than momentary, for if he rises up to heaven in the pride of his heart and his head touches the clouds, at the end he is cast out like a dung-heap. The joy of a hypocrite lasts only a moment, for however great his self-adulation and complacency throughout his life, and however much he adorns himself with good deeds to be seen and praised by the world, in the end nothing remains but sorrow and pain. You may say: 'There are few like this, and none are so blind that they would mistake vain self-love for love of God.' As to this I cannot say, and would not if I could; but this I can tell you, that there are many who are hypocrites although they think they are not, and there are many who are afraid of being hypocrites although they certainly are not. Which is the one and which the other God knows, and none but He. Whoever has a humble fear will not be deceived, and whoever thinks himself secure may easily fall. For Saint Paul says: *Qui aestimat se aliquid esse cum nihil sit, ipse seducit* (Gal. vi, 3). Whoever thinks himself to be something when he is nothing, deceives himself.

CHAPTER 60: *How impulses of pride and vainglory in good people are only venial sins*

ON the other hand men or women who devote themselves to the contemplative life surrender their own wills and offer themselves wholly to God with a full general resolution never to sin willingly by pride, nor to take vain delight in themselves, but to delight in God alone with all their powers.

But if after this surrender of the will to God they are still troubled by frequent impulses of pride, and momentarily yield to them without recognizing them as such, their sin is only venial. For instance, this is the case when having recognized this vain self-love for what it is, they correct themselves and steel their wills to resist it. When they ask mercy and help of God, our Lord in His mercy is quick to forgive this sin of self-love, and He will reward their efforts to resist it. Such is the graciousness shown by our Lord to all who are His especial servants and chosen friends. These include all who for His love gladly and freely forsake all the sins of the world and the flesh, and give themselves body and soul to His service with all their powers, as do enclosed anchorites and true Religious, who for the love of God and the salvation of their souls enter some Order approved by Holy Church. And if there are some who at first entered Religion with worldly motives – such as food and lodging – yet if they repent and amend their motives so as to serve God, then as long as they hold to this intention and pursue it as fully as their frailty permits, they are true Religious. And whoever they may be and whatever their position in Holy Church – whether priests, clerics, laymen, widows, wives, or young girls – if for love of God and desire for salvation they will sincerely and fully renounce all desire for worldly honours and pleasures, and restrict their worldly affairs to a bare minimum, they are God's true servants. And if they willingly offer themselves to God's service by devout prayer, holy thoughts, and other good works both bodily and spiritual, and if they steadfastly persevere in this intention, they are God's especial servants in Holy Church. And by means of this goodwill and intention, which is God's gift to them, they will increase in grace and charity in this life, and will have an especial reward in the joys of heaven. Their place will be higher than of that other chosen souls who did not offer themselves soul and body, inwardly and outwardly, to God's service as fully as they did.

All these, whom I call God's servants and chosen friends, although at times through frailty or ignorance they may take pleasure in impulses of vainglory, do not commit mortal sin by this pleasure because the pleasure that they feel prevents their reason and will from recognizing these impulses. For the general intention established in their hearts to please God and forsake all sin when they recognize it preserves them during these impulses, as in all others that spring from frailty, and it will preserve them as long as they firmly maintain this intention.

CHAPTER 61 : *How different states in the Church have differ-ent rewards in heaven: of two rewards, supreme and secondary*

FOR your consolation and that of all who have embraced the state of an enclosed anchoress, as well as those who by the grace of God have entered any Religious Order approved by Holy Church, I will say further that all those who by the mercy of God shall be saved will have an especial glory and reward for their lives in the joys of heaven, a reward above that of other souls, however holy, who did not share their state in Holy Church. This glory is incomparably greater than all the glories of this world, and if you could but see it, you would not ex-change it for all the glory of the world even if you could enjoy it without sin, nor would you wish to change your state of anchoress or Religious, or lessen your especial reward in heaven. This is called an accidental reward, but lest others misunder-stand what I mean, I will define it more clearly. You should understand that amid the joys of heaven there are two rewards which God gives to chosen souls. One is supreme and principal, and consists in loving and knowing Him in proportion to the degree of charity granted by God to the soul while living in this mortal body. This is the best and supreme reward, for it is God Himself, and is granted to all souls that are saved, whatever their status and calling in Holy Church, and is proportionate to the greatness of their charity. For he who loves God with the greatest charity in this life, whatever his status, whether simple or learned, secular or religious, will have the highest reward in the glory of heaven, for he will have the deepest love and knowledge of God, and this is the supreme reward. As to this reward, it may happen that some man or woman of the world, lord or lady, knight or squire, merchant or ploughman will have a higher reward than some priest or friar, monk or canon, or enclosed anchoress. And why? Surely because he has a greater love for God.

The other reward is secondary, and God gives this for special good works which a man does voluntarily over and above what he is bound to do. The doctors of the Church mention three things in particular: martyrdom, preaching, and virginity. These three things are excellent, and since they surpass all others, they will have a special reward known as an aureole. This is an exceptional honour special sign ordained by God to reward outstanding achievements, and it is given in addition to the supreme reward of the love of God, which is given to them and to others alike. This applies to other exceptional good works, which if they are done sincerely, are specially acceptable in the sight of God and commended by Holy Church. Such include the enclosure of an anchoress by the authority of Holy Church, and the entering of an approved religious Order. In the judgement of the Church, the stricter the Order the better. After and beneath these comes the taking of priestly orders, either to care for men's souls and to administer the Sacraments of Holy Church, or from a personal desire to please God and to help one's fellow-Christians by the Sacrifice of the precious Body of our Lord Jesus Christ. When these are done sincerely for God's sake, these are special and excellent works, approved by Holy Church and acceptable in the sight of God, and everyone will receive the particular reward that is his due. On account of his status a bishop and prelate will receive a higher accidental reward than all others, as is shown in Holy Scripture by the prophet Daniel, when he says: *Tu autem vade ad praefinitum tempus, et requiesces, et stabis in sorte tua in finem dierum* (Daniel xii, 13). That is to say, when the angel had shown Daniel the secrets of God, he said: Go to the rest of your bodily death, and you shall stand in your place as a prophet at the last day. And as Daniel will assuredly stand as a prophet at the day of judgement, and enjoy the honour and precedence of a prophet as well as the supreme reward of the love and sight of God, so you will stand in your own place as an anchoress, a Religious as a Religious, and so with other high callings, and will receive honour above others at the day of judgement.

CHAPTER 62: *A short address on humility and charity*

Now from what I have said, if I have made it clear, you will find it a comfort in your way of life and a help in learning humility. For although it be true that if you come to heaven you will receive the special reward for your state of life, there may be many a wife and woman living in the world who will be nearer to God than you, and who will love Him more and know Him better than you despite your way of life. This will put you to shame unless you labour to acquire as full and perfect a degree of charity as anyone living in the world. For if by the gift of God you attain only the same degree of charity as one who remains in a worldly occupation, you will have the same degree of the supreme reward; but in addition to this you will receive the particular reward and honour belonging to your own calling, which he will not have. If, then, you wish to grow in grace, forget your calling – for it is nothing in itself – and direct all your desires and efforts to acquiring charity, humility, and other virtues. All depends on this.

CHAPTER 63 : *How one may learn the extent of one's pride*

I HAD nearly forgotten this image, but I will now return to it. If you wish to learn the extent of your pride, you may test yourself in this way. Consider truthfully and without sparing yourself whether the praise, respect, and favour of worldly men and others is enjoyable to you. Does it fill you with vain pleasure and self-satisfaction? Do you secretly think that men should praise your life and respect your opinions above those of others? And if, on the contrary, people criticize and belittle you, thinking you a fool or a hypocrite, or if they slander and libel you falsely, or trouble you unreasonably in any other way, do you feel a hearty dislike for them and a great unwillingness to endure shame or disgrace in the eyes of the world? If so, this is proof that you have great pride in this dark image, however holy you may appear in the eyes of men. For although these impulses are only slight and venial, they show clearly that great pride lies hidden in your inmost heart, as a fox lurks in his earth. These and many other impulses arise from this image, and so much is this so that you can hardly do anything good without some admixture of pride or self-conceit. Thus pride spoils all your good deeds and makes them displeasing in the sight of God. I do not say that they are rendered useless by this element of pride, but they are not so pleasing to God as they would be were they inspired by simple and sincere humility. Therefore if you wish to attain to the love of God with purity of heart, you must refuse to allow yourself to take pleasure in vainglory through a deliberate assent to pride, and check any involuntary pleasure in it arising from natural frailty. You must strive to eradicate every trace of it. But you cannot do this unless you are prompt and ready to guard your heart, as I will tell you later.

CHAPTER 64: *On anger and envy, and their branches*

EXAMINE this image closely, and you will find two limbs attached to it, envy and anger. From these spring many branches, which obstruct the love and charity that you should have toward your fellow-Christian. The branches of anger and envy are these: hatred, evil suspicion, false and rash judgement, resentment, disdain, calumny, wrongful accusation, unkindness, backbiting, dislike, anger, resentment against those who despise or speak evil of you, pleasure at their troubles, animosity against sinners and those who will not act as you think they should, together with a strong desire – disguised as charity and righteousness – that they should be well punished and chastised for their sins. Such feelings may appear good, but if you examine them closely, you will find them directed against the individual rather than his sin. But you must love the man, however sinful he may be, and hate the sin, in whomsoever it appears. Many are misled in this matter because they prefer the bitter to the sweet, and darkness to light. As the prophet says: *Vae vobis, qui dicitis malum bonum, et bonum malum; ponentes lucem tenebras et amarum in dulce* (Isa. v, 20). Woe to those who say that evil is good and good is evil, and mistake light for darkness and bitter for sweet. This is what people do when instead of hating the sin of the fellow-Christian and loving him as a person, they hate the person instead of the sin and think that they hate the sin. This calls for discernment in those who wish to act rightly.

CHAPTER 65: *That it is a great achievement to love men sincerely while hating their sin*

IT is no achievement to watch and fast until your head aches and your body sickens, nor to go to Rome and Jerusalem on your bare feet, nor to rush about preaching as though you expected to convert everybody. Nor is it an achievement to build churches and chapels, to feed the poor, or to build hospitals. But it is a great achievement for a man to be able to love his fellow-Christian in charity, and to be discerning enough to hate his sin and yet love the sinner. For although all the above actions are good in themselves, they are done by good men and bad alike, for everyone could do them if he had the desire and the means. So I do not consider it any achievement to do what everyone can do. But only a good man can love his fellow-Christian in charity while hating his sin, and he can only do it by the grace of God and not through his own efforts. As Saint Paul says: *Caritas Dei diffusa est in cordibus nostris per Spiritum Sanctum, qui datus est nobis* (Rom. v, 5). The love of God is shed abroad in our hearts by the Holy Spirit which is given to us. It is therefore the more precious and the more difficult to come by. Without this all other good actions do not make a man good or worthy of heaven: this alone can make him good and his actions worthy of reward. All other gifts of God are common to good and bad alike, but this gift of charity is granted only to good and chosen souls.

CHAPTER 66: *That men will have different rewards for the same actions*

For love of God a good man fasts, watches, goes on pilgrimage, and renounces worldly pleasures sincerely and without pretence. He will have his reward in heaven. A hypocrite does the same things out of empty self-esteem, and receives his reward in this life. Similarly, a true preacher of God's word, filled with charity and humility, sent by God and commissioned by Holy Church, will have a special reward for his preaching known as the aureole. But a hypocrite or a heretic, who has neither humility nor charity, and is not sent by God or Holy

Church, will receive the reward for his preaching here. And a good man living in the world builds churches, chapels, abbeys, and hospitals and does other good acts of mercy for the love of God. He will have his reward in heaven, not for these actions in themselves, but for the goodwill and charity given him by God which moved him to do them. Another man may do the same good actions out of vanity, to win honour and praise from the world and to gain a good name for himself; he also has his reward here. In all these instances the determining factor is that one has charity and the other has none. Which is the one and which the other God knows, and He alone.

CHAPTER 67: *That all seemingly good actions should be regarded as such, excepting those of heretics and excommunicates*

THEREFORE we should love and respect all men in our hearts, and approve all their actions that seem good, although in God's sight those who do them may be bad. But it is otherwise in the case of an avowed heretic or of a person who has been publicly excommunicated. We should be careful to avoid meeting or speaking with them, and we should condemn their doings however good they may appear, so long as they remain rebels against God and Holy Church. Therefore should an excommunicated man of the world build a church, or give food to the poor, regard his action as unprofitable, for so it is. And should an avowed heretic, who is a rebel against the Church, preach and teach, then although he may convert an hundred thousand souls, he gains no merit from it. For such people are openly out of charity, and without it no actions have any merit. It is for this reason that I say that it is a great achievement for a man to love his fellow-Christian in charity. This is shown clearly in Saint Paul's words: *Si linguis hominum loquar et angelorum, caritatem non habuero, nihil sum; et si habuero omnem fidem, ita ut montes transferam, caritatem non habeam, nihil sum. Et si noverim mysteria omnia, nihil sum; et si distribuero omnes facultates meas in cibos pauperum, et tradidero corpus meum ita ut ardeam, caritatem autem non habuero, nihil mihi prodest* (I Cor. xiii, I). In praise of charity Saint Paul said: If I speak the languages of all men and of angels and have no charity, I am nothing. And if I have such great faith that I can move mountains and carry them away and have no charity, I am nothing. And if I understand all mysteries, without charity I am nothing. And if I give all that I have to the poor and my body to the fire to be burned and have no charity, I have no profit in it. Saint Paul's words make it clear that a man may perform all kinds of corporal good works without possessing charity, and that charity is nothing else but the love of God and of our fellow-Christian.

CHAPTER 68: *That no good deed can assure a man's salvation without charity, and that God only grants His gift of charity to the humble*

How can any sinner alive, whoever he may be, take any pleasure or feel any confidence in himself on account of anything that he can achieve through his bodily powers or natural reason? For nothing is of any value without love and charity towards his fellow-Christian, and this charity cannot be acquired by any personal efforts. It is the free gift of God granted to humble souls; as Saint Paul says: Who can presume to say, 'I have charity', or 'I am in charity'? Indeed, no one can say it with certainty unless he is perfectly and sincerely humble. Other people may think and hope that they are in charity by various indications, but one who is perfectly humble knows it, and can truthfully say so. Saint Paul had this humility for he said of himself: *Quis separabit nos a caritate Dei? Tribulatio? An angustia?* etc. (Rom. viii, 35). Who shall separate us from the love of God? Tribulation or anguish? And he answers himself, saying: No created thing shall separate us from the charity of God which we have in Christ Jesus. Many do deeds of charity without possessing charity, as I have said; for to reprove a sinner at the right moment to bring about his amendment is a deed of charity, but to hate the sinner instead of his sin is contrary to charity. One who is truly humble can distinguish one from the other, but no one else. Even a man with all the moral virtues of the philosophers could not do it. He would hate the sin in other men – for he hates it in himself – but he could not love the sinner in charity for all his philosophy. And if a man had great knowledge of theology but lacked true humility, he would make mistakes and confuse one with the other. Only humility is worthy to receive this gift from God, but it is one which cannot be acquired through human knowledge.

But perhaps you find my statement charity cannot be acquired by any action that you can perform somewhat alarming, and say: 'What can I do then?' On this point I say that it is true that there is nothing so hard to acquire by your own efforts as charity: on the other hand, there is no gift of God that can be so readily obtained as charity, for God gives no gift so freely, so gladly, and so frequently as charity. 'How then shall I obtain it?' you may say. Be meek and humble in spirit, and you shall have it; and what is easier than to be humble? Surely, nothing. So it is clear that there is nothing more readily obtained than charity, and you have therefore no reason to fear. Be humble, and you shall receive it.

Saint James the Apostle says: *Deus superbis resistat, humilibus dat gratiam* (Jas. iv, 6). God resists the proud, but gives grace to the humble. This grace is in fact charity, for you will receive charity in proportion to your humility. If your humility is imperfect – in your will, and not merely in your feelings – then your charity will be imperfect. Yet this is good, for it is sufficient for salvation; as David says: *Imperfectum meum viderunt oculi tui* (Ps. cxxxix, 16). Lord, your merciful eyes saw my imperfection. But if your humility is perfect, you will receive perfect charity, and this is best. We must needs have humility if we are to be saved, and we must desire it. So if you ask me who is perfectly humble, I can only say that a man is humble when he truly knows and feels himself to be what he is.

CHAPTER 69: *How we may know much anger and envy is hidden in our hearts*

Now turn again to this image, if you wish to know how much anger and envy is hidden in your heart unknown to yourself. When impulses of anger and envy against your fellow-Christian rise up in your heart, examine and watch yourself closely. The stronger these feelings and the more you are moved to gloomy bitterness or ill-will, the greater is this image. For the more impatiently you grumble, whether against God because of any trouble, sickness, or infirmity He sends you, or against your fellow-Christian, the less is the likeness of Jesus reformed in you. I do not say that such grumblings and instinctive reactions are mortal sins, but I do say that they prevent purity of heart and quietness of conscience. As a result you cannot attain to perfect charity, which is essential to the contemplative life. My purpose in all that I say is that you should not only cleanse your heart from all mortal sins, but also as far as possible from venial sins, so that by the grace of Jesus Christ the sources of sin within you may be in part removed. For although you may feel no ill-will towards your fellow-Christian for a time, you cannot be sure that the sources of sin within you are destroyed, because you are not yet in full possession of the virtue of charity. Let him only annoy you by an angry or shrewd word, and then see whether your heart is fully rooted in charity. The more you are moved to ill-will against him, the further you are from perfect charity towards your fellow-Christian; the less you are moved, the nearer you are to charity.

CHAPTER 70: *How to ascertain whether you love your fellow-Christian, and how to follow Christ's example in this matter*

IF you are not moved to anger and open dislike of a person, and feel no secret hatred which makes you despise, humiliate, or belittle him, then you are in perfect charity with your fellow-Christian. And if, the more he shames or harms you in word or act, the more pity and compassion you feel towards him, as you would feel towards one who was out of his right mind, then you are in perfect charity. And if you feel that you cannot find it in your heart to hate him, knowing love to be good in itself, but pray for him, help him, and desire his amendment – not only in words as hypocrites can do, but with heartfelt love – then you are in perfect charity with your fellow-Christian. St Stephen possessed this perfect charity when he prayed for those who stoned him to death. And Christ called for this charity in all who desire to follow Him perfectly when He said: *Diligite inimicos vestros, benefacite his qui oderunt vos, orate pro persequentibus et calumniatoribus* (Matt. v, 44). Love your enemies and do good to those who hate you; pray for those who persecute and slander you. Therefore, if you desire to follow Christ, imitate Him in this matter. Learn to love your enemies and all sinners, for they are all your fellow-Christians. Remember how Christ loved Judas, who was both His deadly enemy and a wicked man. How patient Christ was with him, how kindly, how courteous and humble to one whom He knew to be worthy of damnation. Despite this He chose him to be His apostle, and sent him to preach with the other apostles. He gave him power to work miracles, He showed him the same loving friendship in word and deed as the other apostles. He washed his feet, He fed him with His precious Body, and taught him as He did the other apostles. He did not openly expose or rebuke him, nor did He despise or speak ill of him, although He might justly have done all these things. And to crown his crimes, at Jesus' arrest Judas kissed Him and called Him his friend. Christ showed all this charity to one whom He knew to be a traitor; yet in everything that He did there was no pretence or insincerity, but pure love and true charity. For although Judas, because of his wickedness, was unworthy to receive any gift from God or any sign of love, it was nevertheless right and fitting that our Lord should show Himself in His true nature. For He is love and goodness, and therefore shows love and goodness towards all His creatures as He did towards Judas. I do not say that He loved Judas for his sins, or that He loved him as one of His chosen, as He loved Saint Peter. But He loved him inasmuch as he was His creature, and gave him proofs of His love, if only he could have responded to them and amended.

Follow Jesus in this matter if you can, for although your body is enclosed in a cell, nevertheless in your heart, which is the seat of love, you should be able to attain some degree of this love for your fellows of which I have spoken. Anyone who thinks himself a perfect follower of Christ's teaching and way of life – as some do, inasmuch as they preach and teach and are poor in worldly goods as Christ was – but who cannot follow Christ in having love and charity towards all, both good and bad, friends and foes, without pretence or flattery, contempt, anger, or spiteful criticism, is indeed deceiving himself. The more closely that he thinks he is following the way of Christ, the further he is from it; for Christ Himself said to those who wished to be His disciples: *Hoc est praeceptum meum, ut diligatis invicem sicut dilexi vos* (S. John xiii, 34). This is My commandment, that you love one another as I have loved you. For if you love as I loved, then you are My disciples.

But now you may ask, 'How am I to love the bad as well as the good?' I reply that you must love both good and bad with charity, although not for the same reason; and I will now explain how you are to love your fellow-Christian as yourself. Now you must love yourself only in God and for God. You love yourself in God when you are in a state of grace: but you love yourself solely because you love the goodness and virtue that God gives you. Then you love yourself in God, because you do not love yourself, but God. You love yourself because God loves you, and were you in a state of mortal sin and longed to be made good and virtuous, you would not love yourself as you are, but as you would wish to be. It is exactly in this way that you should love your fellow-Christians. If they are good and holy, you must love them in God with charity, for the reason that they *are* good and holy; for then you love God's goodness and righteousness in them, and you love them more than if they were in a state of mortal sin. As for your enemies, and others who are clearly not in a state of grace, you must love them too, not for what they are, nor as if they were good and holy, for they are not; but you must love them for God's sake, hoping that they will become good and holy. You are not to hate anything in them except whatever is contrary to righteousness, and that is sin. This, as I understand it, is the teaching of Saint Augustine. Only one who is sincerely humble, or desires to be, is capable of loving his fellow-Christian.

CHAPTER 71: *How to discover the extent of your inward covetousness*

TAKE this image and examine it thoroughly; you will discover that although it had seemed small, covetousness and love of worldly things form a large part of it. You have renounced riches and great possessions in this world, and are vowed to enclosure; but have you renounced all love for these things? I do not suppose that you have yet succeeded, for it is easier to renounce worldly goods than to renounce all love for them. It is possible that you have not yet rid yourself of covetousness, and that it affects you in little ways, so that you want a penny instead of a pound, and a halfpenny instead of silver. This is a naïve exchange, and you are not much good at business. This is a childish example, but it has a deeper significance. If you do not believe me, test yourself and find out whether you still take delight in possessing and keeping any small things that you still have, and whether such pleasure sometimes fills your heart. Or do you have a longing for something that you do not possess, and does this longing occupy your mind so that it prevents a pure desire for virtue and for God? If so, it is proof that there is covetousness in this image. And should you require more definite proof, see what happens when anything is taken from you, whether by force, or borrowing, or in some other way, so that you cannot recover it. Are you vexed, angry, or disgruntled because you want the thing and cannot have it? And are you angry with the person who has it, because he could return it but will not? This is proof that you love worldly property, for this is how worldly people behave. When their property and money are taken from them they are distressed and angry, and they take all possible action against those who have taken it. You do this secretly in your heart, but God knows of it, and you are more guilty than a man of the world, because you have formally renounced all love of worldly things; but he has not, and it is therefore permissible for him to try to regain his property by all lawful means. You may perhaps point out that you must have certain necessities in your way of life as well as a man in the world. I readily grant this, but you should not depend on them, take pleasure in possessing them, or be distressed if you lose them. For as Saint Gregory says: 'The extent of your distress at losing a thing reveals the extent of your love for it when you possessed it.' Therefore, if you were pure in heart and had a true desire for spiritual things, accompanied by a small degree of spiritual insight, you would free yourself from dependence on earthly things and would not cling to them. To desire and to possess more than you reasonably require is a serious fault. And to desire something that you require is also a fault, although less serious. But to possess and use what you need is no fault provided that you are not attached to it. Many who are vowed to a state of poverty are blind to this fact, and it cripples their love of God. I do not accuse any particular individuals, nor do I blame any particular occupation, for there are good and bad in every walk of life. But there is one thing that I would like to say to all who are vowed to a life of voluntary poverty, whether Religious or secular, and whatever their rank: So long as their affections are bound up with and dependent on any earthly thing that they may possess or wish to possess, they cannot possess or experience a pure love and vision of spiritual things.

Saint Augustine, speaking to God, says: 'Lord, a man loves Thee but little if he loves anything as well as Thee.' (*Confessions* x, 29.) For the more you love and desire any earthly thing, the less is the love of God in your heart; for although this love of earthly things does not exclude charity unless it is so strong that it stifles the love of God and their fellow-men, it certainly obstructs and diminishes the fervour of charity in them, and deprives them of that special reward for perfect poverty that would be theirs in heaven. This is a great loss if only they could realize it. For one who can recognize how good, how precious, how noble, and how permanent this reward is would not wish to lessen the least reward that he might obtain in heaven in exchange for all earthly pleasures and possessions, even if he could enjoy them without sin. God knows I am speaking of things in which I myself fail, but I beg you and others to strive after them by the grace of God, for it would be a comfort to my heart to know that, though I do not attain this degree of charity myself, I might see it in you or in others who have received more plentifully of His grace than I. But since deep-rooted covetousness is so serious an obstacle to feeling the love of God in the soul, consider how much greater an obstacle it is in men and women of the world, whose minds and activities are constantly devoted to making money and amassing worldly possessions. They can find no pleasure except in earthly things, nor do they wish to do so, because they do not look for it elsewhere. I will say no more of them at present, because I am not addressing them in this book. But I do say that if they could and would understand what they are doing, they would not behave in this way.

CHAPTER 72: *On gluttony, sloth, and lust*

ALTHOUGH this image is obscure, you can see still more in it; carnal self-love revealed in gluttony, spiritual indolence, and lust. These carnal desires make men like beasts, and debar them from the inward enjoyment of God's love and the clear perception of spiritual things. You may object that since food, drink, and sleep are necessities and you cannot use them without pleasure, this pleasure cannot be sinful. I reply that if you use food, drink, and such like with moderation and take no more pleasure in them than is natural, employing them to support your spiritual life, I certainly agree that there is no question of sin: you know how to use these things rightly, and need have no scruples. I myself am very far from this knowledge, and further still from using it rightly, for nature requires one to eat, but the knowledge of how to eat rightly can only be acquired by grace. Saint Paul possessed this knowledge through grace, as he says himself: *Ubique in omnibus institutus sum; et satiari, et esurire, et abundare, et penuriam pati. Omnia possum in eo qui me confortat* (Phil. iv, 12). I am guided in all things, knowing when to go hungry and when to eat; I can face plenty and poverty alike. I can do all things through Him who strengthens me. And Saint Augustine says to God: 'Lord, You have taught me to use food as a medicine.' (*Confessions* x, 31.) Hunger is due to the weakness of nature, therefore in so far as the pleasure that accompanies food is natural and necessary, it is not sinful. But when this pleasure deteriorates into gluttony and wilful craving, it becomes sinful. So the secret of self-mastery lies in having the wisdom to distinguish necessity from gluttony. These are so intermingled that one accompanies the other, and it is difficult to allow one as necessary and to denounce the other as wilful gluttony, since the latter often has the appearance of necessity. Were a man able to take food and drink as he would take a medicine in sickness, he would have the knowledge to distinguish between gluttony and necessity. Nevertheless, since necessity is the root of this sin, and necessity itself is not sinful – for however holy a man may be, he must eat, drink, and sleep – the desire for pleasure that passes for necessity but goes beyond it is not so serious a sin. For a man seldom commits mortal sin through gluttony unless he is already guilty of other mortal sins: when this is the case, the lesser sin may easily become mortal. For this much is certain, that one whose sole aim and object is to gratify his bodily desires, who loves food and drink, who seeks no other form of happiness, and who would if possible always occupy himself with these carnal pleasures, is in a state of mortal sin. Such a person loves his own body more than he loves God. One who lives in a state of mortal sin through pride or envy is blind, and is such a slave to the devil that for the time being he has lost the full use of his free will. Consequently he cannot effectively resist his bodily desires, but devotes himself to them like a beast to carrion. Being in mortal sin, his will is not directed firstly toward God, and the gluttonous desires to which he yields may easily become mortal sins because he makes no general or particular effort to resist them.

But the will and intention of one who is in a state of grace and charity is always directed toward God, whether asleep or at wake, eating or drinking, or whatever he is doing, as long as it is not something sinful in itself, and in his will he chooses God before all else. Such is his love for God that rather than displease Him he would forgo all the pleasures of this world. And although this intention is only general, the grace of our Lord Jesus is so powerful that even if his frailty causes him to fall into a desire and liking for food and drink – either by eating too much, too often, with too much gusto, too daintily, or before the appointed time – yet it preserves him from mortal sin. This remains true as long as he remains in charity in other matters, and maintains his general intention in all that he does. Especially is it true if he confesses his weakness, asks for mercy, and sets his will to resist all such desires of the flesh. God is good and merciful, and He is quick to forgive these venial sins of gluttony in a soul that is humble; for temptations to gluttony, inasmuch as they arise from natural bodily needs, are the hardest sins to avoid, and are more excusable and less dangerous than others. Consequently you cannot attack the root of this sin as you must that of all others. For the root of this sin is simple necessity, which cannot be escaped unless you go to extremes and destroy the need, as some foolish folk do, when they should instead avoid the thief and spare the honest man; in other words, avoid unreasonable desire and wilful love of pleasure while maintaining the body that nature gave them. But against other sins you must take resolute action, in order to destroy not only the mortal and graver venial sins, but also, as far as possible, the roots from which they spring.

CHAPTER 73 : *How the roots of lust must be destroyed by spiritual means rather than physical*

PURSUING this reasoning, bear in mind that although you cannot live without food and drink, you can if you are resolved to live without lust, and be all the better for it. You must not only shun the act, which is mortal sin, but also any deliberate inward pleasure in it; for while this is venial sin, it can sometimes become mortal. You must also attack its roots in order to destroy all sinful impulses and desires of the body. But this attack on the roots of sin must be made by spiritual means, by prayer and spiritual virtue, and not by bodily penance alone. For you can be certain that although you may watch and fast, use the scourge and do all that you can, you will never acquire purity and chastity except by the help of God and His grace of humility. Indeed, you might kill yourself before you could destroy your sinful inclinations and feelings in mind or body by physical penance. But by the grace of Jesus working in a humble soul the roots of sin can be cut and destroyed, and its source dried up. And this is true chastity of body and soul.

CHAPTER 74 : *How a man must exert himself to overcome all sinful impulses, especially those to spiritual sins*

THE same may be said of pride, covetousness, and other sins of this nature, for you could live without any need to be proud or covetous; you must therefore destroy all tendencies to them as far as you can. But in attacking gluttony you must set yourself to prune away all temptations to excess, while sparing their natural origin. A man is half-blind if he attempts to

resist temptations to bodily pleasure in food and drink with
greater energy and zeal than he resists temptations to pride –
which is treated lightly because it seems harmless – or to envy,
anger, covetousness, and lust. For he does not realize the deprav-
ity of such spiritual wickedness as pride and covetousness in the
sight of God. Could a man but realize how depraved pride and
covetousness are in the sight of God, and how contrary they
are to His will, I am sure that he would have a greater loathing
for all impulses of pride and for the vain pleasure that men take
in them. He would fear and fight more strongly against envy
and anger towards his fellow-men than against temptations to
gluttony and lust. However, people do not always realize this,
for they are usually more afraid of a temptation to bodily sin,
and are more sorry and grieved about it, than of temptations to
vainglory and other spiritual sins. But they are wrong in this
matter, for if they would only understand what Holy Scripture
and the great teachers say, they would find it as I say. However,
I cannot cite their statements now.

CHAPTER 75: *How hunger and physical distress greatly hinder
spiritual progress*

I AM not saying that those who indulge in gluttony and lust
are guiltless of sin, since I am fully aware that all these are
sins to a greater or less degree according to the measure of wilful indulgence, together with other circumstances. But I wish
you to recognize and assess every sin as it is; that is, recognize
all spiritual sins as grave, and carnal sins as less grave. But you
must hate and avoid all sins, whether spiritual or carnal, with
all your strength. For be assured of this, that bodily desires and
unbridled pleasure in food and drink, or in any other pleasures
that exceed our reasonable needs, are a serious obstacle to the
soul that desires purity and spiritual joy in God, although they

are not always great sins in one who is in a state of charity. You must therefore guard against them at all costs. The soul cannot experience true inward joy until the body has been largely deprived of its sensual pleasures. So if you desire to attain purity of heart, you must resist unreasonable bodily desires, but you should not attack their natural origin, such as hunger, which you are bound to feel and to satisfy at proper times. You must strengthen yourself against it by taking the medicine of food in the same way as you would take the proper medicine against a bodily ailment, so that you may serve God in greater freedom of body and soul.

You can be sure that unless he is given abundant grace, anyone who wishes to devote himself to the spiritual life will find himself greatly hindered in his attempt to attain spiritual knowledge and experience if he deliberately allows himself to suffer the pangs of hunger; and if he goes to extremes in fasting, it will be his own fault if he suffers from stomach complaints, headache and similar bodily ailments. For bodily pain, whether due to penance, illness or overwork, does not always prevent fervour towards God in devotion, but often increases it; nevertheless, I am sure that it prevents fervour of love in contemplation, because this cannot be acquired or experienced of set purpose, and is only possible in great tranquillity of body and soul. Therefore act reasonably in all that you do, and treat your body sensibly; then let God send what He pleases, whether it be health or sickness. Accept everything with cheerfulness, and do not willingly complain against God.

CHAPTER 76: *Remedies against indiscreet eating and drinking*

ACCEPT my advice, then, and take your food as it comes; make reasonable provision for it if necessary, and take it cheerfully as you need it. But beware lest greed accompanies need, and avoid excess as well as deficiency of food. And if, when you have fed, your conscience warns you that you have eaten too much or too little, and you become troubled or discouraged on that account, lift up your heart to our Lord Jesus, confessing yourself a wretched creature, and asking His forgiveness. When you have done this, the more shortly the better, do not trouble yourself any further about it. And do not strain yourself in an effort to destroy these impulses completely; it is not worth your while, for you will never succeed. Turn instead to some other occupation, physical or spiritual, as you feel disposed, so that you may make greater progress in other virtues such as humility and charity.

You can be certain that anyone who directs all his desires and efforts to nothing except humility and charity, and is always longing to acquire them, will by so doing grow in all the other virtues such as chastity and abstinence, although he may give them little thought at the time. He will grow stronger in them in a single year than he would do in seven without this desire, although he were to strive continually against gluttony, lust, and the like, and scourge himself daily from dawn to dusk.

CHAPTER 77: *How the ardent desire and pursuit of humility and charity enable a man the sooner to acquire all other virtues*

ACQUIRE humility and charity, then, and if you devote all your efforts to this end, you will be fully occupied. If you acquire them, they will be an inward rule and guide, so controlling your food, drink, and other bodily needs that you will need no advice from anyone. You will have no doubts or fears, nor will you be troubled by anger, depression, lust, or folly, and you will enjoy the peace of an easy conscience and a tranquil mind. I have said more than I intended on this subject, but act on my advice if you can, and I know that God will prosper your efforts.

From what I have said you may now see in part how seriously this image hinders your progress. The Gospels describe how Abraham spoke to the rich man in the depths of Hell: *Chaos magnum inter nos et vos firmatum est, ut hi qui volunt transire ad nos non possint, neque inde hic transmeare* (Luke xvi, 26). There is a great gulf – that is to say, a thick darkness – between us and you, so that we cannot come to you, nor you to us. This dark image in your soul and mine may also be called a great gulf, because it prevents us from coming to Abraham, that is Jesus, and it prevents Him from coming to us.

CHAPTER 78: *On the five bodily senses*

LIGHT your lamp and see the five windows in this image through which sin enters into your soul. As the prophet says: *Mors ingreditur per fenestras nostras* (Jer. ix, 21). Death comes in at the windows. These windows are the five senses, through which your soul, contrary to its true nature, goes out and seeks its pleasure and support in earthly things. Through the eye it looks for strange and beautiful things, and through the ear new and wonderful things, and so with the other senses. By employing these faculties deliberately and without discretion, in vain pursuits, the soul is greatly hindered in the exercise of its inward and spiritual faculties. So you must close and shutter these windows, and only open them when necessary. This would not be very difficult once you clearly understood the nature of your soul and its potential beauty were it not stifled under the black influence of this vile image.

CHAPTER 79 : *How lack of knowledge causes the soul to seek outward pleasures through the five senses*

BECAUSE you do not understand your own soul, you neglect your inner life and seek outward consolations like a creature without reason. In Holy Scripture God says to a chosen soul: *Si ignoras te, O pulchra inter mulieres, egredere et abi post vestigia gregum sodalium tuorum, et pasce haedos tuos* (Cant. i, 8). O fairest of women, if you do not know yourself, go out and follow in the footsteps of your companions' flocks, and feed your kids. As if to say: O soul, beautiful by nature, made in the likeness of God but frail as a woman in your body because of original sin, since you do not know yourself and do not understand that your inward delight should be in the Food of Angels, you wander out in your bodily senses seeking satisfaction and pleasure like a beast of your flock. As a result of this fare, your thoughts and affections are unclean like goats.

CHAPTER 80 : *How the soul should seek its needs inwardly from Jesus, and not from outward things*

IT is a shame to act in this way, so return home to yourself and remain there. Do not wander abroad begging for the food of swine. If you still wish to be a beggar, beg inwardly of your Lord Jesus, for He is rich indeed, and is more ready to give than you to ask. Do not wander about like a beast from the flock any longer, or like a worldly person who has not pleasure in anything except his bodily senses. If you do this, your Lord Jesus will supply all your wants. He will take you into His wine cellar and allow you to taste of His wines, for He has many casks from which to choose. Thus in Holy Scripture a chosen soul speaks with joy of our Lord: *Introduxit me rex in cellam vinariam* (Cant. ii, 4). The king led me into his wine-cellar. In other words: When I forsook the drunkenness of bodily desire and worldly pleasure, which are like wormwood, and sought the king of all bliss, the Lord Jesus led me in. He first led me into myself, so that I might see and know myself; then He brought me into His cellar, transporting me out of myself into Him, and He gave me to taste of His wine, which is His own spiritual sweetness and heavenly joy. These are not my own words, wretched sinner that I am, but the words of the Spouse of Christ in Holy Scripture. I quote them in order that you may withdraw your soul from outward things, and follow her example as closely as you can.

CHAPTER 81 : *How the windows of the imagination need to be closed, as well as those of the senses*

YOU may say that you are already doing this. You see and hear nothing of worldly affairs, and you do not employ your bodily senses more than necessary. This is why you are enclosed. If you are indeed doing this, you have closed a large window in this image, but you are not yet safe, because you have not closed the hidden openings of your imagination. Although you cannot see me with your eyes, you can still see me in your imagination, and the same applies to all material things. So if you deliberately allow yourself to consider the vanities of this world, or to think of comfort and ease, then although your soul may remain within you as far as the bodily senses are concerned, it is in fact lured far away by these vain fancies.

You may perhaps ask whether it is any great sin for a soul to consider such things, either with the senses or in the imagination. My answer is that I do not think that you should ask such a question, for anyone who truly desires to love God does not enquire whether one sin is greater than another. He regards anything that hinders him from loving God as a great sin, and nothing as sinful except what is evil and obstructs his love of God. And what is sin but separation from God or neglect of Him? I do not say that an obstacle of this kind will be so dangerous to him as a mortal or venial sin, nor do I deny that he can distinguish between mortal and venial sin, and especially avoid the former.

CHAPTER 82: *When the use of the senses or imagination is mortal sin, and when venial*

NEVERTHELESS, I shall answer your question more fully, because your wish for guidance impels me to say more than I had originally intended. Our Lord says in the Gospel: *Homo quidam fecit coenam magnam et vocavit multos. Et misit servum suum hora coenae dicere invitatis ut venirent. Primus dixit: Villam emi; rogo te, habe me excusatum. Secundus dixit: Juga boum emi quinque, et eo probare illa. Et tertius dixit: Uxorem duxi, et ideo non possum venire* (Luke xiv, 16–20). A man made a great supper and invited many guests, and sent his servant at supper-time to those who were invited. The first excused himself from coming because he had bought a farm; the second also excused himself because he had bought five yoke of oxen and was going to try them; the third, because he had married a wife. Setting aside the first and the last, I will comment on the man who bought the oxen. These five yoke of oxen represent the five senses which we have in common with animals like the ox. Now the man who was invited to the supper was not rebuked because he bought the oxen, but because he went to try them and therefore could not come. Similarly, I say that to possess these senses and use them as necessary is not sinful, but if you go to try them by taking vain pleasure in creatures, this is sinful.

And if you choose that pleasure as the final joy and satisfaction of your soul, and wish for no happiness beyond such worldly vanity, this is mortal sin. For you choose this pleasure as your god, and you will therefore be excluded from the supper. Saint Paul forbade us employ our senses in this way when he said: *Non eatis post concupiscentias vestras.* You shall not indulge your lusts or deliberately pursue pleasures. And anyone who is already guilty of mortal sins will not escape mortal sin in this respect, although he does not realize it. But I trust that this does not apply to you. Nevertheless, if through frailty you take pleasure in such vanities through the senses, but despite this keep yourself in charity in other respects, not choosing such pleasure as the ultimate satisfaction of your soul but always desiring God above all things, then this sin is venial, and its guilt is greater or less according to circumstances. You will not be excluded from this supper because of such venial sins, but you will not be able to enjoy the delights of this supper during this life unless you make every effort to resist these venial sins. For although venial sins do not destroy charity, they undoubtedly lessen its fervour and our feeling of it in the soul.

CHAPTER 83: *How a man or woman vowed to the life o. religion should conduct themselves toward visitors*

YOU may say that you cannot avoid hearing about worldly matters because all kinds of people often come to talk with you, and sometimes tell unedifying tales. I answer that conversation with your fellow-men cannot do you any great harm, and is sometimes helpful if you employ it wisely, for in this way you may test the reality of your love towards your fellow-men, whether it is great or small. Like all other Christians, it is your duty to have a true love for your fellows, and when possible to show this love in practice as well as you are able. And although you are an enclosed anchoress and unable to leave your cell to seek opportunities of helping your fellow-men by acts of mercy, you are still bound to love them all in your heart, and to show clear signs of this love to all who come to you. So when someone wishes to speak to you, whoever it may be, and you have no idea who and what he is, or why he comes, always be ready and willing to find out what he wants. Do not be aloof, or keep him waiting a long time. Think how ready and glad you would be if an angel came from heaven to speak to you. Be equally ready and willing to speak to your fellow-Christian when he visits you, for until you have asked him, you do not know who he is, why he comes, or what he may want of you or you of him. And although you may be at prayer and re-luctant to abandon it, thinking that it is not proper to leave God in order to speak to man, I do not think you would be right in this instance, for if you are wise, you will not leave God by so doing. You will find Him, possess Him, and see Him as fully in your fellow-man as in prayer, but it will be in a different way.

If you have a true love for your fellow-men, it will be no hindrance to your prayer if you talk with them discreetly, and I think that your discretion should be exercised in this way. When someone comes to you, ask him humbly what he wants. If he comes to tell you his troubles and receive comfort, give him a ready hearing and allow him to say what he wishes to ease his heart. When he has ended, comfort him as kindly and lovingly as you can, but do it briefly. If he then proceeds to tell idle tales or gossip about other people's doings, make little com-ment and do not encourage him: he will soon get tired of it and depart. Should one of the clergy come to instruct you, respect his office and listen to him humbly. If his words are helpful, ask any questions you wish, but do not presume to instruct him: it is not proper for you to instruct a priest except in necessity. If his words afford little help, answer little and he will soon take his leave. And should anyone come to bring you a gift, seek your advice, or receive instruction, speak kindly and humbly to them all. Do not rebuke anyone for their faults; it is not your responsibility unless you happen to know the person well and are sure that he will take it from you. In short, if you think that your advice will be of spiritual service to your neighbour, say what you will if he will listen. Otherwise keep silence, and people will soon cease to trouble you. This is my advice; do better if you can.

CHAPTER 84: *How the limbs of this image in the soul, defiled by the seven deadly sins, can be destroyed*

FROM what I have said, you may now realize how dark this image is; not that I have described it fully, for I cannot. Nevertheless, from what little I have said, you can see more if you look carefully. But you may say: 'How do you know that I bear within me such an image as you describe?' In reply I quote the words of the prophet: *Inveni idolum mihi* (Hosea xii, 8). That is, I have found within me a false image, which men call an idol, horribly disfigured and deformed by the wickedness of all the sins of which I have spoken. These sins have drawn me away from purity of heart and perception of spiritual virtues, and plunged me into bodily cravings and worldly vanities too numerous to mention. For this I am truly repentant, and I beg for mercy. And because of this inward sorrow which I feel more keenly than I can say, I am in a better position to tell you about your own image. For we all spring from Adam and Eve, who were clothed in the skins of beasts, as Holy Scripture says: *Fecit Dominus Adae et uxori ejus tunicas pelliceas* (Gen. iii, 21). God made clothes of skins for Adam and his wife, as a sign that for his sin he was reduced to the level of the beasts. And we are all born in this animal clothing, which conceals and disfigures our true likeness.

CHAPTER 85: *The limbs of this image of sin*

THIS is an ugly image to look at. Its head is pride, for pride
is the first and principal sin. As the wise man says: *Initium
omnis peccati superbia* (Ecclus. x, 15). Pride is the beginning of
all sin. The back part is covetousness; as Saint Paul says: *Quae
retro sunt obliviscens, in anteriora me extendo* (Phil. iii, 13). I will
forget all worldly things that are behind me, and reach forward
to eternal things. The breast, in which is the heart, is envy,
which is not a bodily sin but comes from the devil. As the wise
man says: *Invidia diaboli mors introivit in orbem terrarum. Imitantur
illum omnes qui ex parte ejus sunt.* Through the devil's envy death
came into the world, and all who are of his party follow him in
it. The arms of this image are anger, for a man gives vent to his
anger with his arms, contrary to Christ's commandment in the
Gospel: *Si quis percussit te in unam maxillam, praebe illi et alteram*
(Matt. v, 39). If a man strikes you on one cheek, you are not to
strike back at him, but offer him the other. The belly of this
image is gluttony, as Saint Paul says: *Esca ventri, et venter escis;
Deus hunc et has destruet* (1 Cor. vi, 13). Food for the belly, and
the belly for food: God will destroy both the belly and the food.
That will be at the end of all things, when God restores His
chosen and judges the reprobate. Its legs are lust, of which Saint
Paul says: *Non exhibeatis membra vestra iniquitatis ad peccatum*
(Rom. vi, 13). You shall not yield your limbs, and especially
your secret parts, to be the means of sin. The feet of this image
are sloth, and so the wise man tells the soul to bestir itself to
good works. *Discurre, festina, suscita amicum tuum* (Prov. vi, 3).
Bestir yourself to good works quickly; make haste, for time
is passing, and rouse your friend, who is Jesus, by devout
prayer and meditation. Now you know about the limbs of this
image.

CHAPTER 86: *Of what the image of Jesus and the image of sin consist*

THIS is not the image of Jesus. It is more like the image of the devil, for the image of Jesus consists of virtues – humility, perfect love, and charity. But this image and its limbs consist of a false and carnal love of self. Both you and all men, whoever they may be, bear this image inwardly until it is partly destroyed by the grace of Jesus. David seems to refer to this in the psalms: *Verumtamen in imagine pertransit homo; sed et frustra conturbatur* (Ps. xxxix, 6). Meaning that although in the beginning man was made in the image of God, stable and steadfast, nevertheless because of sin he now passes through this life bearing the image of sin, which makes him unstable and troubled. Saint Paul also speaks of this image: *Sicut portavimus imaginem terreni hominis, sic portemus imaginem caelestis* (I Cor. xv, 49). If we desire to come to the love of God, having formerly borne the image of Adam the earthly man, which is the image of sin, we must henceforward bear the image of Jesus the heavenly man, which is the image of virtue.

CHAPTER 87: *How we must crucify this image of sin, and quicken the image of Jesus*

WHAT are we to do with this image? I answer in the words of the Jews to Pilate about Christ: *Tolle, tolle, crucifige eum* (S. John xix, 15). Take this body of sin and crucify it. That is, destroy this image and slay the false love of sin in yourself. As Christ's body was slain for our sins, so if you wish to be like Christ, slay your bodily desires and lusts. As Saint Paul says: *Qui autem Christi sunt, carnem suam crucifixerunt cum vitiis et concupiscentiis* (Gal. v, 24). Those who are followers of Christ have crucified and subdued their flesh, that is, the image of sin, with all its lusts and unreasonable desires.

Slay pride, break it down and establish humility. Break down anger and envy, and replace them by love and charity towards your neighbours. Instead of covetousness cultivate poverty of spirit, and instead of sloth foster fervent devotion and a glad readiness for all good works. Replace gluttony and impurity by temperance and purity of body and soul. This is what Saint Paul recommended when he said: *Deponentes veterem hominem cum suis actibus, qui corrumpitur secundum desideria erroris; et induite novum hominem, qui secundum Deum creatus est in sanctitate et justitia* (Eph. iv, 22). Put off the old man – which is the sinful image of the old Adam, with all its limbs corrupted by wrongful desires – and put on the new man – which is the image of God – by holiness, righteousness, and the perfection of virtue. Who will help you to destroy this image? None but the Lord Jesus Himself. In His might and in His Name you will destroy this idol of sin. Pray to Him earnestly and with longing, and He will help you.

CHAPTER 88: *The advantage of guarding the heart, and the close attachment of the soul to what it loves*

TRY to be recollected in heart, and follow the advice of the wise man who said: *Omni custodia serva cor tuum, quia ex ipso procedit vita* (Prov. iv, 23). Do your utmost to guard your heart, for out of it comes life. This is true, for when it is well guarded, wise thoughts, pure affections, and ardent desire for virtue and charity, and for the joys of heaven come from it, and cause the soul to live a life of blessedness. If, on the contrary, it is not well guarded, then as our Lord says in the Gospel: *De corde exeunt cogitationes malae, quae coinquinant hominem*

(Matt. xv, 19). Evil thoughts and impure desires come from the heart and defile a man. If these are mortal sins they injure the life of the soul, or if they are venial they weaken or sicken it. For what is a man but his thoughts and his loves? These alone make him good or bad. The more you love and know God, and the better you love your neighbour, the greater is your soul; and the less you love Him, the less your soul. And if you do not love Him at all, your soul is worthless, for while it has no capacity for goodness, it has great capacity for sin. If you want to know what you really love, examine your thoughts, for your mind dwells on what you love, and your thoughts will mostly be on what your heart loves best. If you love God deeply, you will like to think constantly of Him, and if you love Him little, then you will think of Him little. So direct your thoughts and affections rightly, and you will be virtuous.

CHAPTER 89: *How the image of sin is to be destroyed*

BEGIN, then, to destroy this image. Consider yourself and your wretched condition, as I have said. But when you come to realize how proud, vain, envious, gloomy, covetous, unspiritual, and full of corruption you are, also, how little knowledge or experience of God you have, while in worldly matters you are clever, quick, and interested – in short, if you realize that you are as full of sin as a hide is of meat – do not be too greatly discouraged. When you have done all this, lift up your heart in longing desire to your Lord Jesus, and ask His help. Earnestly implore Him to help you bear the heavy burden of this image, or else to destroy it for you. Think how shameful it is for you to fill yourself with the swine's food of worldly pleasures when you should be seeking the spiritual joys of heaven. If you do this, you will be beginning to attack the foundations of sin within you, and it may be that this will bring you pain and sorrow, for you will come to understand that no soul can live without great pain unless it can find rest and pleasure either in its Creator or else in creatures. So when you turn from self with a fervent desire to feel the presence of your Lord Jesus, and withdraw your love from all material things and from dependence upon bodily feelings, you will find that you are still burdened by self. It will seem to you that all created things are trying to hold you back, and all these things that once pleased you will turn to pain and weariness. When you have thus forsaken self and cannot readily find comfort in Jesus Christ, your soul must needs suffer pain. Nevertheless, endure this pain for a time, steadfastly holding to the bare longing for Jesus only. Desire nothing but Him. Let nothing distract you from this. Do not seek for external consolations during this time, for it will not last long: our Lord is near, and He will soon bring comfort to your heart. He will help you to bear with your body and its corrupt nature, and will destroy this false image of self-love in you by the merciful power of His gracious presence. This will not take place at once, but little by little, until you are to some degree reformed in His likeness.

CHAPTER 90: *How to control impulses of pride and other vices*

AFTER such a complete uprising against your self-love, you will be able to control yourself more wisely, gently, and easily, and to guard your thoughts and feelings more carefully, so as to distinguish between the good and the bad. And if afterwards you should feel any stirring of pride, be on your guard at once, and give it no chance to survive. Grasp it, crush it, and despise it; expose it to every possible contempt. Do not spare it or listen to it, however plausible it may seem, for it is false however true it may seem to be. As the prophet says: *Popule meus, qui te beatum dicunt ipsi te seducunt, et in errorem mittunt* (Isa. iii, 12). Which is to say: My people, those who tell you that you are blessed and holy deceive you and lead you astray. And if you do this often and thoroughly, you will by the grace of God soon stop much of the spring of pride and greatly abate your vain delight in it, so that you will hardly feel it. And when you do feel it, it will be so weak and nearly dead that it will do you little harm. Your soul will catch a glimpse of the fair beauty of humility, and come to desire and love it for its own sake. You will be glad to be judged as you are, and if need arises you will willingly endure scorn and reproof for love of what is right. Similarly, when you feel moved to anger or despair, or ill-will to your neighbour, beware of it, however reasonable it may seem. Be on the alert to restrain it, lest the natural instincts seize control. Do your utmost not to yield to it in word or deed, and whenever it revives, strike it down again. Slay it with the sword of the fear of God, and it will not hurt you. Remember that if you set your will and reason to resist these impulses of pride, vainglory, envy, and such like directly you are aware of them, you will kill them even though they linger in the mind against your wish and are not easily dislodged. Do not fear them, for although they may rob your soul of peace, they cannot defile it. Treat all evil impulses of covetousness, spiritual lethargy, gluttony, and impurity in the same way, and let your reason and will be always quick to reject and despise them.

CHAPTER 91: *What best helps a man to know and obtain what he needs, and destroys sin in him*

You will be able to do this better and more easily if you firmly set your heart on one thing, that is, on our Lord Jesus Christ alone, who is the blessed one, both God and Man. Let Him be the sole object and inspiration of your soul's desire, and the light of your heart. Have a deep and reverent fear of displeasing Him, and a great desire to please God, to love Him, know Him, see Him, and possess Him in some measure here by grace, and to enjoy Him fully in the bliss of heaven. If you cherish this desire for Jesus Christ, it will enable you to judge what is sinful and what is not, what is good and what is better. Hold fast to it, and it will teach you all you need to know, and obtain for you all that you want. Therefore, whenever you fight against the root of sin in general or any sin in particular, hold fast to this desire, and fix your mind upon Jesus Christ for whom you long rather than upon the sin which you are fighting. If you will do this, Jesus Christ will fight for you, and destroy sin in you. You will attain your purpose much sooner if you do this than if you were to set aside this humble desire for God alone, and devote your attention to crushing sinful desires in the expectation that you can destroy them by self-discipline alone. You will never succeed in this way. Do as I have said, and better if you can, and I am confident that by the grace of Jesus you will put the devil to shame, and crush all these evil desires so that they will do you little harm. This is the way to break down and destroy the image of sin which distorts the true image of Christ in you. Humility and charity will fashion you to the likeness of Jesus in His Humanity, and will at length transform you to the true likeness of Jesus in His Godhead. You will have only a glimmering of it here in contemplation, but in the bliss of heaven it will be yours in the fullness of reality.

Saint Paul speaks of this conformity to the likeness of Christ: *Filioli, quos iterum parturio donec Christus formetur in vobis* (Gal. iv, 19). My dear children, whom I bear as a woman bears her child until Christ is formed in you. You have conceived Christ by faith, and He lives in you in so far as you possess the good-will and desire to serve and please Him. But He is not yet fully formed in you by perfect charity, nor you in Him. Therefore

Saint Paul bore you, me, and other Christians with pain, as a woman bears her child, until Christ is fully formed in us, and we in Him.

CHAPTER 92: *How a man is to be conformed to the likeness of Christ, and Jesus formed in him*

WHOEVER imagines that he can attain to the full state and practice of contemplation in some other way – that is, without continual recollection of the precious Humanity and Passion of Jesus Christ, and the pursuit of all virtues – does not come in by the door, and will therefore be cast out like a thief. I do not deny that by the grace of God a man may sometimes have some foretaste and limited experience of contemplation, for some have been granted this early in their spiritual life, but they cannot retain it permanently. For Christ is both the door and the porter, and no one may enter unless he shares His life and bears His sign. As He Himself has said: *Nemo venit ad Patrem nisi per me* (John xiv, 6). No man comes to the Father except through Me. Meaning that no one can come to the contemplation of the Godhead until he is first conformed by perfect humility and charity to the likeness of Jesus in His Humanity.

CHAPTER 93: *Why this book was written, and how the person for whom it was written should use it*

NOW I have told you a little about the contemplative life as I see it, and of the ways in which grace leads us to it. And although I cannot fully experience and practise what I have been saying, I hope that my words – such as they are – will rouse me out of my negligence to do better than I have done hitherto. My other purpose is to inspire you and others who have entered the contemplative life to devote yourselves to it more actively and humbly by such simple words as God's grace has enabled me to say. Therefore, if anything that I have said in this book brings you some encouragement, or moves you to a deeper love of God, then thank God, for it is due to His grace and not to my words. But if it brings you no help, or does not suit your needs, do not study it for too long. Put it aside till another time, and give yourself to prayer or some other occupation. Use it as it suits you; do not read it all at once. And do not take all that I have written too literally. But wherever after due thought you feel that I have dealt inadequately with some matter, whether through poor command of English or through faulty reasoning, please correct it, but only where necessary.

Lastly, what I have written does not apply to anyone living the active life, but only to you and others who live the contemplative life.

The grace of our Lord Jesus Christ be with you.   Amen.

BOOK TWO

CHAPTER 1: *How the soul of every good man reflects the image of God*

SINCE YOU HAVE ASKED TO HEAR MORE about the image which I previously described to you in part, I will gladly accede to your wishes, although I do so with some apprehension. But by the help of our Lord Jesus Christ, in whom I place my whole trust, I will deal with the matter somewhat more fully.

First of all, if you wish to know plainly what I mean by this image, I mean nothing but your own soul; for your soul, and mine, and that of every rational being is an image, since it is the image of God. As the Apostle says: *Vir est imago Dei*. Man is the image of God, created in His likeness, not as regards his bodily form, but in his inner powers. As Holy Scripture says: *Formavit Deus hominem ad imaginem et similitudinem suam*. That is, the Lord God formed the soul of man in His own image and likeness. It was this image of which I was speaking. In its original state the soul, made in the image of God, was beautiful and glorious, filled with burning love and spiritual light. But through the sin of Adam it was disfigured and deformed into a different likeness, as I said before. For it lost this spiritual light and heavenly support, and fell into grievous darkness and a perverted longing for this wretched life. It was exiled and cast out from the heritage of heaven which it would have enjoyed had it stood firm: it was cast down into the sorrows of this earth, and later into the prison of hell, doomed to remain there for ever. It would never have been able to return from that prison to its heritage in heaven had it not been restored to its original form and likeness. But this restoration could not have been effected by any human being, for every man was in the same unhappy plight, and none was able to help himself, much less anyone else. Therefore it could only be done by one who is more than man, that is, by God Himself. And it was fitting that if man were to be saved, God Himself should reform and restore him to the happiness for which in His eternal goodness He had first created him. By God's help I will tell you how man's soul may be, and is, reformed in the likeness of Him who first created it; this, indeed, is my main intention in this book.

CHAPTER 2: *How God's justice requires that sin cannot be forgiven unless amends are made*

THE justice of God requires that a sin cannot be forgiven unless all possible amends are made for it. Now it is clear that all mankind, in the person of the first man Adam, sinned so grievously against God when it disobeyed His explicit decree and yielded to the evil suggestions of the devil, that it justly deserved to be banished from His presence and condemned to hell for eternity. Indeed, in accordance with God's justice, it could not receive forgiveness unless amendment and full satisfaction were first made for it. But no one who was only a man of Adam's line could make this expiation, for the sin and affront to God were of such magnitude that it was beyond the power of man to make amends for it. And there was a further reason, in that one who has sinned and wishes to make amends ought to restore to the person whom he has offended all that is his due, irrespective of what his offence has been, and should in addition give something over and above what he owes as an atonement for his offence. But mankind has nothing to offer God in atonement for its sin beyond what it already owes Him. Whatever good deed a man might do, whether in body or soul, could only be his duty. For as the Gospel says, it is the duty of every man to love God with all his heart, with all his soul, and with all his strength (S. Luke x, 27); more than this he cannot do. Nevertheless, such an action could not suffice to restore mankind, nor could a man do even this unless he could first be re-formed himself. Therefore if man's soul were to be re-formed, and the effects of his sin repaired, it was necessary that the Lord God Himself should reform this image and make atonement for this sin, since man himself could not do it. But God could not do this in His divinity, for God could not, and was not obliged to, expiate man's sin by suffering pain in His divine nature. It was therefore necessary that God Himself should assume our sinful human nature and become man. But He could not do this by the normal process of human generation, for it was not possible for the Son of God to be born of any woman known by man. It was therefore necessary for Him to become man by a generation effected by the grace and operation of the Holy Spirit in a pure virgin, full of grace, our Lady Saint Mary. And so it was done. For our Lord Jesus Christ, the Son of God, became man, and through His precious death and suffering for us He made satisfaction to the heavenly Father for man's guilt. He had the power to do this because He was God, and owed nothing Himself, except in so far as He was also man, born of the same race as Adam who first sinned. And so, although he owed no debt for Himself, because He could not sin, yet of His own free will He assumed the debt of man's sin, and in His infinite mercy took human nature for man's salvation. For the truth is that no man except our blessed Lord Jesus could ever offer God anything of his own that he did not already owe Him. He alone could offer God one thing that He did not owe of Himself, and this one thing was His own precious life, which He offered by His willing acceptance of death for love of the truth. He was under no obligation to do this. He was bound to do all things to the glory of God during his life on earth, but He was not obliged to suffer death for love of justice. He was under an obligation to act with justice, but He was under no obligation to die, for death is the penalty incurred by man for his sin. But the Lord Jesus never sinned, and could not sin; consequently He did not incur the penalty of death. Therefore, since He chose to die, although under no obligation to do so, He offered to God something more than He owed. And since this was the noblest and most meritorious action ever performed by man, it was fitting that through it the sin of mankind should be forgiven. For in Jesus mankind found a man of its own race untouched by sin, who was able to make expiation for its sin and offer to God all that was His due and more. Since, then, our Lord Jesus Christ, God and man, died in this way to save the souls of men, it was fitting that their sin should be forgiven, and that man's soul, created by God in His own image, should be re-formed to His true likeness and restored to the joys of heaven.

For the Passion and precious death of our Lord are the means whereby the soul of man is re-formed, and without them we could never have been restored to His likeness nor come to the joys of heaven. Blessed may He be in all that He has done! Now by the merits of His Passion the flaming sword of the Cherubim that drove Adam from paradise is sheathed, and heaven's eternal gates stand open to all who desire to enter. For in His person Jesus is both God and King of Heaven in the glory of the Father; while as man He is the porter at the gate, ready to receive every soul who desires to be re-formed to His likeness here in this life. For now every soul that so desires may be re-formed in the likeness of God, for its sin is forgiven, and expiation for its original guilt has been made through Jesus. Nevertheless, although this is true, all souls do not receive the benefits of His precious Passion, nor are they restored to His likeness.

CHAPTER 3 : *How there are two kinds of people who are not reformed by the merits of the precious passion of our Lord Jesus Christ*

Two kinds of people are not reformed by the merits of the Passion; those who do not believe in it, and those who do not love it. Jews and pagans do not receive the benefits of the passion because they do not believe in it. They do not believe that Jesus, the son of the Virgin Mary, is Son of God; while pagans do not believe that the sovereign Wisdom of God would become man, and in His humanity suffer the pains of death. Therefore the Jews regard the preaching of the cross and passion of Christ as nothing but a scandal and a blasphemy, while to the pagans it is an illusion and a folly. But true Christians accept it as a revelation of the sovereign Wisdom of God, and of His great power. Thus Saint Paul said: *Praedicamus vobis Christum crucifixum, Judaeis quidem scandalum, gentibus autem stultitiam: ipsis autem vocatis, Judaeis atque Graecis, Christum Dei virtutem et Dei sapientiam* (1 Cor. i, 23). That is: we preach to you what we believe, that Jesus Christ the Crucified, the son of Mary, is Son of God and the sovereign Wisdom and power of God. To Jews and pagans who do not believe in Him, Jesus is a scandal and a folly. By their unbelief they render impossible the re-formation of their souls, and if they continue in their unbelief they will never be saved, nor come to the joys of heaven. For it is the truth that from the beginning of the world to the end, no one was ever saved – nor will be saved – except through a belief in Jesus Christ and His coming, whether this belief be general or explicit. For the chosen people who lived under the dispensation of the Old Testament before the Incarnation had faith in Christ, believing that He would come and reform the souls of men. They held this faith either explicitly, as did the patriarchs, prophets, and other holy men, or else implicitly and in a general way, like children or other simple and imperfect souls who had no specific knowledge of the mystery of the Incarnation. Similarly, all chosen souls under the dispensation of the New Testament have faith in Christ as having already come. They hold this faith either explicitly and by conviction, as in the case of spiritual and educated people, or else in a general way as in the case of children who die baptized, or other simple and unlearned people who have been brought up within Holy Church. Since this is the truth, it seems to me a serious mistake for anyone to say that Jews and pagans may be saved by keeping their own law, although they do not believe in Jesus Christ as the Church believes. Because these hold that their own beliefs are good and sound and sufficient for their salvation, and seem to perform many good deeds in this faith, it is sometimes assumed that they will be saved, and that if they knew that the Christian faith was better than their own, they would renounce their faith and accept it. But this is not sufficient, for Christ, God and man, is both the way and the goal; He is the mediator between God and man, and no one can be reconciled to God or come to the joys of heaven except through Him. Therefore those who do not believe that He is both God and man can never be saved nor reach heaven. There are others who do not love Christ or His passion, and whose souls are not re-formed in His likeness. These are insincere Christians, who have no charity, and who live and die in mortal sin. Such people seem to believe that Jesus is the Son of God, and that His passion avails for man's salvation, and they accept all the other articles of the faith; but their faith is still-born and dead, for they do not love Jesus, nor do they wish for the fruits of His passion. They cling to their sins, and to a false love of the world till their dying day. They are not restored to the likeness of God, but are doomed to the pains of hell for eternity, like Jews and pagans, but their pains are much more severe, inasmuch as they knew the true faith and did not observe it. For this is a much graver sin than ignorance.

If, then, you wish to learn which souls are re-formed here in this life to the image of God by the merits of Christ's passion, it is only those who believe in Him and love Him. In these souls God's image, which was deformed by sin into that of an evil beast, is restored to its original form, and to the dignity and honour which it once enjoyed. And no soul can be saved or come to the joy of heaven unless it has been restored and re-formed.

CHAPTER 4: *How man's soul, which is God's image, may be restored to His likeness in this life*

YOU may now ask how it can be true that this image of God, which is man's soul, can be restored to His likeness here in this life. It would seem to be impossible, for were it restored it would possess a sound understanding, clear vision and pure ardent love of God and spiritual things at all times, such as it enjoyed at its creation. But as you are well aware, no one has these things in this life, and you yourself admit that you are very far from such a position. Your thoughts, your reason, and the affections of your soul are so immersed in earthly things that you have little perception of spiritual things. You cannot feel any reformation in yourself, but are so stifled by this dark image of sin that despite all your efforts, wherever you turn you feel yourself degraded and defiled by the sinful impulses that spring from it. It does not seem to you that the flesh is yielding to the spirit, either as regards your spiritual faculties or your bodily feelings. It must therefore appear to you that this image cannot be reformed; or if it can, you enquire how this reformation can take place.

To this, I answer that there are two ways in which this image of God, which is man's soul, may be reformed: one reformation is complete, and the other partial. Complete reformation cannot be effected in this life, but will take place later in the joy of heaven. The soul of man will then be fully restored, not to that state in which it was created, nor yet to that which it might have attained had it remained sinless: but by the great mercy and infinite goodness of God it will be brought to an even greater happiness and higher joy than it could have attained had it never fallen. For God Himself will occupy and fill the soul, which will then have no desire for anything but Him. It will view humanity in the Person of Jesus, exalted above the angels and united to the Godhead. Jesus, God and man, will be all in all; He alone and none but He. As the prophet says: *Dominus solus exaltabitur in illa die* (Isa. ii, 11). In that everlasting day our Lord Jesus will be exalted, and He alone. Man's body also will be glorified, for it will receive the precious gift of immortality with all its blessings. Both soul and body will receive more blessings than I can describe, but this will be in heaven, and not in this life. For although the passion of our Lord will bring about this full restoration of man's soul, it was not His purpose to grant it immediately after His passion to all His chosen who were living at the time, but to reserve it until the Last Day. This He did because in His mercy our Lord Jesus predestined certain souls to salvation, and at the time of His passion their number was not complete. It was therefore necessary that a certain time should elapse through successive generations before this number could be complete. For if every soul that believed in Him had received this blessing, and had been fully restored immediately after the death of our Lord, every person then living would have accepted the Faith in order to receive this blessing. Human generation would then have ceased, and we who are now living and others after us who have been chosen by God would not have been born, and our Lord would not have completed the number of His chosen. But since this could not be, God pro-

vided a better plan for us in that He reserved the perfect reformation of man's soul until the Last Day. As Saint Paul says: *Deo
pro nobis melius providente, ut non sine nobis consummarentur.* That
is: God provided better for us in delaying our restoration than
in granting it then, in order that the chosen souls who preceded
us should not reach perfection before us. There is also another
reason, because man at his creation was granted free-will, and
had a free choice whether to enjoy God or not; but since at first
he rejected God and became a wretched apostate, it was reasonable that should man subsequently be restored, he should again
be granted the same free choice that he once had. He would
have to choose whether to reap the benefits of his restoration or
not. And this may be a reason why man's soul was not fully
restored immediately after the passion of our Lord Jesus Christ.

CHAPTER 5: *How the soul may be restored to the likeness of
Christ in two ways, by faith or by experience*

THIS likeness can be partially restored, but such restoration
must take place during this life, otherwise it can never be
attained, nor will the soul be saved. This reformation comes
about in two ways; one is by faith alone, the other is by faith
and experience. The first – reformation by faith alone – is sufficient for salvation, but the second earns a high reward in
heaven. The first may be secured without difficulty and in a
short time, but the second can only be won after a long time
and with great spiritual effort. The first may be had while the
image of sin is still active within us; for though a person may
be conscious of nothing but sinful impulses and carnal desires,
yet if he does not willingly assent to them, he may be reformed
by faith to the likeness of God. But the second type of reformation eradicates from the soul all carnal impulses and worldly
desires, and allows no imperfections to survive. The first

reformation takes place in souls who are entering upon and progressing in the spiritual life, and in those leading the active life, while the second is reserved for perfect souls and for contemplatives. By the first reformation the image of sin is not destroyed, and its influence is not lessened; but the second reformation destroys the former influence of this image of sin, and fills the soul with new grace through the working of the Holy Spirit. Therefore the first is good, and the second is better; but the third – which takes place only in heaven – is the best of all. We will begin by considering the first and second, and will later come to the third.

CHAPTER 6: *How a soul may lose its likeness to God and its chance of reformation through two kinds of sin, original and actual*

Two kinds of sin cause a soul to lose its likeness to God; the first is called original, being the first sin, and the other is called actual, being sin deliberately committed. These two sins exclude a soul from the joys of heaven and condemn it to the eternal pain of hell, unless by the grace of God it is restored to His likeness before it passes out of this life. Nevertheless, there are two remedies against these two sins, by means of which a deformed soul may be restored. The remedy against original sin is the sacrament of Baptism, and that against actual sin is the sacrament of Penance. The soul of an unbaptized child bears no likeness to God because of original sin; it is nothing but an image of the devil and a brand of hell.* But as soon as it is baptized, it is reformed into the likeness of God, and through virtue of the faith of Holy Church it is transformed from the likeness of the devil and made like an angel of heaven. The same applies to Jews and pagans, who until they are baptized are nothing but the bond-slaves of hell. But when they abjure their errors, humbly accept the truth in Christ, and receive Baptism by water and the Holy Spirit, they are at once re-formed into the likeness of God. The Church regards this reformation as so complete that were they to die immediately after Baptism, they would pass directly to heaven without de-lay, and would never experience the pain of hell or purgatory. This privilege would be theirs through the merits of the Passion of Christ.

CHAPTER 7: *How a soul that has lost the likeness of Christ through mortal sin can be fully restored to it by recourse to the sacrament of Penance*

IF any Christian who has lost the likeness of God through mortal sin and disobedience to His commandments is moved by grace to heartfelt contrition and sorrow, with a sincere de-sire to forsake sin, and if he is firmly resolved to live a godly life, he should if possible receive the sacrament of Penance, or if he cannot, he should at least wish to do so. Once this is done, the soul of this person, formerly distorted by mortal sin into the likeness of the devil, is restored by the sacrament of Penance to the likeness of God. God is of great kindness and infinite mercy, for He is willing to forgive every kind of sin, and is swift to grant abundant grace to a sinner who asks His mercy. He does not wait until severe penance has been performed or bodily suffering endured before He forgives, but He does re-quire that the soul should detest and resolve to forsake its sin, and turn to Him with all its love. This is what He asks, and for this He gives grace. And when He sees that the soul responds, He immediately forgives its sin and restores the soul to His like-ness. So the sin is forgiven, and the soul will not be damned; but the penalty incurred by sin is not fully removed unless the contrition and love of the sinner are sufficiently great. The

sinner must therefore confess to his spiritual father, accept the
penance allotted him, and perform it willingly, in order that
both the sin and its penalty may be removed before he passes out
of this life. This requirement of Holy Church is a reasonable
one, and it is greatly to the good of man's soul that although
the sin is forgiven by virtue of contrition, the penitent should
if possible make full confession to his priest, since this is evidence of his humility and of his desire to make full satisfaction.
It is the proof and pledge of forgiveness, which he needs to con-
vince his enemies. For if some man whose life was forfeit had
been pardoned by his earthly king, he would require a written
pardon in order to live in security among his fellow citizens.
Similarly in the realm of the spirit, if a man has offended the
King of heaven by mortal sin and deserves to forfeit his life, he
does not obtain full security by offering his contrition to God
in secret: he requires if possible some evidence from the
Church, and it is the sacrament of Penance which is both the
proof and evidence of his forgiveness. For since he has sinned
both against God and His Church, it is fitting that he should
receive forgiveness from the one and a pledge of it from the
other.* This is one reason why confession is necessary. Another
reason is that the reformation of the soul depends upon faith
and not upon natural feelings, so that a rough and simple
man of the world who cannot easily understand anything but
tangible things would feel no assurance that his sins were forgiven unless he were to possess outward proof. This proof is
afforded in confession, through which he is assured of forgiveness if he does all that he can. This is the Church's teaching as I
understand it. And a further reason is this. Although forgiveness does not depend principally upon confession, but upon
heartfelt contrition and abandonment of sin, I am sure that there
is many a soul who would never have felt contrition nor abandoned sin had it not been for confession. For in confession it
often comes about that the grace of compunction visits a soul

which had never before experienced it, but was always cold, dry, and insensible. And since confession is of such benefit to most Christians, the Church has required that all Christians should confess their sins at least once a year to their spiritual father and receive absolution for them, even though they may have already felt deep contrition for them. But if everyone were as diligent in avoiding sin, and had reached as deep a knowledge and experience of God as some people have, the Church would not have found it necessary to insist on confession as a vital obligation. But all people are not so perfect; indeed, the majority of Christians are probably far from perfect. Therefore the Church has made confession of general obligation for all Christians who acknowledge the Church as their mother and obey her precepts. If, as I believe, this is true, then it is a serious error for anyone to say that it is neither necessary nor right for a sinner to confess his sins to a priest, and that no one is under any obligation to do so. For it follows from what I have said that it is both necessary and beneficial to all souls who are defiled by sin in this life of sorrow, and especially to those who have been distorted from God's likeness by mortal sin. Such souls cannot be restored to His likeness except through the sacrament of Penance, which depends primarily on sincere contrition and sorrow, and secondarily on verbal confession whenever this is possible. In this way the sacrament of Penance restores a sinful soul to the image and likeness of God.

CHAPTER 8: *How a soul reformed through the sacrament of Penance must hold firmly to the Church's faith*

BUT this reformation depends upon faith and not upon feelings, for while it is a property of faith to believe what one cannot see, it is also a property to believe what one does not feel. But one whose soul is restored to God's likeness by the sacrament of Penance does not feel any change in himself, either physical or spiritual. His feelings are the same as before, and he experiences the same sinful impulses, the same passions and worldly desires as formerly. Nevertheless, he must believe in his restoration to God's likeness, although he cannot feel or see it. But if he receives grace and keeps a close watch on himself, he may well feel sorrow for his sin and realize that his will is turning away from sin towards holiness of life. But he does not see the reformation of his soul, or feel how by the secret working of God's grace it is wonderfully and imperceptibly changed from the foulness of a devil to the fairness of an angel. He cannot see this process, but he must believe in it; and if he believes in it, then his soul is really reformed.

The Church holds that by the right reception of the sacrament of Baptism the soul of a Jew, a pagan, or a new-born babe is reformed to the likeness of God by the secret and imperceptible working of the Holy Spirit, although bodily temptations will be experienced as strongly after Baptism as before. Similarly, by the humble and right reception of the sacrament of Penance, the soul of an unworthy Christian, who has lived his whole life in mortal sin, is imperceptibly reformed and his will re-directed by the hidden power and gracious action of the Holy Spirit. This power works swiftly, correcting a stubborn soul in a moment, and transforming its spiritual ugliness into invisible beauty. It changes a servant of the devil into a son of joy, and promises a former prisoner of hell a place in the kingdom of heaven, despite all the carnal inclinations fostered by this sinful image within us. Understand, then, that the sacraments of Baptism and Penance do not entirely stifle or destroy all bodily desires and violent passions, so that the soul is never troubled by such feelings. Were this the case, the soul would be fully restored here to its original dignity at creation; but perfect restoration is not possible in this life. These sacraments, however, possess power to cleanse the soul from all its former sins. If the soul has left the body, it is saved from damnation; if it is still in the body, it is given grace to resist the temptations of sin. It is also preserved in a state of grace, so that no sinful inclinations and passions that it feels, however violent, can harm it or separate it from God so long as it does not willingly consent to them. This is what Saint Paul meant when he said: *Nihil damnationis est iis qui sunt in Christo, qui non secundum carnem ambulant*, etc. (Rom. viii, 1). That is, those souls who are restored to the image of God in faith through the sacraments of Baptism or Penance will not be condemned for feeling this image of sin, so long as they do not yield to evil inclinations or act on them.

CHAPTER 9: *How we should believe that we have received this gift of reformation if our conscience witnesses to our renunciation of sin and our resolve to live a good life*

SAINT PAUL says of this reformation by faith: *Justus ex fide vivit* (Heb. x, 38). The good man lives by faith. That is, one who is justified by Baptism or Penance lives by faith, which enables the soul to be saved and enter the peace of heaven. As Saint Paul says: *Justificati ex fide, pacem habeamus ad Deum* (Rom. v, 1). In other words, between God and ourselves, who are justified and reformed through faith in Christ, there is peace and concord, despite the sinful feelings astir within us. And although this reformation is hidden and cannot be assessed in this life, nevertheless whoever firmly believes in it, diligently mending his ways and never lapsing into mortal sin, will certainly discover the truth of what I am saying when the hour of death approaches and the soul departs from the body. In order to encourage chosen souls who live by faith but are still distressed by this grievous image, Saint John says: *Carissimi, et nunc sumus filii Dei, sed nondum apparuit quid erimus. Scimus quoniam cum Christus apparuerit, tunc apparebimus cum eo, similes ei in gloria* (1 John iii, 2). That is : Dear friends, while we live on earth we are the sons of God, for we are restored to His likeness by faith in Christ : but what we shall be is not yet revealed, and remains unknown. But we know for certain that when our Lord shall appear at the Last Day, we shall appear with Him, and be like Him in everlasting joy. If, then, you wish to know whether or not your soul is restored to the likeness of God, you can be guided by what I have said. Examine your own conscience, and consider the direction of your will, for everything depends on this. If it is turned away from every kind of mortal sin, so that you would not under any circumstances knowingly or willingly break the commandments of God ; and if you have humbly confessed all your former offences against His laws, with a firm resolve to abandon these sins and a true sorrow for having committed them, then I can assure you that your soul is restored by faith to the likeness of God.

CHAPTER 10: *How one whose soul is completely restored to the image of God makes every effort to avoid sin and keep himself in perfect charity with God and his neighbour*

MOST of God's chosen lead their lives reformed in faith alone. They are resolved to avoid all mortal sins, to keep themselves in love and charity with their neighbours, and to obey God's commandments to the best of their knowledge. And whenever evil feelings of pride, envy, anger, lust, or any other grievous sin rise in their hearts, they steel their wills to resist and reject them. Should they involuntarily commit some venial fault through frailty or ignorance, they are so troubled in conscience that they cannot rest until they have confessed and received forgiveness. I am sure that all who live in this way are reformed in faith to the image of God. And if they continue in this reformed state and are found in it at the hour of death, they will be saved and attain full reformation in the joys of heaven, although they may never have experienced any spiritual consolation or special grace of devotion all their lives. For otherwise, if you say that no one can be saved unless they have reached some level of devotion and spiritual experience that is granted only to certain special souls, then few would be saved compared with the multitude lost. It is impossible to imagine that our Lord Jesus Christ would have become man and suffered the bitter pains of death only to save those who are devout and have been granted the grace of spiritual fervour. It would have been a paltry success if He had come so far and humbled himself so profoundly for so few souls. No, His mercy reaches far more widely than that. Nevertheless, if on the contrary you imagine that the passion of our Lord was so precious and his mercy so infinite that no Christian soul will be damned, however great its sin – as some fools suppose – you are greatly mistaken. So take a balanced view of the matter, and believe as the Church believes; that is, that if by the grace of God the greatest sinner alive turns from mortal sin with sincere penitence to serve God, his soul is reformed, and were he to die in that state, he would be saved. For God spoke through His prophet, saying: *In quacumque hora conversus peccator et ingemuerit, vita vivet et non morietur* (Ezek. xviii, 21). As soon as the sinner turns from sin to God and repents, he shall live, and will not suffer eternal death. On the other hand, whosoever remains in mortal sin and refuses to abandon it or amend, is not reformed to the likeness of God. Neither is he reformed if he refuses to accept the sacrament of Penance, or if he does not accept it sincerely for love of God – that is, for love of virtue and purity – but only in deference to public opinion or from fear of hell. If he dies in that sorry state, he will not be saved. His faith will not save him, for his faith is dead and loveless, and is therefore of no use to him. But those whose faith is inspired by even a small degree of love and charity are reformed to the likeness of God. Among such are simple folk who have no special gifts of devotion or knowledge of God such as some spiritually gifted people possess, but who have a general belief in the faith of the Church without a full understanding of it; for in their case this is not necessary. In this faith they do their best to live in love and charity with their neighbours, to avoid all mortal sins, and to perform acts of mercy. All these will win a place in the joys of heaven, for it is written in the Apocalypse: *Qui timetis Deum, pusilli et magni, laudate eum* (Rev. xix, 5). Praise God, all you who fear Him, both small and great.

The great are souls who are growing in grace, or who are reformed in spirit and perfect in the love of God. The small are imperfect souls, men and women in worldly occupations, who have only a child's knowledge of God and very little understanding of Him. But these are reared in the bosom of the Church, and are nourished with the sacraments as children are fed with milk. They should all love God, and thank Him for saving their souls by His infinite mercy and goodness. For Holy Church, who is their Mother and has a tender love for all her spiritual children, prays for them to Jesus her Spouse, and obtains healing for their souls through the merits of His passion. In particular she prays for those who cannot express their own needs in prayer. Thus in the Gospel we are told how the woman of Canaan asked our Lord to heal her daughter who was possessed by a devil, and how at first He refused because she was of an alien race. But she persisted in her request until our Lord granted it, and said to her: 'Woman, great is your faith; be it done as you will.' (Matt. xv, 828.) And her daughter was made whole at that instant. This woman represents the Church, who asks our Lord to help all simple, ignorant souls who are troubled by the temptations of the world, and who cannot speak to God aright with perfect devotion nor contemplate Him with burning love. And although it may seem that our Lord at first refuses her because her children are as it were unknown to Him, yet because of the great faith and merits of the Church He grants her everything that she asks. And so these simple souls who hold fast to the faith of the Church, trust wholly in God's mercy, humbly receiving the sacraments and obeying the laws of the Church, are saved through the prayers and faith of their spiritual mother Holy Church.

CHAPTER 11: *How reformed souls need to fight constantly against temptations to sin: and how a soul may know whether it yields to temptation or not*

THIS reformation in faith is easy to acquire, but not so easy to maintain, so that anyone who is truly reformed to God's likeness must devote much effort to keeping this likeness whole and pure, so that it does not degenerate into the image of sin through weakness of will. A reformed Christian dare not be idle or thoughtless, because the image of sin grips him firmly and constantly offers sinful suggestions, so that unless he is very watchful it is very easy to assent and fall. So he must be always fighting the evil suggestions of this wicked image, for he cannot come to terms with it or comply with its unlawful demands. If he does so, he deceives himself; but if he fights against it he need have little fear of yielding to it, for the struggle itself will dispel any false sense of security. It is right that a man should be at peace with all things except the devil and this sinful image, against which he must fight constantly in mind and body until he has overcome them. But he will not entirely overcome them in this life, while he carries this image with its evil influence within him. I do not deny that by the grace of God it is possible to win the upper hand over this image, to the extent that the soul will not follow or assent to its temptations; but it is not possible to be liberated from it entirely, for no one can avoid feeling the pull of evil suggestions, bodily desires, or vain thoughts in this life.

I think it possible that a soul which is reformed in feeling and transported by love into the contemplation of God may be so remote from the influence of the senses and vain imagination, and temporarily so withdrawn from physical influences that it is conscious of nothing but God; but this condition is not permanent. I repeat that everyone must fight against this sinful image, and in particular any who is reformed only in faith, for he may easily be deceived by it. Saint Paul speaks for such souls when he says: *Caro concupiscit adversus spiritum et spiritum adversus carnem* (Gal. v, 17). A soul restored to the likeness of God fights against bodily impulses roused by this sinful image, and the image resists the will of the spirit. Saint Paul understood this twofold struggle, and said: *Inveni legem in membris meis, repugnantem legi mentis meae, et captivum me ducentem in legem peccati* (Rom. vii, 23). I have found two laws in myself, one in my soul, and another in my body which fights against the former and often makes me the unhappy prisoner of the law of sin. By these two laws I understand him to mean these two images. The law of the spirit is the restoration of the reasonable soul to the image of God, while the law of the flesh is sensuality, which I call the image of sin. A reformed soul lives its life subject to these two laws. As Saint Paul says: *Mente enim servio legi Dei, carne autem legi peccati* (Rom. vii, 25). In my will – that is, in my will and reason – I serve God; but in my body – that is, in my bodily desires – I serve the law of sin. However, although a reformed soul is subject to the law of sin inasmuch as it involuntarily feels temptations to wickedness arising from the corruption of our bodily nature, Saint Paul forbids it to despair, and quotes his own experience: *Non enim quod volo bonum hoc ago; sed malum quod odi, hoc facio. Si autem malum quod odi, hoc facio, non ego operor illud, sed quod habitat in me, peccatum* (Rom. vii, 19, 20). I do not do the good that I wish; that is, I wish to escape the influence of the flesh, but I cannot. And the evil that I hate – that is, the sinful impulses of the flesh – I do. But although I feel them and often take involuntary pleasure in them, I shall not be condemned or held responsible for them, because I hate them. And why? Because they are due to the corruption of this sinful image, and not to my own inclination. In this passage Saint Paul encourages all souls who are reformed in faith not to fear the power of this sinful image and its irrational impulses too greatly, so long as they do not willingly yield to them. Nevertheless, many people who are truly reformed are needlessly troubled on this point. For instance, when they have felt pride, envy, greed, lust, or any other grave sin stirring within them, they are sometimes not sure whether they have yielded to them or not. This is not surprising, for man is weak, and in time of temptation his mind is so troubled and confused that he cannot think clearly or make a free decision; consequently pleasurable desires come upon him unawares, and establish themselves in his mind long before he realizes it. This is why doubts arise in some people, who are not sure whether they have sinned during temptation or not.

On this point, I think that a person can find out whether he has consented or not in the following way. A man may be tempted to some sin which appeals so strongly to his senses that it affects his judgement and obsesses his imagination. But if he controls himself and refuses to yield to these sinful desires, finding them so distasteful that if he could put them out of mind he would do so: and if, when the temptation has passed, he is glad to be rid of it, he may rest assured that however strongly his senses pressed him to sin, he did not yield or commit any mortal sin. But the best safeguard for a simple person who is weak and simple is that he should avoid over-confidence, and should not assume that sensual impulses of this kind are blameless, for he might easily lapse into carelessness and false security. On the other hand, he should not be over-scrupulous or naïve, imagining that all these impulses are mortal or grave venial sins. Neither of these opinions is true. So let him regard them all as sins or faults and be sorry for them, without trying to discover whether they are mortal or venial. But if his conscience is seriously troubled he should visit his confessor without delay, and reveal them to him either in general or particular. He should make especial mention of any temptation that is beginning to take root in and possess his heart, drawing it down to sin and worldly vanities. And when he has received absolution, let him trust firmly in God's forgiveness, and cease to trouble his mind as to whether his sins were mortal or venial. Let him instead devote more attention to guarding himself against them in the future. If he does this, he will find peace of conscience.

But some people are so worldly-minded and stupid that they would like to feel, hear, or see the forgiveness of their sins in the same way as they feel or see a material object; and because they cannot do so, they are so doubtful and uncertain that they cannot rest. This is foolish, because faith comes before feeling, and when our Lord healed a paralysed man, he said: *Confide, fili, dimittuntur tibi peccata tua* (Mark ii, 5). Son, believe firmly that your sins are forgiven. Since forgiveness comes spiritually and invisibly by the grace of the Holy Spirit, He did not tell the man to see or feel that his sins were forgiven, but to believe. In the same way, if a man desires peace of conscience he must first do whatever he can without feeling any spiritual assurance of forgiveness. If he does this, he will by the grace of God afterwards feel and understand that it is so. The prophet said: *Nisi credderitis, non intelligetis.* Unless you first believe, you cannot understand. For belief comes first, and understanding follows. This understanding, which may be called the sight of God when the result of grace, can only be possessed by a soul of great purity. As our Lord says: *Beati mundo corde, quoniam ipsi Deum videbunt* (Matt. v, 8). Blessed are the pure in heart, for they shall see God. Meaning that they will see God, not with their eyes but inwardly, with their understanding purified and enlightened by the grace of the Holy Spirit to see truth. But no soul can attain this purity unless it first possesses a firm faith. As the apostle says: *Fide mundans corda eorum* (Acts xv, 9): that is, God purifies the hearts of his chosen through faith. So a person must first believe that his soul has been reformed through the sacrament of Penance, although he cannot see it, and he must resolve to live rightly and virtuously as his faith requires, so that he may in due time come to recognize and feel this reformation within him.

CHAPTER 12: *Although the soul is reformed, this image remains both lovely and ugly during this life: and how reformed and unreformed souls differ in their secret reactions*

THE soul of man is both lovely and ugly: lovely in so far as it is reformed in faith to the likeness of God, but ugly in so far as it is still corrupted by the carnal impulses and senseless urges of this sinful image. It can be ugly and bestial, and it can be lovely and angelic; ugly in its bondage to sensuality, but lovely in its search for truth by reason. It is ugly in its carnal desires, and lovely in its will to good. So the chosen soul is both lovely and ugly, and Holy Scripture says: *Nigra sum, sed formosa, filiae Jerusalem, sicut tabernacula Cedar et sicut pelles Salomonis* (Cant. i, 5). I am black but lovely, daughters of Jerusalem, as the tents of Kedar and as the fleeces of Solomon. Meaning: the angels of heaven – that is, the daughters of Jerusalem on high – do not despise me because I am black, for although my skin is black as the tents of Kedar, inwardly I am lovely as the fleeces of Solomon, for I am reformed to the likeness of God. Kedar means black, and represents the devil: Solomon means peace, and represents our Lord Jesus Christ, for He is peace and the lover of peace. Solomon's fleece represents a holy angel, in whom

God dwells unseen, just as life is hidden within the skin of a living body. So an angel is compared to a fleece. A chosen soul may therefore say with humble trust in God and with a glad heart: Although my body is outwardly blackened by sin, like an unregenerate soul that is the dwelling of the devil, yet by faith and good will I am inwardly beautiful as an angel from heaven. Elsewhere the Scripture says: *Nolite considerare me quod fusca sum, quia decoloravit me sol* (Cant. i, 6). Disregard my blackness, for the sun has darkened me. The sun blackens the body outwardly, but not inwardly, and this is a parable of earthly life. So the chosen soul says: Do not condemn me because I am black, for my blackness is all external. It is due to touching and bearing this image of sin, but it is not a blackness of soul. And although a chosen soul, reformed in faith, inhabits this sinful body, is subject to the same bodily desires, and acts outwardly in the same way as an unregenerate soul, so that people cannot see any difference between them, yet there is a great difference in the sight of God. But the power to discern one from another belongs to God alone, and is beyond the knowledge and experience of man, so that we should never condemn a man for any action, the intention of which may be good or evil. For an unreformed man is so obsessed by love of the world and so concerned with bodily pleasures that he is entirely satisfied with such things and secretly desires nothing better than to enjoy them for ever. He is insensible to the influence of grace, which would render this earthly life distasteful and move him to desire the joys of heaven. One might almost say that a man in this state does not so much carry this sinful image as be carried by it, like a man who is so ill and weak that he cannot support himself and is carried on a stretcher. For a sinful man is so weak and enfeebled through lack of grace that he cannot move hand or foot to do good, nor can he resist the smallest temptation when it comes, but succumbs to it like a beast to carrion. Although one whose soul is reformed employs his bodily senses and is aware of their influence, at heart he despises them, and would never rest content with them. He shuns this temptation as he would the bite of an adder, and desires if possible to rest in God and offer the love of his heart to Him. Sometimes this desire is strong in him, and he longs to exchange the tedious pleasures of this life for the joys of life everlasting. Although aware of this image, a man in this state is not carried by it like a sick man, but has to carry it. However, grace gives him strength to endure and wear his body with its sinful impulses without being harmed or defiled by them, because he does not love, consent to, or practise things that are mortal sins, as do unregenerate souls.

This was literally fulfilled in the Gospel in the case of the paralytic man who was too weak to walk and was carried to our Lord in a litter. When Jesus saw his trouble, He said in His goodness: *Surge et tolle grabatum tuum, et vade in domum tuam* (S. John v, 8). Rise, take up your bed, and go to your house. The man did so and was made whole. And just as he carried on his back the bed which previously carried him, so it may be said spiritually that a soul reformed in faith carries the image of sin which previously carried him. Therefore do not be too worried about the blackness that you have acquired through carrying this image of sin. Be confident in spite of the shame and regret you feel when you look at it, and despite the sneers of your spiritual enemies who whisper in your heart, 'Where is your Lord Jesus? What are you looking for? Where is the beauty of which you speak? What do you feel except blindness and sin? Where is the image of God which you say is reformed in you?' Take comfort and be strong in faith, as I have already said: if you are, this faith will empower you to crush all the temptations of your enemies. Saint Paul said: *Accipe scutum fidei, in quo tela hostis nequissima poteris extinguere* (Eph. vi, 16). Take the shield of firm faith: with it you will be able to put out all the burning darts of your enemy.

CHAPTER 13 : *On three types of people; those who are re-formed, those who are unreformed, and those who are reformed both in faith and feeling*

YOU will realize from what I have already said that people are of various types according to the varying states of their souls. Some are not reformed to the likeness of God, and some are reformed only in faith, while some are reformed both in faith and feeling.

For you must understand that the soul has two faculties. One is called sensibility, that is, the faculty of perception through the senses, which man shares with the animals. When this sensibility is not rightly directed and controlled, the image of sin arises; for if the senses are not ruled by the reason, the result is sin. The other faculty is called reason, and this itself has two powers, the higher and the lower reason. The higher may be termed male, since it should exercise control, and it is in this faculty that God's likeness exists, for it is only through this faculty that the soul knows and loves Him. The lower faculty may be termed female, and should obey the higher reason as woman obeys man. Its function is to understand and control mundane things, to employ them with discretion as necessary, and to reject whatever is not essential. It must always watch, respect and follow the higher rational faculty. Now a man who lives only to gratify his bodily desires like an unreasoning animal, and who has neither knowledge of God nor desire for virtue and holy living, but is blinded by pride, gnawed by envy, dominated by greed, and corrupted by lust and other grave sins, is not reformed to the likeness of God. For such a man is entirely satisfied with and subject to the image of sin. But one who fears God and refuses to obey the dangerous impulses of the senses keeps control over worldly things, and makes it his aim to please God in all that he does. In this way the soul is reformed to the likeness of God in faith, and although it experiences the same temptations as the other soul, they cannot harm it since it does not surrender to them. But a soul which receives grace to resist all sensual temptations, both mortal and venial, and is not even disturbed by them, is reformed in feeling. For it follows the higher powers of reason, and is enabled to see God and spiritual things, as I shall explain later.

CHAPTER 14: *How sinners come to resemble the animals, and are known to be lovers of this world*

WRETCHED is the man who does not recognize the true worth of his soul, and has no wish to do so. For with the exception of the angels, whom it resembles, the soul is the highest of God's creations, and is superior to all other incarnate beings. Therefore man cannot find true rest except in God, and he should love and desire Him alone, seeking only to be reformed to His likeness. But because he does not understand this, man tries to find rest and pleasure in creatures inferior to himself. Yet man acts contrary to nature and reason if he leaves God, the supreme good and source of all life, unsought, unloved, unknown, and unworshipped, and seeks rest and pleasure in the passing pleasures of the world. But this is what is done by all who love this world, and who seek happiness in this wretched life alone. Some find pleasure in pride and conceit, and having lost all reverence for God, they labour night and day to win the honour and praise of the world. Nothing matters to them so long as they win it and excel all others, whether in scholarship or technical skill, in reputation and fame, in riches and respect, in influence and authority, in estate and dignity. Some take delight in wealth, and make it their sole object to amass vast possessions. Their hearts are so set on this that they think of nothing but how to obtain it. Some love to gratify their bodily cravings in gluttony and lust, some in one way and some in another. And those who act in this vile manner degrade man's noble nature, and lower themselves to the level of beasts.

Pride turns a man into a lion, for he wishes to be feared and respected by everyone, and will not allow anyone to thwart his wishes by word or act. And if anyone resists his presumption he is furious, and sets on him like a lion does on a lesser beast. One who behaves in this way is no true man, and is acting contrary to man's true nature, so that he is changed into a lion. Envy and anger turn men into dogs. They bark at their neighbours, and bite them with wicked and malicious words; they harass those who have done them no harm, and harm them in body and soul contrary to God's laws. Some people become like asses, because they are slothful in the service of God, and unwilling to show any kindness to their neighbour. They are ready enough to hurry away to Rome for worldly profit and honours, or to win popular approval. But when it is a matter of spiritual gain, of the good of their own souls, or of God's glory, they are soon bored. They do not really want these things, and if they do anything at all, they only make a grudging gesture. Some people are so obstinately ignorant and ill-mannered that they are like swine. They have no fear of God, and only seek to gratify the lusts and desires of the body. They have no respect for the dignity of human nature, and make no attempt to be guided by reason or to control the irrational impulses of their physical nature. When bodily temptation arises, they yield to it at once, and revel in it like swine. Treacherous and covetous people who rob their neighbours of their worldly goods by threats and oppression become like ravening wolves. False and deceitful people who live by trickery and guile become like foxes.

All such people, and others like them, live in no fear of God, but break His commandments, distort His likeness in them, and make themselves like beasts: indeed, they are worse than beasts, and resemble the devils in hell. But unless those who live in these ways are reformed before their souls part from their bodies at the hour of death, their sin-blinded eyes will then be opened to the truth, and they will receive the punishment due to their wickedness. And because the image of God has not been restored in them through the sacrament of penance, and they have been reformed neither in faith nor feeling in this life, they will be accursed and cast out from the face of our Creator, doomed to lie in the depths of hell with the devil for ever. Saint John says in the Apocalypse: *Timidis et incredulis, et execratis et homicidis, fornicatoribus, veneficis, idolatris et omnibus mendacibus, pars illorum erit in stagno ardenti igne et sulphure* (Rev. xxi, 8). Those who are proud and unbelieving, accursed, murderers, lustful and covetous, poisoners, idolaters, and liars will all receive their dues in the pit of hell burning with fire and brimstone. If those who love the world would often consider how transitory it is, and how all improper love will be severely punished, they would soon learn to despise the worldly delights to which they are at present devoted. They would lift up their hearts to God in love, and do all in their power to be reformed to His likeness before they passed out of this life.

CHAPTER 15: *How those who love this world hinder the reformation of their souls in various ways*

BUT certain of these people say: 'I would gladly love God, be good, and renounce love of the world if I could, but I have not the grace to do so. If I had the same grace as a good man I would live as he does; but since I have not this grace, I cannot do it.' I reply that it is quite true that they have no grace, and therefore remain in their sin and cannot escape it. But this will not help them, nor does it excuse them before God, because it is their own fault. They hinder themselves so greatly and in so many ways that the light of grace cannot shine in them nor dwell in their hearts. Some of them are so obstinate that they do not desire grace or a good life, for they realize that if this were the case they would have to give up their love and desire for worldly things. And they do not wish to do this, because these things are so pleasant to them that they do not wish to forgo them. They would furthermore have to undertake works of penance, such as fasting, keeping vigils, praying and other practices which discipline the body and subdue its sinful inclinations. And they cannot do this because it appears so painful and unpleasant to them that they are frightened to think of it. As a result these cowardly and unhappy people continue in their sins.

Some would seem to desire grace, and begin to prepare themselves for it. But their wills are extraordinarily weak, for they immediately yield to any temptation that arises, although it is clearly contrary to the laws of God. They are so accustomed to giving way that resistance to sin seems impossible to them, and this imaginary difficulty gradually saps their will-power and destroys it.

Some, again, feel the influence of grace when their conscience pricks them for their evil life and prompts them to abandon it. But this suggestion is so painful and displeasing that they refuse to entertain it. They run away and forget it if they can, seeking outward distraction in creatures so as not to feel this inward pricking of conscience.

Besides these there are some who are so blind and brainless that they think there is no life beyond the present, and that man's soul is no different to that of an animal, but dies with the body like that of a beast. So they say: 'Let us eat, drink, and make merry. We are certain of this life, and know of no other heaven.' And there are wretches who hold these views inwardly, but do not say it outwardly. It is of such people that the prophet says: *Dixit insipiens in corde suo, Non est Deus* (Ps. xiv, 1). The fool has said in his heart, There is no God. Every wretch who loves sin and makes this world the sole aim and delight of his soul is such a fool. He does not utter the words 'There is no God', for when he prospers he speaks of God with reverence, and says 'Blessed be God.' And when he has a grudge against God or his neighbour, he will swear by God's blessed Body, or by any of His parts. But in his mind he denies God, for he imagines that God cannot see his sin, or that He will not punish him so severely as Holy Scripture says. Or he may think that God will forgive his sin although he does not abandon it; or that no Christian will be damned however evil his life; or that if he fasts in honour of Our Lady, or says a certain prayer daily, or hears two or three Masses a day, or performs some action that is outwardly in honour of God, he will never go to hell, however gross his sin and despite his refusal to abandon it. This type of man says in his heart, 'There is no God,' but, as the prophet says, he is a fool, and will find by painful experience that He whom he forgot or ignored in times of prosperity is God indeed. *Sola vexatio dabit intellectum auditui,* says the prophet (Isaiah xxviii, 19). Suffering alone will bring understanding. For one who does not understand this now, or refuses to understand it, will do so well enough when he comes to die.

CHAPTER 16: *Those who love this world are advised what to do if their souls are to be reformed before they die*

ALTHOUGH such people are fully aware that they are not in a state of grace and are in mortal sin, they do not care; they are not sorry, nor do they give the matter a thought. They pass their time in worldly pastimes and pleasures, and the further they are from grace, the more hectic their pursuits. Perhaps some are even glad that they have no grace, so that they may, as it were, feel more free to gratify their desire for worldly pleasures, as though God were asleep and could not see them. This is one of the gravest errors, for by their perverseness they prevent the light of grace entering their souls. For the light of grace shines on all spiritual beings, ready to enter where it is welcomed, just as the sun shines on all material things wherever it is not prevented. Thus Saint John says in the Gospel: *Lux in tenebris lucet, et tenebrae non comprehenderunt* (S. John i, 5). The light of grace shines in the darkness – that is, on the hearts of men darkened by sin – but the darkness does not welcome it. In other words, these blind hearts do not receive this light of grace or profit by it. Just as a blind man is bathed in sunlight when he stands in it, but cannot see it or walk by it, similarly a soul blinded by mortal sin is bathed in this light of grace, but is none the better for it, because he is blind and does not or will not realize his blindness. The greatest obstacle to grace is a person's refusal to admit his own blindness because of pride; or if he does realize it, he ignores it and continues to enjoy himself as though all were well with him.

I urge all who are blinded and enslaved by the love of the world in this way, and those in whom the true beauty of human nature is distorted, to consider their souls and prepare them to receive grace as well as they can. If they so desire, they may do it in this way. Once they realize that they are not in a state of grace and are burdened by mortal sin, let them consider what peril and loss they are incurring by being out of grace and alienated from God. There is nothing to prevent them falling into the depths of hell save the single thread of this physical life by which they hang. And what can be snapped more easily than a single thread? Were their breathing to cease, as may easily happen, the soul would at once depart and find itself in hell for ever. If they would consider this, they would tremble for fear of God's justice and of His strict punishment for sin. They would grieve and be sorry for their sins and lack of grace, and implore God to grant them grace. And if they did so, grace would be given them. It would drive away all darkness and hardness of heart, and all weakness of will; it would give them strength to abandon the false love of the world where it leads to mortal sin. For there is no soul in this life so estranged from God by a perverse following of mortal sin that it cannot be corrected and restored by grace to purity of living if only it will humbly surrender its will to God, amend its ways, and sincerely ask His grace and forgiveness. It must accept full responsibility for its own guilty state, and not try to blame God. For Holy Scripture says: *Nolo mortem peccatoris, sed magis ut convertatur et vivat* (Ezek. xxxiii, 11). God says: I do not desire the death of a sinner, but rather that he should turn to Me and live. And it is the will of our Lord that the most obstinate and misguided sinner living should be reformed to His likeness if he will but amend his life and seek for grace.

CHAPTER 17: *How reform of feeling and faith cannot be achieved all at once; it is effected by grace after a long time and with much bodily and spiritual effort*

As I said previously, this reformation in faith can be achieved quite easily. Reformation in faith and feeling must follow; this is not so easily attained, and comes only after patient and prolonged effort. For all God's chosen are reformed in faith, although they may still remain in the lowest degree of charity; but reformation in feeling comes only to souls who reach a state of perfection, and it cannot be achieved all at once. A soul can reach it only through great grace and by prolonged spiritual effort, but it must first be healed of its spiritual sickness. Its bitter passions, bodily desires, and unregenerate feelings have to be burned out of the heart by the fire of desire, and new feelings of burning love and spiritual light have to be infused by grace.

Then the soul begins to draw near to perfection and reformation in feeling.

The soul's progress is like that of a man who has been brought near to death by bodily illness. Although he may be given medicine which restores him and saves his life, he cannot immediately get up and go to work like a man in full health. His bodily weakness prevents this, so that he has to wait a good while, continue with his medicine, and carefully follow his doctor's instructions until his health is fully restored. Similarly in the spiritual life, although one who has been brought near to spiritual death by mortal sin can be restored to life by the medicine of the Sacrament of Penance, and saved from damnation, he is not at once healed of all his passions and worldly desires, nor is he capable of contemplation. He must wait a long time and take good care of himself, and he must order his life so as to recover full health of soul. However, if he takes the medicines of a good doctor and uses them regularly and with discretion, he will be restored to spiritual vitality all the sooner, and will attain reformation in feeling.

Reformation in faith is the lowest state of chosen souls, and below this level they cannot well be; but reformation in feeling is the highest state attainable by a soul in this life. But a soul cannot suddenly leap from the lowest to the highest state, any more than a man who wishes to climb a high ladder and sets his foot on the lowest rung can at the next instant fly to the top. He has to mount each rung in succession one after the other until he comes to the highest. So it is in the spiritual life. No one is suddenly endowed with all graces, but when God, the source of all grace, helps and teaches a soul, it can attain this state by sustained spiritual exercises and wisely ordered activity. For without His especial help and inner guidance no soul can reach a state of perfection.

CHAPTER 18: *One reason why comparatively few souls achieve reformation in faith and feeling*

You may say that since our Lord is so good and gracious, and bestows His gifts so freely, it is surprising that so few souls come to be reformed in feeling, compared with the vast number who do not. It might seem that He is estranged from those who by faith have become His servants, or that He has no regard for them; but this is not true. I think one reason why people are so seldom reformed in feeling is that many who have been reformed in faith do not make a whole-hearted effort to grow in grace, or to lead better lives by means of earnest prayer and meditation, and by other spiritual and bodily exercises. They think it sufficient to avoid mortal sin, and continue to live in the same way. They say that it is enough for them to be saved, and they are content with the lowest place in heaven, wanting nothing higher.

It is possible that some of the elect who lead an active life in the world behave in this way, and this is not altogether surprising, because they are so busy with necessary worldly matters that they cannot devote proper attention to spiritual progress. This is a perilous condition, for they are rising and falling, up and down all day, and never attain any stability in their attempt to lead a good life. However, their way of life affords some kind of excuse. But there are others who have no need to be occupied in worldly business, and who do not have to work very hard to support themselves – for instance, religious of both sexes who vow themselves to a state of perfection in a religious order, or layfolk who are naturally capable and intelligent. People like these could achieve a high state of grace if they set themselves to do so, and they are all the more culpable if they remain idle and make no attempt to grow in grace, or to attain the love and knowledge of God.

It is most dangerous for a soul that is reformed in faith alone to make no effort to seek God and grow in grace, nor to engage in spiritual activity. It may so easily lose ground already gained, and fall back again into mortal sin. For while the soul remains in the body it cannot stand still; it must either grow in grace or relapse into sin. It behaves like a man drawn up out of a pit, who refuses to leave the edge once he is out. He is certainly a fool, for a little gust of wind or a single incautious movement on his part will send him headlong in a worse condition than before. But if he moves right away from the edge and stands on firm ground he will be much safer, even should a great storm arise. It is similar in the spiritual life with one who has been drawn up out of the pit of sin by reformation in faith. If he thinks himself safe enough once he is no longer in mortal sin, refusing to step away, and staying as close as possible to the brink of hell, he is a fool, for at the smallest temptation of the devil or the flesh he falls into sin again. But if he leaves the pit – that is, if he makes a firm resolve to grow in grace, and makes a real effort to win it by prayer and meditation, and by other good works – then although he may undergo violent temptations, he will not easily relapse into mortal sin.

Since grace is good and brings blessing it amazes me when a person who has so little grace that he could hardly possess less, says: 'I have enough; I need no more.' But although a worldly man may have more possessions than he needs, I never hear one say, 'I have enough; I need no more.' He will always want more and more, and devote his whole mind and resources to obtaining more, because his greed is insatiable. Much more, then, should a chosen soul desire spiritual treasures which last for ever and fill the soul with blessing. The wise soul will never cease to desire grace, however much it may already possess, for whoever desires most will obtain most. Indeed, in so doing it will earn great riches and grow in grace.

CHAPTER 19: *Another reason for this failure, and how an unwise reliance on outward forms of devotion sometimes hinders souls from receiving greater grace*

ANOTHER reason is this. Some who are reformed in faith adopt a certain rule of life in both spiritual and worldly matters in the early days of their conversion, and imagine that they must always observe it without change, even although grace may reveal a better. They think that this rule will always be best for them, so that they love it and it becomes such a routine that, once they have fulfilled its obligations, they are quite content, and imagine that they have done great things for God. And should anything occur to interrupt their established routine, although for a reasonable cause, they are discouraged, angry, and troubled in conscience, as though they had committed a mortal sin. Those who behave in this way make it difficult for themselves to receive greater graces because they regard perfection as being dependent on certain outward forms of devotion, and in so doing they mistake a halfway sign for the end of the road.

Outward forms of devotion followed by people at the beginning of their conversion are good, but they are only ways and means leading to perfection, so that anyone who thinks that perfection consists in the carrying out of some bodily or spiritual observance that he learned at his conversion, who remains quite content with this, and who looks no further ahead, will largely halt his own spiritual development. In a very simple craft a mere apprentice can become proficient and understand everything as well on the first day as he will twenty years later. But in a noble and skilled craft the apprentice who makes no progress at all must be either dull-witted or perverse. But the service of God is the noblest of all crafts. It demands the greatest skill, and is the highest and hardest in which to attain perfection. It is also the most profitable and richly rewarding to one who can practise this craft rightly. So it is evident that apprentices who never acquire any knowledge of it are either dull-witted or perverse.

I am not condemning these forms of devotion used by beginners, whether inward or outward, for I know them to be good and helpful. But I would have them regarded simply as aids to spiritual development, to be used only until such time as beginners discover something better. And when the soul discovers something better and more spiritual, which withdraws it a little from the influence of the body, the senses, and the imagination, then if the earlier practices prove a hindrance, they should be abandoned as soon as this can be done without causing scandal or distress to other people, and the soul should follow the way to which it feels drawn. But if neither form of devotion interferes with the other, then whoever wishes to do so may use both. In this matter I am not alluding to devotions enjoined by the Church or by monastic rule, or to those that are imposed as a penance, but only to those undertaken voluntarily.

The prophet teaches us in the Psalms: *Etenim benedictionem dabit legislator, ibunt de virtute in virtutem, videbitur Deus deorum in Sion* (Ps. lxxxiv, 7). The Lawgiver shall give his blessing; they will progress from virtue to virtue, and the God of gods will appear in Sion. Meaning that the Lawgiver, that is our Lord Jesus Christ, will give His blessing, and grant His gifts of grace to chosen souls, calling on them to renounce sin, and restoring them to His likeness by good works. With the help of His grace they will progress from virtue to virtue until they come to Sion, that is, to contemplation, in which state they will see the God of gods. They will see clearly that there is but one God, and that nothing exists apart from Him.

CHAPTER 20: *How perfection can only be attained by constant effort and by purification of the desires*

Now you may say that since reformation in faith alone is an elementary and precarious state from which there remains the danger of a fall, and since reformation in feeling is so high and secure a state for those who can reach it, you wish to learn the best way to attain this goal, and whether there is anything in particular which helps one to win this grace of reformation in feeling. My answer is that you are well aware that anyone who wishes to reach purity of heart and awareness of God has to fight with determination and constancy against all the capital sins. Not only must they fight pride and envy, but all the others, together with those that spring from them, as I have already explained in the first Book, because all passions and bodily desires hinder purity of heart and peace of conscience. It is also necessary to establish all virtues, not only chastity and temperance, but also patience, gentleness, charity, humility, and all others. This is not effected in one particular way but in many ways, which differ according to individual dispositions. It is sometimes fostered by prayer, meditation, and good works, while a person may sometimes prove himself by enduring hunger, thirst, cold, shame, disgrace, and other troubles for love of virtue and truth. You already know this, for you read it in every book that deals with the Christian life, and everyone who tries to fire men's souls with the love of God speaks of it. So it seems that there is no special exercise or method by which alone a soul may attain this grace. It depends chiefly on the grace of our Lord Jesus, and upon great personal efforts, all of which are little enough in themselves.

One reason for this fact may be that our Lord Jesus Himself is the supreme Master of this craft and the supreme healer of

spiritual sickness, without whom we can do nothing. It is therefore reasonable to require that a man should follow and practise what He teaches and inspires. But a master who can only
teach his pupil one lesson has little knowledge to impart, and a
doctor who prescribes one medicine for all ailments has little
learning. So our Lord Jesus, who is so wise and good, reveals
His wisdom and goodness to His disciples in different ways,
and gives to each soul the particular remedy best suited to its
need. A further reason is that if there were one particular way
by which a person might come to the perfect love of God, a
man might imagine that he could attain it by his own efforts,
in the same way that a merchant makes his profit by his own
effort. But the love of God cannot be attained in this way, for
one who wishes to serve God wisely and love Him perfectly
must desire God as his sole reward. But no creature can deserve
to possess God through its own unaided efforts, for even if the
physical and spiritual exertions of a single man were to equal
those of all creation, he would not on that account deserve God
as his reward. For God is supreme bliss and infinite goodness,
and immeasurably transcends everything that mankind can
merit, so that He cannot be won by any man's own efforts, like
some material reward. God is free, and gives Himself to whom
He wills and when He wills, and not for any particular achievement or at any particular time. For though a person may do his
utmost throughout his life, he can never attain the perfect love
of Jesus until the Lord Jesus Himself freely gives it. On the other
hand, He gives this love only to those who exert themselves to
the utmost, and would do even more if they could.

It seems clear, then, that neither grace alone without full support from the soul, nor a soul's individual efforts unsupported
by grace, can bring it to reformation in feeling – a reformation
grounded in perfect love and charity. But God's grace allied to
man's effort fosters the blessed fervour of perfect love in a soul,
a grace only granted in its fullness to a soul that is truly humble,

and stands in awe of God. Consequently one who is not humble and zealous cannot attain this reformation in feeling, since one who is not completely humble cannot see himself as he is. For instance, he may do all the good deeds that he can, and he may fast, watch, wear a hair shirt, and practise all kinds of bodily penance; he may perform all the outward works of mercy for his neighbour, or all the inward duties of prayer, contrition, and meditation; but if he rests content with these and relies on them, regarding them so highly that he presumes on his own merits and thinks himself good, gracious, holy, and virtuous, he still lacks humility. Even though he says and thinks that all that he does is due to God's grace and not to himself, he still lacks humility, because he will not yet renounce all credit for his good deeds, nor make himself truly poor in spirit and know himself to be nothing. And until grace enables a soul to recognize its own nothingness, and, having seen the truth in Jesus, to drop all pretence of personal merit for its good actions, it is not perfectly humble.

What is humility but truthfulness? There is no real difference. For grace enables a humble soul to see that Jesus does everything, and that the soul itself does nothing but allow Jesus to work through it as He wills. But one who is guided solely by human reason and is unaware of any alternative form of guidance finds it very hard – indeed, almost impossible and unreasonable – to do good actions and then to ascribe all merit for them to Jesus and discount his own part. Nevertheless, one who has a spiritual perception of truth knows this to be wholly true and completely reasonable. Indeed, anyone having this perception will never do less good on this account, but will be spurred to a greater and more wholehearted activity both in body and soul. This may be one reason why some people strain and torture their unhappy bodies with harsh penance all their lives, and are constantly reciting prayers, psalms, and other devotions, but never come to feel the love of God in their souls, while others seem to do so in a short time and with less strain. The reason is that the former lack this humility of which I speak.

On the other hand, a person who takes no action at all cannot experience this grace. The idle man thinks to himself, 'Why should I bother? Why should I pray or meditate, watch or fast? Why should I undertake bodily penance in order to win this grace when it cannot be obtained except by the free gift of grace? I shall continue as I am, a man of the world, and I shall not adopt any of these bodily or spiritual exercises until God gives it. For if He is willing to give it, He does not require me to do anything; and however much or little I do, He will give it me. And if He does not will to give it, I shall never obtain it however hard I try.' But anyone who adopts this attitude can never be fully reformed, because he deliberately chooses worldly idleness, and renders himself incapable of receiving the gift of grace. He refuses to rouse himself either spiritually to a lasting desire and longing for Jesus, or physically to perform his exterior duties. So he cannot receive this grace.

Therefore one who has no real humility and will not bestir himself either inwardly alone, through deep fervour, lasting desire, and regular prayer and meditation, or else through both inward and outward activities, cannot be spiritually reformed to the likeness of God.

CHAPTER 21: *How one who wishes to reach Jerusalem, the City of Peace, which represents contemplation, must have faith, be very humble, and endure troubles of body and soul*

SINCE you wish to learn some way by which you can approach this reformation, if the Lord Jesus gives me grace I will tell you what I consider the shortest and simplest way. To explain it, I will use the simile of a good pilgrim.

A man once wished to go to Jerusalem, and since he did not know the way, he called on another man who, he hoped, knew the way, and asked him for information. This other man told him that he would not reach it without great hardship and effort. 'The way is long,' he said, 'and there is great danger from thieves and bandits, as well as many other difficulties which beset a man on this journey. Furthermore, there are many different roads which seem to lead towards it, but every day men are killed and robbed, and never reach their goal. But I can guarantee one road which will lead you to the city of Jerusalem if you will keep to it. On this road your life will be safe, but you will have to undergo robbery, violence, and great distress.'

The pilgrim replied: 'I do not mind how much hardship I have to undergo on the road, so long as my life is spared and I reach my destination. So tell me all you know, and I faithfully promise to follow your instructions.' The other answered, 'I will set you on the right road. See that you carry out my instructions. Do not allow anything that you may see, hear, or feel on the road to delay you. Do not stop for it, look at it, take pleasure in it, or fear it. Keep on your way without halting, and remember that your goal is Jerusalem; that is what you want, and nothing else. If you are robbed, beaten, insulted, and treated with contempt, do not retaliate if you value your life. Resign yourself to such injuries and disregard them, lest you suffer worse things. And if people delay you with foolish tales and lies in order to distract you and make you abandon your pilgrimage, turn a deaf ear to them and make no reply save that you wish to reach Jerusalem. And if people offer you gifts or provide opportunities for you to enrich yourself, disregard them: keep your mind constantly on Jerusalem. If you will keep to this road and do as I have said, I guarantee that you will not be killed, and that you will arrive at the place for which you long.'

Spiritually interpreted, Jerusalem is the vision of peace, and symbolizes contemplation in the perfect love of God. For contemplation is nothing other than the vision of Jesus, who is our true Peace. Therefore if you really desire to attain this blessed vision of true peace and to be a true pilgrim to Jerusalem, I will set you on the right road as far as I can, although I have never been there myself. The beginning of this high road that you must travel is reformation in faith, which, as I have already said, is grounded in humility, faith, and the laws of the Church. And if you have been reformed by the Sacrament of Penance according to the laws of Holy Church, you can rest assured that, despite your earlier sins, you are on the right road. If you wish to make swift and substantial progress along this road, you must constantly bear in mind two things, humility and love. That is, I am nothing, and I want only one thing. Fix the true meaning of these words permanently in your subconscious mind and purpose, so that they will guide you even when you are not thinking of them. Humility says, 'I am nothing, I have nothing.' Love says, 'I desire one thing only, which is Jesus.' When deftly touched by the finger of reason, these two strings, secured by the thought of Jesus, make sweet harmony in the harp of the soul, for the lower you strike on one, the higher the sound on the other. Under the influence of humility, the less you feel that you are or possess, the greater will be your love and longing for Jesus. I am not speaking merely of the kind of humility that a soul feels at the sight of its own sin or weakness, or of the sorrows of this life, or when it sees the better lives of other Christians; for although this kind of humility is sound and wholesome, it is still of an elementary and worldly type, not pure, gentle, and perfect. I am speaking rather of the humility that a soul feels by grace as it contemplates the infinite Being and wondrous goodness of Jesus. And if you cannot yet see this with the eyes of the soul, do believe in its reality. For having once caught a glimpse of His Being, whether by true faith or by spiritual experience, you will see yourself not only as the most wretched of men but as worthless, even though you had never sinned. This is perfect humility, for in comparison to Jesus, who is All, you are nothing. You should also realize that you possess nothing, like a vessel that stands empty, incapable of filling itself; for however many good works you perform, spiritual or bodily, you have nothing until you feel the love of Jesus within you. It is this precious liquor alone that can fill your soul, and no other. And since this alone is so precious and noble, you must realize that whatever you may have or achieve is of no value or satisfaction without the love of Jesus. Put everything else behind you and forget it; only then can you have what is best of all.

A real pilgrim going to Jerusalem leaves his house and land, wife and children; he divests himself of all that he possesses in order to travel light and without encumbrances. Similarly, if you wish to be a spiritual pilgrim you must divest yourself of all that you possess; that is, both of good deeds and bad, and leave them all behind you. Recognize your own poverty, so that you will not place any confidence in your own work; instead, be always desiring the grace of deeper love, and seeking the spiritual presence of Jesus. If you do this, you will be setting your heart wholly on reaching Jerusalem, and on nothing else. In other words, set your heart wholly on obtaining the love of Jesus and whatever spiritual vision of Himself that He is willing to grant, for it is to this end alone that you have been created and redeemed; this is your beginning and your end, your joy and your bliss. Therefore, whatever you may possess, and however fruitful your activities, regard them all as worthless without the inward certainty and experience of this love. Keep this intention constantly in mind and hold to it firmly; it will sustain you among all the perils of your pilgrimage. It will protect you from thieves and robbers – that is, from evil spirits – for although they may rob and assault you with different temptations, your life will always be safe. In short, do as I tell you, and you will escape out of all dangers and arrive speedily at the city of Jerusalem.

Now that you are on the road and know your proper destination, you must begin your journey. The departure consists entirely of spiritual – and when necessary, bodily – activity, and you must direct this activity wisely in the following way. I regard any activity that you undertake as excellent provided that it suits your particular calling and conditions of life, and that it fosters this high desire for the love of Jesus, and makes it more sincere, more comforting, and more productive of all virtues. It may be prayer, meditation, reading, or working, but so long as the activity is one which deepens the love of Jesus in your heart and will, and withdraws your thoughts and affections from worldly trivialities, it is good. But should it grow stale and lose its value, and you consider that some other activity would be more beneficial and bring greater grace with it, then adopt it and abandon the earlier one. For although the desire and longing of your heart for Jesus should be constant and unchanging, you are at liberty to vary your spiritual exercises in order to stimulate this desire, and they may well be changed when you feel that grace moves you to do so.

The relation of spiritual activities to desire is similar to that of sticks to fire. For the more sticks are laid on the fire, the greater is the fire : similarly, the more varying spiritual exercises that a man performs to stimulate his desire for God, the stronger and more ardent it will be. Therefore, if you are free and are not bound by any particular obligation, consider carefully which activity is best suited to you, and which most fosters your desire for Jesus, and undertake it. Do not deliberately bind yourself to an unchangeable routine which would prevent your heart loving Jesus freely should you receive a special visitation of grace. For I will tell you which activities are always good and essential. Any custom is good provided that it tends to foster virtue and prevent sin. Such a custom should never be abandoned, for you must always try to cultivate humility, patience, temperance, purity, and all other virtues. But any custom that prevents the adoption of a better should be abandoned as soon as time and circumstances permit. For instance, if someone is accustomed to recite a certain number of rosaries, or meditate in a certain way for a fixed time, or watch, or kneel for a set time, or observe any other outward custom, such customs should sometimes be set aside when there is reasonable cause, or if greater grace is given by other means.

CHAPTER 22: *How anyone on this road will have to fight enemies, and how he must conquer them by the knowledge of our Lord Jesus, by sacramental confession, sincere contrition, and satisfaction*

YOU are now on the road, and you know how to proceed. But beware of enemies who will set themselves to obstruct you if they can. Nothing distresses them more than your desire and longing for the love of Jesus, and their whole purpose is to uproot this from your heart, and turn you back again to the love of earthly things. Your chief enemies are the bodily desires and foolish fears which the corruption of human nature stirs up in your heart, and which would stifle your desire for the love of God and take full possession of your heart. These are your deadliest enemies. There are also others, for evil spirits employ all their tricks to deceive you. But you have one remedy, as I told you before. Whatever they say, do not believe them; keep on your way, and desire nothing but the love of Jesus. Let your answer always be, 'I am nothing, I have nothing, I desire nothing but the love of Jesus.'

Your enemies may begin by troubling your mind with doubts, hinting that your confessions have been invalid; that some old sin lies unremembered and unconfessed in your heart; that you must give up your desire, go back to the beginning, and make a full confession. But do not believe their lies, for you have received full absolution. Rest assured that you are on the right road, and there is no need for you to ransack your conscience about the past: keep your eye on the road and your mind on Jerusalem. And if they tell you, 'You are not worthy to enjoy the love of God, so why hanker after what you cannot have and do not deserve?', carry on and take no notice of them. Reply, ' I desire the love of God not because I am worthy, but because I am unworthy; for if I had it, it would make me worthy. And since I was created to this end, although I may never enjoy it, I will still desire it, pray for it, and hope to attain it.' If your enemies see that your courage and determination to succeed is growing, they will begin to fear you.

However, so long as you are on the road they will not cease to harass you; at one time they will intimidate and threaten you, at another they will try to flatter you and seduce you, to make you abandon your purpose and turn back. 'If you persist in this desire for Jesus and continue in your first fervour, you will ruin your health or suffer from delusions and fits, as some do. Or you will beggar yourself, or suffer some injury, and no one will be willing to help you. Or the devil may put such subtle temptations in your way that you cannot resist them. For it is a dangerous course for anyone to forsake the world completely, and give himself entirely to the love of God, seeking nothing but His love, because he will encounter many perils of which he knows nothing. So turn back and forget this desire which you can never fulfil, and behave like other people in this world.'

Such are the arguments of your enemies, but do not believe them. Hold firmly to your desire and reply always that you desire to have Jesus and to be at Jerusalem. They will realize that you are so determined that you will not yield to sin or illness, delusions, fits, doubts, temptations, hardship or poverty, life or death. You want one thing and one only, so turn a deaf ear to all their suggestions and continue regularly with your prayers and other spiritual exercises as your superior or spiritual director advises. Then your enemies will be furious, and close in on you. They will begin to rob you, beat you, and put you to all the shame they can. This occurs when all that you do, however good, is condemned and misrepresented by others. You will find that everything you wish to do to further your bodily or spiritual progress will be prevented or obstructed by others, and all your most reasonable intentions frustrated. They will engineer all these things to rouse you to anger, dislike, and ill-will towards your neighbour.

But in the case of these difficulties and all others that may arise, employ this remedy. Fix your thoughts on Jesus, and do not allow any trouble to disturb you or occupy your attention. Remember what you have learned: You are nothing, you have nothing, and loss of worldly goods is nothing, for you desire nothing but the love of Jesus. So continue both your journey to Jerusalem and your present exercises. But if, through the illwill or malice of the devil, your own frailty causes you to be harassed by the troubles that beset this mortal life, regain your peace of mind as soon as possible; stop worrying about difficulties, and continue with your work. Do not allow your enemies the advantage by brooding over your difficulties.

CHAPTER 23: *A general remedy against the evil influences of the world, the flesh, and the devil*

IN due course your enemies will realize that you are unshake-able, and that you cannot be angered, depressed, or greatly affected by anything that they may do or say. When they find that you are fully resolved to face everything that may come to you, whether pleasure or pain, honour or disgrace, and that your thoughts and desires are directed to the love of God alone, they will be very crestfallen. They will then proceed to tempt you with flattery and tickle your vanity. They will remind you of your good deeds and virtues, telling you that everyone praises you and speaks of your holiness, and how they all love and honour you for your holy life. They do this to trick you into believing them, taking pleasure in this foolish conceit, and becoming self-satisfied. But if you are wise you will treat all these exaggerations as the falsehoods and flatteries of an enemy who offers you a drink of poison disguised as honey. So refuse it, and say simply that you wish to be at Jerusalem.

Such are the difficulties that you will encounter, or others like them, arising from the world, the flesh, and the devil; there are more than I can enumerate now. For so long as a man allows his mind to roam freely over a wide range of subjects, he is not aware of many difficulties. But as soon as he directs his whole mind and desire to a single objective, desiring to possess it, see it, know it, and love it – that objective being Jesus Himself – he will certainly encounter many distressing obstacles. For everything that he encounters other than the object of his desire is a hindrance. I have given you some examples of this, and I add in general that any experience – whether natural or diabolic in origin, pleasant or painful, bitter or sweet, enjoyable or frightening, happy or sad – which withdraws your mind and desire from the love of Jesus to the vanities of the world, destroys the longing of your soul for Him, and preoccupies your thoughts, must be disregarded, rejected, and given short shrift.

If you have some mundane duty to do for yourself or your neighbour, get it finished as soon as possible, so that it does not preoccupy your mind. If it is not essential and does not concern you, leave it alone; do not let it worry you, but put it out of mind. Say to yourself, 'I am nothing, I have nothing, I desire nothing but the love of Jesus.' Focus your mind on this desire, strengthen and maintain it by prayer and other spiritual exercises. Never let it go, and it will lead you on the right road, and preserve you in all dangers. Although you must face them they will not overwhelm you, and I am sure that your desire for the Lord Jesus will bring you to love Him perfectly.

On the other hand, whatever pursuit or spiritual exercise fosters and strengthens your desire for Jesus, detaches your mind from worldly desires and concerns, and kindles a deeper, fuller love of God – whether it be prayer or meditation, silence or speech, reading or listening, seclusion or company, walking or sitting still – continue to employ it for as long as it is helpful. And as regards your food, drink, and sleep, behave sensibly, and follow the guidance of your superior as a pilgrim does. For in however great a hurry the pilgrim may be, he must eat, drink, and sleep from time to time. Do the same, for although sometimes it may delay you, at others it will help you on your way.

CHAPTER 24: *How a soul conformed to the likeness of Jesus desires nothing but Him: and how he puts this desire in the soul, and Himself desires your soul*

IF you wish to learn the nature of this desire, it is in fact Jesus Himself. He implants this desire within you, and is Himself both the desire and the object of your desire. If you could only understand this, you would see that Jesus is everything and Jesus does everything. You yourself do nothing; you simply allow Him to work within your soul, accepting sincerely and gladly whatever He deigns to do in you. For although you possess the power of reason, you are nothing but an instrument in His hand. Therefore when your mind is touched by His grace and you feel yourself moved by a strong desire to please and love Jesus, you can be sure that Jesus is within you, for it is He whom you desire. Fix your eyes on Him, for He does not come in bodily form but invisibly, with the hidden presence of His power. See Him spiritually if you can; trust Him and follow Him wherever He goes, for He will guide you on the right road to Jerusalem, which is the vision of peace in contemplation. For this was the prophet's prayer to his Father in heaven: *Emitte lucem tuam et veritatem tuam; ipsa me deduxerunt, et adduxerunt in montem sanctam tuam, et in tabernacula tua* (Ps. xliii, 3). Father in heaven, send out your light and your truth, that is Your Son Jesus: and He will lead me by desire to Your holy hill and to Your dwelling; that is, to the experience of perfect love and to the height of contemplation.

Of this desire the prophet says: *Memoriale tuum Domine in desiderio animae. Anima mea desiderat te in nocte, sed et spiritus meus in praecordiis meis* (Isa. xxvi, 8). Lord Jesus, the thought of You is imprinted in the desire of my soul, for my soul has desired You in the night, and my spirit has longed for You in all my meditations. And I will tell you why the prophet says that he desired God in the night, and what he means by it. You are aware that the night is an interval of time between two days; for when one day is ended, another does not follow at once, but first there comes the night and separates the days. Sometimes the night is long and sometimes short, and then comes another day. But the prophet was alluding not only to this temporal night, but to spiritual night. Understand, then, that there are two periods of day or light; the first is a false light, and the second a true. The false light is the love of this world, which is inherent in man through the corruption of his nature; the true light is the perfect love of Jesus experienced in man's soul by grace. The love of this world is a false light, because it is transitory and impermanent, and so fails to fulfil its early promise. It was this light which the devil promised to Adam when he tempted him to sin, saying: *Aperientur oculi vestri, et eritis sicut dii* (Gen. iii, 5). Your eyes will be opened, and you will be like gods. In this particular he spoke the truth, for when Adam had sinned, his inward vision and spiritual light was withdrawn and his outward eyes were opened, so that he felt and saw a new light of bodily pleasure and love of the world previously unknown to him. And so he saw a new day, but it was an evil day. This was the day that Job cursed when he said: *Pereat dies in qua natus sum.* Perish the day on which I was born! It was not the day in the course of the year ordained by God that he cursed, but the day made by man, that is, the state of concupiscence and love of the world into which he was unwittingly born. It was this day and light of which he asked God that it should perish and come to nothing.

But the everlasting love of Jesus is true day and blessed light, for God is both love and light, and He is everlasting, so that one who loves Him dwells in everlasting light, as Saint John says: *Qui diligit Deum manet in lumine* (1 John ii, 10). Whoever loves God dwells in light. But anyone who realizes that the love of this world is false and transitory, and therefore wishes to abandon it and seek the love of God, cannot at once experience His love, but must remain awhile in the night. He cannot pass suddenly from one light to the other, that is, from the love of this world to the perfect love of God. This night is nothing other than a complete withdrawal of the soul from earthly things by an intense desire to love, see, and know Jesus and the things of the spirit. This is a real night, for just as night is dark, hiding all created things and bringing all bodily activity to a halt, similarly one who sets himself to think of Jesus and to desire His love alone must try to withdraw his thoughts and affections from created things. In so doing his mind will be set free and his affections liberated from enslavement to anything of a nature inferior to his own. If he can do this, then it is night for him, for he is in darkness.

But this is a night pregnant with good, a glowing darkness, for it shuts out the false love of this world and ushers in the dawn of the true day. Indeed, the darker this night, the nearer the true day of the love of Jesus, for the further the soul in its longing for Jesus retires from the clamour of worldly desires and impure thoughts, the nearer it approaches to experiencing the light of His love. Indeed, it is very close. This seems to be what the prophet meant when he said: *Cum in tenebris sedero, Dominus lux mea est* (Micah vii, 8). When I sit in darkness, the Lord is my light. That is, when my soul is withdrawn from all sinful inclinations as though asleep, then our Lord is my light, for then in His grace He draws near to show me His light. However, this light is sometimes full of pain, and sometimes pleasant and consoling. When one who is deeply contaminated by sin wishes to enter this darkness it is at first painful to him, for grace has not as yet accustomed him to it; so he tries to fix his mind and will on God as best he can, and to think of Him alone. And because he finds this difficult, he is troubled. Sinful habits, with the memory of former worldly affections, interests, and doings crowd in upon him with such force that his soul is dragged back to them, and he is unable to escape their influence as quickly as he would wish. So this darkness is full of pain for him, and especially at times when he has little grace to help him. Nevertheless, if this is so in your case do not be too discouraged, and do not overstrain yourself as though you could force these thoughts out of your mind, for you cannot do it. Therefore wait for God's grace, persevere, and do not overtax yourself. If you can do so gently and without forcing them, guide the desires and powers of your soul towards Jesus. Understand that when you desire Jesus and wish to think of nothing but Him, but cannot do so properly because of worldly thoughts crowding into your mind, you have in fact left the false daylight and are entering this darkness. But you will not find this darkness peaceful because it is strange to you, who are not yet enlightened and cleansed. Therefore enter it often, and by the grace of God it will gradually become easier and more peaceful. Your soul will become so free, strong, and recollected that it will have no desire to think of anything worldly, while no worldly thing will prevent it from thinking of nothing. This darkness will then bring blessing to the soul.

By 'thinking of nothing' I mean that the soul attains recollection, stability, and integrity, so that it cannot be compelled against its will to think of, or be drawn towards, any sinful, vain, or worldly thing. The soul may then be said to think of nothing, because its thoughts are not attracted to earthly things. This nothing brings a rich reward, and this night full of great consolation to the soul that desires the love of Jesus. For it is undisturbed by any earthly thoughts, and is free to think of Jesus alone. For although the soul has banished all thoughts of the world, it is actively engaged in the contemplation of Jesus.

What, then, is the nature of this darkness? It arises solely from a grace-inspired desire to have the love of Jesus. This desire and longing for the love of God, to see Him and to possess Him, drives out of the heart all worldly considerations and affections. It moves the soul to recollection, and to ponder how it may come to this love; in this way it brings it into this precious nothing. But the soul is not in complete darkness and nothingness during this time, for although it conceals it from the false light it does not entirely conceal it from the true light. For Jesus, who is both love and light, is in this darkness, whether it brings pain or peace. He is at work in the soul, moving it to anguish with desire and longing for the light, but not as yet allowing it to rest in love, nor showing it His light. This state is called night and darkness, because the soul is hidden from the false light of the world, and has not yet fully enjoyed the true light, but is awaiting the blessed love of God which it desires.

If you want to know when you are in this secure darkness and when not, you may test the matter in this way, and in this only. When you feel that your will is wholly set on seeking God and thinking of Him alone, ask yourself whether you wish to possess anything in this life for its own sake, or to use any creature to gratify your bodily senses. If your eye answers, 'I do not wish to see anything,' and your ear, 'I do not wish to hear anything,' and your mouth, 'I do not wish to taste anything, or to speak of earthly things.' If your nose answers, 'I do no wish to smell anything,' and your body, 'I do not wish to feel anything,' and if, lastly, your heart says, 'I do not wish to think of earthly matters, or to give my love to any creature; I wish if I can to think of and love God alone'; and when all your bodily powers respond thus – as may easily happen if you receive grace – then you have penetrated some distance into this darkness. For although unprofitable thoughts and fancies may enter your mind, and bodily desires distract you, nevertheless you remain in this blessed darkness so long as you do not allow your thoughts to dwell on them. For these foolish fancies that take your mind unawares disturb this darkness and trouble the soul, because it wishes to be free of them, but cannot. But they do not deprive this darkness of its value, for it is by this means that the soul will come to find peace in the darkness. For when the soul is released awhile from the distraction of all empty thoughts, and rests quietly in its simple desire and longing for Jesus and a spiritual glimpse of His presence, then this darkness is peaceful. And although this state of rest lasts but a short while, it brings great blessing to the soul.

CHAPTER 25: *How the desire of Jesus felt in this glowing darkness conquers every evil inclination, and enables the soul to see the spiritual light of the heavenly Jerusalem, that is, of Jesus*

THIS darkness and night, then, springs solely from the soul's desire and longing for the love of Jesus, combined with a blind groping of the mind towards Him. And since it brings so much blessing and peace to the soul, albeit of short duration, how much better and more blessed must it be to experience

His love, to be bathed in His glorious and invisible light, and to see all truth. It is this light which a soul receives as night passes and day dawns. It was this night to which I think the prophet alluded when he said: *Anima mea desideravit te in nocte* (Isa. xxvi, 9). My soul has desired Thee in the night. For although the process may be painful, it is much better for the world to be hidden from view than for the soul to be out among the false pleasures of the world, which appear so attractive and desirable to those whose eyes are blind to the light of the spirit. For when you are in this darkness you are much nearer to Jerusalem than when you are living in that false light. So respond wholeheartedly to the stirrings of grace, and learn to live in this darkness. When you grow accustomed to it, you will soon find peace, and the true light of spiritual knowledge will grow within you; not all at once, but imperceptibly and little by little. As the prophet says: *Habitantibus in regione umbrae mortis, lux orta est eis* (Isa. ix, 2). Light has shone upon those who dwell in the land of the shadow of death. The light of grace has risen, and will shine on those who dwell in the shadow of death, that is, in the darkness that resembles death. For just as death destroys a living body and all its powers, so the desire to love Jesus that is experienced in this darkness destroys all sins, sensual desires, and impure thoughts. And by the time this takes place you are fast nearing Jerusalem. You have not yet reached it, but you will be able to see the city in the distance before you come to it because of the twinkling rays of light shining from it. For remember that although your soul dwells in this peaceful darkness, untroubled by thoughts of the world, it is not yet at the end of its journey, for it is not yet clothed in light or wholly ablaze with the fire of love. It is fully conscious of something beyond itself which as yet it neither knows nor possesses, but it has an ardent longing for it. The object of its longing is nothing other than the vision of Jerusalem, which resembles the city that the prophet Ezechiel saw in his vision.

He describes (Ezech. xl) how he saw a city set on a hill sloping toward the south, which measured no more than a rod in length and breadth, that is, six cubits and a palm. But when he was brought into the city and looked about him, he thought it very spacious, for he saw many halls and rooms, both public and private, with gates and porches outside and in, and more buildings than I can describe many hundred cubits in length and breadth. It was extraordinary to him that this city which was so spacious within appeared so small when he stood outside. This city symbolizes the perfect love of God, set on the hill of contemplation. To a soul that has no experience of it but has a sincere desire for it, the city appears small, no longer than a rod, which is six cubits and a palm. Here six cubits represent man's struggle for perfection; the palm, a little experience of contemplation. He sees clearly that here is a reward that transcends anything that human efforts can attain, in the same way as the palm extends beyond the six cubits, but he cannot be sure what it is. But if he can enter the city of contemplation, he then sees much more than he discerned at first.

CHAPTER 26: *How one may recognize the false lights caused by the trickery of the devil from the true light of knowledge which comes from Jesus*

BEWARE of the devil who walks at noon, and who makes his false light appear to come from Jerusalem. For the devil knows that our Lord Jesus shows the light of truth to those who love Him, so he shows a false light in place of the true light to deceive the unwary. However, the soul can distinguish the light of truth that comes from God from that which is an illusion of the devil. I will illustrate this by an example taken from the heavens.

Sometimes there appears in the sky a ray of light that seems to be the sun itself, but is not; and sometimes the sun itself appears. The distinction between the two is this. The false sunlight appears only between two black rainclouds. Because the sun is near, a light shines from behind the clouds which looks like the sun itself, but is not. The true sun shines only when the sky is clear, or at least not overcast by black clouds. Now to apply this illustration: some people seem to forsake the love of the world and wish to attain the love of God and the light of understanding, but they are not willing to pass through this darkness that I have mentioned. They will not look at themselves honestly and humbly, and examine their former life and present sinful state, nor recognize their own nothingness before God. They make no effort to enter upon an interior life, and put aside all worldly things. They will not stamp out the sinful impulses of pride, envy, anger and such like that arise in their hearts by constantly reaching out to Jesus in prayer and meditation, silence and tears, and in other spiritual and corporal exercises as devout and holy people have done in the past. But directly they have outwardly forsaken the world – or soon after – they imagine that they are holy, and able to understand the inner meaning of the Gospels and holy scripture. And provided that they can fulfil the commandments of God literally and avoid bodily sin, they think that they love God perfectly. So at once they want to preach and instruct everyone else, under the misapprehension that they have received the grace of understanding and perfect charity by a special gift of the Holy Spirit. They are even more strongly impelled to do this when they feel themselves suddenly endowed with great knowledge after little previous effort on their part, or with what seems to be fervent love which drives them to preach truth and righteousness to their fellow-men. They regard this as a grace from God, a blessed light granted to themselves before all others. But if they examine these things carefully, they will realize that this light of knowledge and fervour does not come from the true Sun, that is our Lord Jesus, but from the noonday devil who makes his spurious light resemble the sun. You can recognize this imposter by the example I have given.

This light of false knowledge shown by the devil to a soul in darkness is always seen between two black rainclouds. The higher cloud is presumption and self-conceit, while the lower is oppression and depreciation of our neighbour. So whatever appearances of knowledge and fervour may shine in a soul, if they co-exist with presumption, conceit, and disregard for our neighbour, it is not the light of grace given by the Holy Spirit, even though the knowledge may be true in itself. If it comes suddenly, it is of the devil; and if it comes after prolonged study, it is the fruit of man's own mental powers. So we can tell clearly when this false light of knowledge is not the light of the true sun.

Those whose knowledge comes from these sources are full of spiritual pride. They are so blinded by this spurious light that they regard their own conceit and disobedience to the laws of Holy Church as perfect compliance with the Gospel and laws of God. They imagine that the following of their own inclination is freedom of spirit, and as a result errors and heresies pour from them like rain from black clouds. For their preaching gives rise to controversy and quarrels, and to contentious denunciation of other people and their ways of life. Yet they claim to be moved solely by charity and zeal for righteousness. But this claim is false, for Saint James the Apostle says: *Ubi enim zelus et contentio, ibi inconstantia et omne opus pravum. Non est sapientia haec desursum descendens a Patri luminum, sed terrena, animalis et diabolica* (S. James iii, 16). Wherever there is envy and contention there is instability and all kinds of evil at work. Therefore the knowledge that breeds such sins does not come down from God, the Father of Light, but is earthly, bestial, and devilish. So this false light can be distinguished from the true by these by-products of pride, presumption, disobedience, anger, scandal, and other sins. For the true Sun does not display Himself to bestow mental light and perfect charity upon the soul unless the sky is first bright and free from clouds; that is, unless the conscience is first cleansed in this darkness by the fire of a burning desire for Jesus, which cauterizes and destroys all evil impulses of pride, vainglory, anger, envy, and other sins in the soul. As the prophet says: *Ignis ante ipsum praecedet, et inflammabit in circuitu inimicos ejus* (Ps. xcvii, 3). Fire shall go before Him; that is, the loving desire for Jesus will go before Him in a man's soul, and will burn up all His enemies, that is, destroy all his sins.

For unless a soul's self-esteem is first humbled by fear, and well tried and essayed in this fire of desire and purified from all its stains by devout prayers and other spiritual exercises over a long period, it cannot endure the brilliance of spiritual light, nor can it receive the precious elixir of the perfect love of Jesus. But once it is purified and transformed by this fire, it can absorb the gracious light of spiritual knowledge and perfect love from the true Sun, Jesus Christ. In this connection Holy Scripture says: *Vobis qui timetis Dominum orietur sol justitiae* (Mal. iv, 2). The true Sun of Righteousness, that is our Lord Jesus, will shine upon you who fear Him; that is, on humble souls who acknowledging their own weakness, esteem themselves less than their neighbours, and cast themselves down before God. They know that they themselves are nothing, and they attain perfect humility through reverent fear and constant contemplation of God.

Upon these souls the true Sun will rise and illumine their minds to know truth, and will kindle their affections with burning love, so that they burn and shine. Under the influence of this heavenly Sun they will burn with perfect love and shine with the knowledge of God and spiritual things, for they will then be reformed in feeling. So one who does not want to be deceived must first humble himself and hide within this darkness from all interference by other people, and try to forget the world entirely. He must follow Jesus with constant desire, seeking Him in prayer and meditation. For I know that the light that succeeds this darkness is sure and true. It shines from the true Sun in the city of Jerusalem to light the way for a soul struggling in darkness and calling for light, and gives it comfort in its trouble. For I do not think that a false light ever succeeds true darkness. In other words, if a man sincerely and wholeheartedly sets himself to forsake the love of the world, and by grace comes to feel and know himself as he is, and continues humbly in this realization, he will not be deceived by any errors, heresies, or delusions. For all these enter by the gate of pride, and if pride is locked out, they will find no foothold in the soul. And although they may come and seek admission, they will not be able to enter. For the grace experienced by a soul in this darkness of humility will teach it the truth, and show it that all such approaches are moves of the devil.

CHAPTER 27: *How a soul led by grace into this glowing darkness receives great benefits, and how one should prepare oneself to enter it*

THERE are many devout souls who by grace enter this darkness and attain self-knowledge, but who do not yet fully understand this process. This ignorance tends to hinder their progress. They often feel their thoughts and affections withdrawn from earthly things, and they are brought into a state of deep peace, untroubled by unprofitable thoughts or bodily sensations. They enjoy such freedom of spirit that they can think of Jesus in peace, and offer Him their prayers and psalms with great joy and sweetness for as long as the frailty of human nature will permit. They are quite certain that this experience is good, but they are not sure what it is. So I would say to all such souls that although such an experience may only be short and seldom had, it seems to be a genuine phase of this darkness which we have been discussing. For it consists firstly of self-knowledge, and then of self-transcendence through a burning desire to see Jesus; or more accurately, the experience is itself a spiritual perception of Jesus. And if they can remain in this peace, or by grace make it such a part of themselves that they can readily and freely re-possess or retain it as they will, they will never be overcome by the temptations of the devil, nor be subject to errors and heresies. They are now standing at the threshold of contemplation, able and ready to receive the perfect love of Jesus. Therefore whoever has this gift should acknowledge it with humility, preserve it with care, and cultivate it with zeal, so that nothing in existence can prevent his entry into contemplation whenever he can. Provided that he is a free agent and can do whatever he wishes without causing scandal or distress to his neighbours, he should forget and ignore everything that might prevent contemplation. For I do not think that he can readily attain this peace unless he receives great grace and submits himself entirely to its guidance. And this is just what he should do, for grace must always be free to work – free from obstacles caused by sin and worldliness, and free from all things which, although not sinful, nevertheless impede its action.

But if one who has not yet received this fullness of grace desires to attain this spiritual knowledge of Jesus, he must do his utmost to dispose himself to it, and to remove all obstacles to grace. He must learn to die to the world, and wholeheartedly renounce all love of it. First of all he must renounce pride, both worldly and spiritual, desiring neither honour nor recognition from the world, renown nor fame, position nor rank, authority nor power, worldly knowledge nor skill, estates nor riches, fine clothing nor outward display – nothing, indeed, which might cause him to be respected above other men. He must desire none of these things, and if they are given him let him accept them with fear, so that if he cannot be poor both outwardly and inwardly, he can at least be so inwardly. He should wish to be forgotten by the world, so that however rich or clever he may be, he receives no more attention than the poorest man alive.

He must not foster self-satisfaction by recalling his own good deeds or virtues, thinking that he is doing better than others because he has renounced the world while others have not done so. This makes him imagine that all is well with him. He must also subdue all feelings of anger, ill-will, and envy towards his neighbour, and avoid causing any unnecessary distress or annoyance by word or act, or giving anyone reasonable cause for anger or complaint. In this way he will be free, owing no obligation to anyone, nor anyone to him. He must also renounce greed, requiring no more than is necessary for bodily sustenance, and considering himself amply rewarded when God moves others to give him anything. He must not rely on worldly possessions, nor on the help and favour of any worldly friends. Let him put his whole trust in God, for if he does otherwise he makes himself dependent on the world, and restricts his freedom to think of God.

He must utterly abandon gluttony and all other sins of the body, and must not indulge in familiarity with women. For there is no doubt that the blind love that sometimes exists between a man and a woman, and which seems good and honest when they have no intention of committing any sin, is impure and sinful in the sight of God. For it is a grave sin for anyone deliberately to set his heart in worldly love on any creature whatsoever when it ought to be set on Jesus, on virtue, and on purity of spirit, particularly if this love is so strong that it fills his mind with restlessness and deprives it of all delight in God. I think that such a choice is sinful even when the person who makes it denies that it is sinful, or when he is so blinded that he will not recognize it as such. He must not indulge his bodily appetites with rich food and drink, but be content with such food as is readily obtainable; for if he is healthy, any simple food will satisfy hunger and maintain the body in normal strength for the service of God. And let him not complain, argue, or be angry about his food, even though he sometimes does not get what he would like.

A man must wholly renounce these and all other sins in will, and when necessary in act, as well as anything else that prevents him giving his mind freely to Jesus. For so long as such obstacles remain, he cannot die to the world nor can he enter the darkness and attain self-knowledge. If he wishes to do so he must do all this as Saint Paul did, who said: *Mihi mundus crucifixus est, and ego mundo* (Gal. vi, 14). The world is slain and crucified to me, and I to the world. Meaning that one who renounces the love of the world, its honours, riches, and all pleasures for the love of God, and who neither loves nor seeks the world, but is content to possess nothing in it – nor would if he could – is indeed dead to the world because it holds no pleasure or attraction for him. If the world passes by and ignores him, pays him no respect, and has no use for him, but forgets him as it would a dead man, then he is dead to the world. Saint Paul was exactly in this position, which must also be that of anyone who wishes to follow him and attain the perfect love of God, for it is impossible to live wholly to God until one first dies to the world.

This death to the world is this darkness; it is the gateway to contemplation and reformation in feeling. There is no other way. There may be many different ways leading souls to contemplation, just as there are different forms of activity to suit man of varying dispositions and ways of life, such as the religious and secular lives. But there is only one gateway to contemplation, for whatever form a man's activity takes, unless it leads him to self-knowledge and humility, and mortifies all love of the world so that he can sometimes feel himself deep in this peaceful darkness where he is hidden from the vanity of

the world and can see himself as he is, then he has not yet
achieved reformation in feeling, nor can he yet enter contemplation. Indeed, he is far from it. And if he tries to enter by any
other gate, he is a thief and a house-breaker, who will be ejected
as unworthy. But one who by grace can humble himself to
nothing and die in this way is at the very door, because he is dead
to the world and lives to God. Of such souls Saint Paul says:
Mortui enim estis, et vita vestra abscondita est cum Christo in Deo
(Col. iii, 3). You are dead – that is, you who for the love of God
renounce all love of the world are dead to the world – but your
life is hidden from worldly men, just as the life of Christ is hidden in the Godhead from the eyes of those who love the flesh.

Our Lord Himself showed us this gateway in the Gospel
when He said: *Omnis qui reliquerit patrem aut matrem, fratrem aut
sororem propter me, centuplum accipiet, et vitam aeternam possidebit*
(Matt. xix, 29). Everyone who for love of Me leaves father or
mother, sister or brother, or any earthly possessions, shall have
a hundred-fold in this life, and afterwards the bliss of heaven.
This hundred-fold that a soul will possess if it forsakes the world
is nothing else than the blessing of this glowing darkness which
I call the gateway to contemplation. For one who is in this
darkness and is hidden by grace from worldly vanities has no
desire for worldly possessions and does not look for them; he
is not worried by them, is not interested in them, and does
not want them, so that he is a hundred times richer than a king
or other person who strives after great wealth. For one who
seeks nothing but Jesus possesses a hundred-fold, for he enjoys
more rest, more peace of heart, more true love and delight in
his soul in a single day than the most covetous man in the
world, who has all its wealth at his disposal, enjoys in his entire
lifetime.

This, then, is a darkness full of blessing, a rich nothingness,
which brings to the soul great spiritual freedom and tranquillity. I think that David was alluding to this night or nothing-

ness when he said: *Ad nihilum redactus sum, et nescivi* (Ps. lxxiii, 12). I was brought to nothing, and I did not know it. That is, the grace that our Lord Jesus sent into my heart has slain and annihilated all love of the world, and I do not know how, for it was by no effort and will of my own, but by the grace of our Lord Jesus alone. Therefore I am certain that one who wishes to have the light of grace and to feel a deep love of Jesus in his soul must leave the false light of worldly love and remain in this darkness. And if at first he is afraid to live in darkness, he should not return to the love of the world, but endure it awhile and put all his hope and trust in Jesus; he will not remain long without spiritual light of some kind. The prophet exhorts: *Qui ambulavit in tenebris, et non est lumen ei, speret in Domino, et innitatur super Deum suum* (Isa. i, 10). Whoever is walking in darkness and has no light – that is, whoever wishes to hide himself from the love of the world and cannot easily feel the light of spiritual love – should not despair or turn again to the world. Let him hope in our Lord and lean on Him, that is, trust in God: let him hold fast to God by desire and stand firm awhile, and he shall have light. For his condition is like that of a man who has been a long time in the sun, and then comes suddenly into a dark house. At first he is like a blind man and sees nothing, but if he waits a little he will soon be able to see about him, at first large objects, then small, and then everything that is in the house. It is the same in the spiritual world. To one who renounces the love of the world and attains self-knowledge by examination of conscience everything at first seems dark and obscure. But if he stands firm and prays earnestly, constantly directing his will to the love of Jesus, he will later be able to see many things, both great and small, of which he previously knew nothing. This seems to be what the prophet promised when he said: *Orietur in tenebris lux tua, et tenebrae tuae erunt sicut meridies. Et requiem dabit tibi Dominus Deus tuus, et implebit animam tuam splendoribus* (Isa. lviii, 10). Light shall spring up for you in the darkness. That is, for you who sincerely abandon the light of all worldly love and plunge yourselves mentally into this darkness there will arise the light of the blessed love and spiritual knowledge of God. 'And your darkness shall become like noonday.' That is, the darkness through which at first your desire and blind faith in God persist will turn into clear knowledge and sure love. 'And the Lord God will give you rest': that is, your bodily desires, your tormenting fears and doubts, and the evil spirits that have hitherto harassed you continually, will all weaken, and their influence will largely cease. You will be made so strong that they will not harm you, because you will be hidden from them and at peace. 'And then our Lord Jesus will fill your soul with light': that is, when you have been brought to this peace of soul you will be able to turn to God more readily, and your sole activity will be to love Him. He will fill all the powers of your soul with rays of heavenly light. So do not be surprised if I call the abandonment of worldly love darkness, for the prophet called it so, saying to a soul: *intra in tenebras tuas, filia Chaldaeorum* (Isa. xlvii, 5). Enter into your darkness, daughter of Chaldaea. That is: Soul, whose love of the world makes you a daughter of Chaldaea, leave it and enter into your darkness.

CHAPTER 28: *How our Lord Jesus leads a soul to be reformed by four different stages: He calls, justifies, honours, and glorifies it*

I HAVE now told you a little about the dispositions necessary for progress towards reformation in feeling. However, I do not suggest that you can achieve this in your own strength, for I know very well that our Lord Jesus alone brings this to completion in whatever way He wishes. For it is He alone who stirs a soul with His grace and brings it first into this darkness and then into light. As the prophet says: *Sicut tenebrae ejus, ita et lumen ejus* (Ps. cxxxix, 12). Just as the light of knowledge and the experience of spiritual love came from God, so also the darkness which is the forsaking of worldly love comes from Him. For He does all things; He creates and re-creates. He creates by Himself alone, but gives us a share in our own re-creation, for He gives us grace, and it is our willing cooperation that effects it. Saint Paul indeed describes the way in which He does this: *Quos Deus praescivit fieri conformes imaginis Filii ejus, hoc vocavit; et quos magnificavit, hos et glorificavit* (Rom. viii, 29). Those whom God predestined to be conformed to the likeness of His Son He called, justified, honoured, and glorified.

Although these words may be applied to all chosen souls that are in the lowest degree of charity and are reformed in faith alone, they apply more particularly to those souls that are reformed in feeling, to whom our Lord God has given grace in abundance and showed especial favour. For these are His own especial sons, who are fully restored to the likeness of His Son Jesus. In these words Saint Paul divides God's work in the soul into four stages. The first stage is that during which the soul is called from worldly vanity, and this is often easy and agreeable. For at the beginning of his conversion a person who is disposed to receive great grace is so suddenly moved in spirit, feels such delight in devotion, and sheds so many tears of compunction that he is inclined to think himself already half in heaven. But this pleasant stage passes away after a time, and is succeeded by the second stage, which is that of justification. This is arduous, for when he begins to make good progress on the road of righteousness, to set his will resolutely against all sin both inward and outward, and to aspire to virtues and the love of Jesus, he encounters many obstacles, both inwardly from the perverseness and obstinacy of his own will, and outwardly from temptations of the devil. As a result he is often greatly tormented, and this is not surprising, for he has so long been twisted by the false love of the world that he cannot be straightened without great heat and pressure, just as a twisted bar cannot be straightened without being plunged into the fire and heated. Therefore our Lord Jesus, seeing what is necessary for a perverse soul, allows it to be tried by various temptations and well tested by spiritual difficulties until all the rust of impurities is burned out of it. Inward fears, doubts and perplexities will almost reduce the soul to despair. It will seem to be forsaken by God and abandoned into the hands of the devil, but it will retain a small secret trust in the goodness and mercy of God. For our Lord Jesus leaves this secret trust in such a soul, however far away He seems to go, and this keeps the soul from despair and preserves it from spiritual harm. It will also be mortified outwardly, and suffer pain in its senses. This may happen through illness, or through bodily torments caused by the devil. Or by the secret will of God the poor soul may have to suffer such pain through the wretched body that it would not know how to endure the body any longer were it not that our Lord Jesus sustains it. And yet the soul would rather endure all this pain than be blinded by the false love of this world. For this would be hell to such a soul, but the suffering of this kind of pain is nothing but purgatory; therefore the soul suffers it gladly and would not avoid it even if it could, because it is of great profit to it. Our Lord does all these things to help the soul, in order to prevent its being absorbed in worldly things and to detach it from love of the senses, so that it can receive spiritual enlightenment.

After this, when the soul has been mortified in this manner and led from love of the world into this darkness, so that it no longer takes the slightest interest or pleasure in the world, but finds it bitter as wormwood, then comes the third stage, that of honour. This is when the soul is partially reformed in feeling, and receives the gift of perfection and the grace of contemplation: it is a time of great peace. It is followed by the fourth stage, that of glorification, when a soul is fully reformed in the bliss of heaven. For there are souls who have been called from sin and justified by passing through various trials by fire and water; these are afterwards brought to honour and later to glory. For our Lord will grant all that they desired here on earth, and more. He will raise them above all other chosen souls to the glory of the cherubim and seraphim, because in this life they surpassed all others in the knowledge and love of God.

Therefore whoever wishes to attain this glory must not be afraid of this justification, for it is the only way to attain it. Through His prophet God spoke words of great comfort to all souls who are tested in the fires of tribulation: *Puer meus non timere, si transieris per ignem, flamma non nocebit te* (Isa. xliii, 2). My son, if you pass through the fire, do not be afraid, for the flame shall not hurt you. It will cleanse you from all the corruptions of the flesh, and enable you to receive the spiritual fire of the love of God. And, as I said earlier, this purification must be completed first, because the soul cannot otherwise be reformed in feeling.

CHAPTER 29: *How beginners and those who are growing in grace sometimes show greater outward signs of love than those who are perfect; but outward appearances are misleading*

BUT you may now say, 'How can this be so?' For there are many souls now turning to God who experience many spiritual graces. Some have a deeper sorrow for sin, while others find increased devotion and fervour in prayer, and frequently receive spiritual enlightenment. Others, too, experience feelings of great warmth and sweetness. Yet these souls never really enter this peaceful darkness of which I have spoken with a fervent desire and a mind constantly absorbed in God. You may ask whether these souls are reformed in feeling or not. It seems that they are, inasmuch as they have these profound spiritual experiences which other people who are reformed only in faith do not have.

On this matter I think that these spiritual experiences, whether they consist of compunction, or devotion, or mental visions, are not the same as those given to a soul by the grace of contemplation. I do not deny that they are genuine, and are given by the grace of God. But the souls that have these experiences are not yet reformed in feeling; they have neither attained perfection nor the burning love of Jesus that may one day be theirs. But it often appears otherwise when such souls feel the love of God more strongly than those who have attained perfection, inasmuch as their emotion is much more evident outwardly, and appears in tears and prayers, prostrations, and ecstatic utterances, and in other physical signs. Indeed, to those who see them they appear to be constantly transported by love. And although I do not think that this is so, I am quite sure that these experiences, and the fervour of devotion and compunction that they feel, are gracious gifts of God given to chosen souls to detach them from the worldly love and bodily desires that have long been established in their hearts. It is only by such perceptible experiences of great fervour that these souls can be detached from these things.

However, the fervour that outwardly appears so intense does not spring solely from the intensity of their love; it also indicates the immaturity and weakness of their souls, which cannot bear God's lightest touch. Such souls are still, as it were, carnal and subservient to the flesh, and have not yet been released from it by mortification. Consequently the least touch of love and the smallest spark of spiritual light sent from heaven into such a soul is so great and comforting, so sweet and delightful, so far above all worldly pleasures that it ever enjoyed, that it is prostrated by it. Furthermore, it is so new, so sudden, and so strange that the soul is unable to endure it, but bursts out and betrays itself in tears, sobbing, and other visible signs of emotion. For when an old cask receives new wine that is working and potent, the cask swells and is nearly at bursting point until the wine has fermented and discharged all impurities. But directly the wine is pure and clear, it matures quietly and the cask remains intact. It is the same with a soul grown old in sin, for when it receives even a little of the love of God, this proves so invigorating and potent that the body would be liable to collapse were it not that God preserves it intact. Even so, the eyes break into tears and the mouth into words; but this is due to the weakness of the soul rather than to the greatness of its love. Afterwards, when all the impurities of the soul have been removed by this ferment, its love is left pure and peaceful. Then both soul and body enjoy greater peace, and the soul has much more love than before although this is less apparent outwardly. For inwardly it is now wholly at peace, and there is little outward indication of fervour. I say therefore of these souls who experience great bodily fervour that, while they have received great grace, they are not yet reformed in feeling, although they have made great progress towards it. For I consider that a man who has been deeply corrupted by sin will not be reformed in feeling unless he is first cauterized and cleansed by deep compunction. Another soul who has never been much corrupted by the love of the world, but has remained innocent of grave sins, may reach this reformation more easily and quietly, and without outward signs of great fervour.

I think the truth is that any consolation and fervour that a soul may experience in the beginning and early days of the spiritual life are as it were food sent from heaven to strengthen it in its struggle. Just as a pilgrim who travels all day without food and drink is nearly overcome by weariness, at last comes upon a good inn where he finds food and drink and is well refreshed for the time; so in the spiritual life a devout soul who wishes to renounce the love of the world and love God, and arranges his affairs accordingly, sometimes prays and labours in body and soul all day long without feeling any comfort or joy in his devotions. Then our Lord, who has pity on all His creatures, sends it spiritual food and comforts it with devotion as He sees fit lest it should perish, lose heart, or fall into depression and complaint. And when the soul experiences any spiritual comfort, and when grace has brought it successfully to the close of another day, it considers itself well rewarded for all its previous trouble and distress.

The same experience befalls other souls who are making progress and are well developed in grace. They often feel the touch of the Holy Spirit in their souls, giving them both an understanding and insight into spiritual things, and a real love for them. But they are not yet reformed in feeling, and are still imperfect. The reason is that these experiences come to them as it were unawares; they come and go before they realize, and they cannot recapture them. They do not know where to seek them nor where to find them, for they are not yet accustomed to these transient experiences. They have not yet mastered themselves by stability of mind and a constant desire for Jesus, and their spiritual eyes are not yet opened to the sight of heavenly things, although they are swiftly nearing this state. Therefore they are not yet reformed in feeling, and they do not yet possess the full gift of contemplation.

CHAPTER 30: *How to attain self-knowledge*

A SOUL that desires to attain knowledge of spiritual things must first know itself, for it cannot acquire knowledge of a higher kind until it first knows itself. The soul does this when it is so recollected and detached from all earthly preoccupations and from the influence of the senses that it understands itself as it is in its own nature, taking no account of the body. So if you desire to know and see your soul as it is, do not look for it within your body as though it were hidden in your heart in the same way that the heart is hidden within the body. If you look for it in this way you will never find it. The more you search for it as for a material object, the further you are from it, for your soul is not tangible, but a living and invisible spirit. It is not hidden and enclosed in your body in the way that a lesser object is hidden and enclosed within a greater; on the contrary, it is the soul that sustains and gives life to the body, and is possessed of much greater strength and virtue.

Therefore if you desire to discover your soul, withdraw your thoughts from outward and material things, forgetting if possible your own body and its five senses, and consider the nature of a rational soul in the same way as you would consider any virtue, such as truth or humility. Similarly, consider how the soul is a living spirit, immortal and invisible, with power in itself to see and know supreme Truth and to love supreme Good, which is God. Once you have grasped this, you have some understanding of yourself. Do not seek this knowledge in any other way, for the more clearly and fully you can study the nature and dignity of a rational soul – what it is, and how it functions – the better you will understand yourself. It is very difficult for an untutored soul, pent in the body, to have a true knowledge of itself, or of an angel, or of God, because it pictures them all in a physical form, and expects in some way to see itself, and so God and spiritual things. But this is impossible, for all spiritual things are perceived and made known to the soul by reason, and not by imagination. And just as reason enables a soul to know that the virtue of justice requires that every man receive his due reward, it can in the same way enable the soul to understand itself.

I do not say, however, that the soul should rest content with this knowledge, but that it should employ it to seek a higher knowledge above itself, that is, of the nature of God. For your soul is a spiritual mirror in which you may see the likeness of God. First, then, find your mirror, and keep it bright and clean from the corruption of the flesh and worldly vanity. Hold it well up above the earth so that you can see it, and our Lord reflected in it. In this life all chosen souls direct their effort and intention to this end although they may not be fully conscious of it. It is for this reason, as I said earlier, that at the beginning and early stages of their spiritual life many souls enjoy great fervour and sweetness of devotion, and seem all afire with love; but this is not the perfect love or spiritual knowledge of God. You can be certain that however intense the fervour felt by a soul – even if it is so intense that the body appears unable to bear it or melts into tears – so long as its conception and experience of God is largely or wholly dependent on imagination rather than on knowledge, it has not yet attained perfect love or contemplation.

Understand, then, that the love of God has three degrees, all of which are good, but each succeeding degree is better than the other. The first degree is reached by faith alone, when no knowledge of God is conveyed by grace through the imagination or understanding. This love is common to every soul that if reformed in faith, however small a degree of charity it has attained; and it is good, for it is sufficient for salvation. The second degree of love is attained when the soul knows God by faith and Jesus in His manhood through the imagination. This love, where imagination is stimulated by grace, is better than the first, because the spiritual perceptions are awakened to contemplate our Lord's human nature. In the third degree the soul, as far as it may in this life, contemplates the Godhead united to manhood in Christ. This is the best, highest, and most perfect degree of love, and it is not attained by the soul until it is reformed in feeling. Those at the beginning and early stages of the spiritual life do not possess this degree of love, for they cannot think of Jesus or love Him as God, but always think of Him as a man living under earthly conditions. All their thoughts and affections are shaped by this limitation. They honour Him as man, and they worship and love Him principally in His human aspect, and go no further. For instance, if they have done wrong and offended against God, they think that God is angry with them as a man would be had they offended him. So they fall down as it were at the feet of our Lord with heartfelt sorrow and ask for mercy, trusting that our Lord will mercifully pardon their offence. And although this practice is commendable, it is not as spiritual as it might be. Similarly, when they wish to worship God they imagine our Lord in a bodily form aglow with wondrous light; then they proceed to honour, worship, and revere Him, throwing themselves on His mercy and begging Him to do with them what He wills. In the same way, when they wish to love God, they think of Him, worship Him, and reverence Him as man, recalling the Passion of Christ or some other event in His earthly life. Nevertheless, when they do this they are deeply stirred to the love of God.

Such devotion is good and inspired by grace, but it is much inferior to the exercise of the understanding, when grace moves the soul to contemplate God in Man. For there are two natures in our Lord, that of God and that of Man. And as the divine nature is higher and nobler than the human, so the soul's contemplation of the Godhead in the manhood of Jesus is more exalted, more spiritual, and more valuable than the contemplation of His manhood alone, whether the soul is thinking of His manhood as passible or glorified. For the same reason the love felt by a soul when grace enables it to contemplate God in man is more exalted, more spiritual, and more valuable than the fervour of devotion aroused by the contemplation of Jesus' manhood alone, however strong the outward signs of this love. For this latter love is a natural love, and the former a spiritual love; and our Lord does not reveal Himself to the imagination as He is, for the frailty of man's nature is such that the soul could not endure His glory.

Nevertheless, in order that the devotion of those souls that are incapable of such elevated contemplation of the Godhead should not be misdirected, but be comforted and strengthened by some form of interior contemplation of Jesus to forsake sin and the love of the world, God tempers the ineffable light of His divinity and cloaks it in the bodily form of Jesus' humanity. He reveals it in this way to the inward vision of the soul, and sustains it spiritually through the love of His precious manhood. This love is so potent that it destroys all love of evil in the soul, and gives it strength to endure bodily penance and other physical hardships whenever necessary for the love of Jesus. This is the way in which the Lord Jesus watches over a chosen soul and shields it from the flames of worldly love. For just as a shadow is formed by light falling on a solid object, so this spiritual shadow is cast over a devout soul by the blessed and ineffable light of God's Being and the human nature united to It. Of this shadow the prophet says: *Spiritus ante faciem nostram Christus Dominus: sub umbra ejus vivemus inter gentes* (Lam. iv, 20). That is, our Lord Jesus in His divine nature is a spirit that cannot be seen by us while we live in the flesh; we must therefore live under the shadow of His human nature as long as we are here. But although it is true that this love which depends upon the imagination is good, nevertheless a soul should desire to have a spiritual love and understanding of His divine nature, and all other bodily contemplations are but means of leading a soul to this. I do not say that we should separate the divine nature of Christ from the human, but that we should love Jesus both as God and man, for in Him God is united to man, and man to God; but this love must be spiritual, not carnal.

Our Lord taught this lesson to Mary Magdalen, who was called to be a contemplative, when He said: *Noli me tangere, nondum enim ascendi ad Patrem meum* (S. John xx, 17). Do not touch Me, for I have not yet ascended to My Father. That is to say, Mary Magdalen had an ardent love for our Lord before His Passion, but her love was more carnal than spiritual. She truly believed that He was God, but she did not love Him primarily as God, for she was not capable of doing so at that time, so that she allowed all her affection and thought to dwell on Him as man. And our Lord did not blame her for this at the time, but greatly commended her. But when He had risen from the dead and appeared to her, she would have honoured Him with the same kind of love as she did before, had not our Lord forbidden her, saying, 'Do not touch Me.' That is, Do not allow the love of your heart to dwell only on My human nature which you see with your bodily eyes, for in that form I am not yet ascended to My Father. That is, I am not equal to the Father, for in My human nature I am less than He. Do not touch Me in My present state, but set your mind and love on that state in which I am equal to the Father, that is, in My divinity. Love Me, know Me, and worship Me as God and man, and not as man only. In this way you shall touch Me, for I am both God and man, and the whole reason why I am to be loved and worshipped is that I am God who took the nature of man. So adore Me in your heart and give Me your love as God. Let your mind worship Me as Jesus, God in man, supreme Truth, supreme Goodness, and blessed Life, for so I am. This, I think, is what our Lord taught her, and this is what He teaches all other souls that are disposed and ready for contemplation.

Nevertheless, some people are not spiritually gifted by nature: for these and others who have not yet been refined by grace it is good for them to foster human love through the imagination in their own way until greater grace is given them. For it is not wise for a person to abandon a good thing until he can discover and use something better. The same may be said of other experiences of a physical nature, such as hearing sweet music, sensations of pleasant bodily warmth, seeing light, or enjoying sweet flavours. These are not spiritual experiences, for spiritual experiences are felt in the powers of the soul, chiefly in the understanding and will, and very little in the imagination. But such experiences are in the imagination, and therefore are not spiritual. Even when good and genuine they are only outward manifestations of the inward grace experienced in the powers of the soul. This can be clearly proved in holy Scripture, where it is said: *Apparuerunt apostolis dispertitae linguae tamquam ignis, seditque supra singulos eorum Spiritus Sanctus* (Acts ii, 3). The Holy Spirit appeared to the Apostles on the Day of Pentecost in the form of tongues of fire, and inflamed their hearts, resting upon each of them. Now it is evident that the Holy Spirit, who is the invisible God Himself, was not to be identified with the tongues of fire nor the sensation of bodily heat; but He was invisibly felt in the powers of their souls, for He enlightened their understanding and kindled their affection by His blessed presence so clearly and ardently that they suddenly possessed the spiritual knowledge of truth and the perfection of love, as our Lord had promised them when He said: *Spiritus sanctus docebit vos omnem veritatem* (S. John xvi, 13). The Holy Spirit shall teach you all truth. The fire and the heat, therefore, were no more than material signs and evidences of the grace inwardly experienced. And as it was with the Apostles, so it is with other souls that are visited and enlightened by the Holy Spirit, and enjoy sensible feelings of consolation as a pledge of interior grace. I do not think that this favour is granted to all perfect souls, but only to those to whom our Lord wills to give it. Other souls as yet imperfect may experience these sensations without having received the interior grace, but it is not good for them to depend overmuch on these sensations. Let them rather make use of them in so far as they help the soul to a more constant recollection of God and to a deeper love of Him. For, as I have already said, these sensations may sometimes be genuine and sometimes illusory.

CHAPTER 31: *The means by which a soul is reformed in feeling, and the spiritual gifts that it receives*

I HAVE now said a little about reform in faith, and have also touched briefly on the soul's progress from that stage to the higher reform in feeling. In so doing I do not intend to limit the ways in which God works to any laws of my own making, nor to imply that God works in a soul in one particular way and no other. This is not my meaning: I say only that I am sure that God does work in this way in some of His creatures. I am certain that He also works in other ways outside my own knowledge and experience. Nevertheless, whether God works in this way or in others, in several ways, over a longer or shorter period, or whether He works powerfully or peacefully in a soul, if all tends to the same end, which is the perfect love of Him, then that way is good. For if God wills to give a particular soul the full grace of contemplation in a single day and without any effort of its own – as well He may – then that soul receives as much grace as it might have received after twenty years of trial and suffering, mortification, and purification. Therefore take my words in their proper sense, and as I intend them to be understood. For now, with God's help, I will speak in greater detail about reform in feeling; its nature, how it takes place, and its spiritual effects in the soul.

Firstly, however, lest you should imagine that this reformation of soul is a mere figure of speech or figment of imagination, I will support what I say by the words of Saint Paul: *Nolite conformari huic saeculo, sed reformamini in novitate sensus vestri* (Rom. xii, 2). That is: You are reformed in faith by grace; henceforward, therefore, do not conform to the ways of the world in pride, covetousness, and other sins, but be reformed in newness of feeling. Here you can see that Saint Paul speaks of reform in feeling, and in another passage he explains what this new feeling consists of: *Ut impleamini in agnitione voluntatis ejus, in omni intellectu et sapientia spirituali* (Col. i, 9). We pray God that you may be filled with the knowledge of His will, with full understanding and with every kind of spiritual wisdom. This is what reform in feeling implies. For you should understand that the soul becomes aware of things in two ways: outwardly through the five bodily senses, and inwardly through the spiritual senses, which are properly the powers of the soul, memory, understanding, and will. When these powers are led by grace to a full understanding of the will and wisdom of God, the soul then attains a new level of spiritual experience. Saint Paul demonstrates the truth of this in another place: *Renovamini spiritu mentis vestrae, et induite novum hominem, qui secundum Deum creatus est in justitia, sanctitate, et veritate* (Eph. iv, 23). Be renewed in soul; that is, be reformed, not in your outward senses, nor in your imagination, but in the higher faculties of the understanding. And put on the new man, which is re-shaped to the likeness of God in righteousness. That is, your reason, which should rightly reflect God's likeness, is to be clothed by the grace of the Holy Spirit in a new light of truth, holiness, and righteousness; it is then reformed in feeling. For when the soul attains a perfect knowledge of God, it is then reformed. Saint Paul says: *Exspoliantes veterem hominem cum actibus suis; induite novum, qui renovatur in agnitione Dei, secundum imaginem ejus qui creavit eum* (Col. iii, 9). Put off the old man with all his doings; that is, put away from you the love of the world and all worldly behaviour, and put on the new man; that is, be renewed in the knowledge of God after the likeness of Him who made you.

From these statements you can see that Saint Paul wishes men's souls to be reformed by the perfect knowledge of God, for this is the new experience of which he is speaking. So with his words as my authority I will deal more fully with this reformation as God gives me grace. For there are two ways of knowing God. One depends principally upon the imagination, and little upon reason; it is the degree of knowledge granted to chosen souls in the early stages of their spiritual life and progress. These souls know and love God in a human and not in a spiritual way, and think of Him, as I have already said, as though He possessed human attributes. This degree of knowledge is good, and is a kind of milk which nourishes them in their spiritual infancy until they are able to come to their Father's table and receive solid food from His hand. The other way to knowledge depends principally upon reason, strengthened and illumined by the Holy Spirit. Here imagination has little place. For reason is the lady, and imagination is her maid, serving her as occasion requires. This knowledge is solid food, nourishment for souls made perfect, and it is reformation in feeling.

CHAPTER 32: *How God opens the eyes of the soul to perceive Him, not all at once, but gradually. An example showing the three stages in a soul's reformation*

WHEN a soul has been called to abandon the love of the world, and has been corrected and tested, mortified and purified as I have described, our Lord Jesus in His goodness and mercy reforms it in feeling as He sees best. He opens the eyes of the soul to see and know Him, bathing it in His own blessed light. He does not do this fully at once, but little by little as the soul becomes able to bear it. The soul does not know God as He is, for no creature in heaven or earth can do this, nor can it see Him as He is, for that vision is granted only in the bliss of heaven. But it recognizes Him as a changeless Being, as sovereign Power, sovereign Truth, and sovereign Goodness, and as the source of blessing, life, and eternal bliss. The soul perceives these truths and many others, but not as a bare, abstract, savour-less theory, as a learned man may know Him solely by the exercise of his reason. For its understanding is uplifted and illumined by the grace of the Holy Spirit to see Him as He is more clearly and fully than can be expressed, with wondering reverence, ardent love, spiritual delight, and heavenly joy.

Although such an experience of God is brief and incomplete, it is so exalted and stupendous that it transports the soul and withdraws all its affections and thoughts from worldly things, so that were it possible it would wish to enjoy it for ever. On this experience and knowledge of God the soul establishes all its interior life, for henceforward it venerates God in man as Truth, reveres Him as Power, and loves Him as Goodness. This experience and knowledge of Jesus, and the sacred love that springs from it, may be called the soul's reforming in faith and love of which I have been speaking. It is reform in faith because it is still obscure in comparison to the full knowledge that it will possess in heaven, for then we shall not only know that God is, but we shall see Him as He is. As Saint John says: *Tunc vide-bimus eum sicuti est* (I John iii, 2). That is: We shall see Him as He is. Nevertheless, this reform is also in feeling, in contrast to the blind knowledge that a soul possesses by faith alone. For as a result of this experience and grace the soul knows something of the divine nature of Jesus, but without this experience the soul believes only in the truth of His divinity.

To illustrate better what I mean, I will describe these three stages in the reform of a soul with an example. Three men are standing in sunlight: one of them is blind, the other can see but has his eyes closed, while the third has his eyes open. The blind man has no means of knowing that he is in sunlight, but be-lieves it if a truthful person tells him so. He represents a soul reformed in faith alone, who believes what the Church teaches about God, but does not fully understand it. This degree of knowledge is sufficient for salvation.

The next man is aware of the sunlight, but does not see it clearly or fully because his eyelids obscure his vision. But he sees a glimmer of bright light through them, and he represents a soul reformed in faith and feeling, and is therefore a contemplative. For by grace he sees something of the divinity of Jesus, although not clearly or fully, because his eyelids – that is, his bodily nature – act as a curtain between him and the divine nature of Jesus, and prevents him from seeing Jesus clearly. But when he is visited by grace he can see through this curtain, and knows that Jesus is God, sovereign Good, sovereign Being, and Source of Life, and that all blessings come from Him. Notwithstanding the limitations of bodily nature, the soul perceives all this by grace, and the purer and finer the soul becomes, and the less it is influenced by the body, the keener its spiritual sight and the stronger its love for the divinity of Jesus. So profound is the effect of this experience of Jesus upon the soul that, even were no other living person to believe in Jesus or love Him, its own faith and love would never lessen, for its own certainty is so absolute that it cannot help but believe.

The third man, who sees the sun clearly, has no need of faith because his vision is clear. He represents a blessed soul who sees the face of Jesus openly in the bliss of heaven, unobscured by the limitations of the body or by sin. Faith is no longer required, and he is therefore fully reformed in feeling.

The soul cannot progress beyond the second stage of reforming in this life, for this is the state of perfection and the road to heaven. Nevertheless, souls who have attained this state are not all alike. For some reach this state only to a limited extent, briefly and infrequently; some remain in it longer and more frequently, and attain a higher level; while some attain a high level and remain in it for long periods when they have received abundant grace. For the soul does not know Jesus perfectly all at once, but little by little. It makes gradual progress, its knowledge of Him grows, and so long as it remains in this life it may increase this knowledge and love of Jesus. Indeed, for a soul that has experienced a little of this union with Jesus, I think that nothing remains but to abandon and ignore everything else, and devote itself entirely to obtaining a clearer knowledge and a deeper love of Jesus, and in Him of all the Blessed Trinity.

As I understand it, this knowledge of Jesus is the opening of heaven to the eyes of a pure soul of which the saints speak in their writings. But this opening of heaven does not imply, as some imagine, that the soul can see in imagination our Lord Jesus sitting in His majesty in a visible light as brilliant as that of a hundred suns. This is not so, for however high man's vision may penetrate, he cannot see the heaven of heavens. Indeed, the higher he aspires beyond the sun in his imagination, the lower he falls beneath it. Notwithstanding, thinking of our Lord in this way is permissible for simple souls, who know no better way of seeking Him who is invisible.

CHAPTER 33 : *How Jesus is heaven to the soul, and why He is called Fire*

WHAT is heaven to a reasoning soul? Surely, nothing other than Jesus, our God. For if heaven is that which is above all things, then God alone is heaven to a man's soul, for He alone is superior to the nature of the soul. Therefore if grace enables a soul to perceive the divine nature of Jesus, it sees heaven itself, for it sees God.

Many people misunderstand certain sayings about God because they do not interpret them in a spiritual sense. Holy Scripture says that a soul that seeks God must lift up its eyes and seek God above itself. Some who wish to follow this injunction understand the words 'above itself' as meaning a higher or nobler level in a worldly sense, in the same way that one element or planet is regarded as superior to another. But this does not apply to spiritual matters, for the soul is superior to all material things, not because of its position in the world but because of the dignity of its nature. Similarly, God is superior to all created things, both spiritual and material, not because of His lofty place in the universe, but because of the spiritual dignity of His Being, blessed and unchanging. Therefore, anyone who desires to seek God wisely and to find Him must not allow his thoughts to soar above the sun and circle the firmament, picturing the majesty of God as the light of a hundred suns. Instead, let him forget the sun and all the firmament, regarding them as inferior to himself, and think both of God and himself on a spiritual plane. If the soul can do this, it then looks beyond itself and sees heaven.

The word 'within' must be understood in the same way. It is commonly said that a soul shall see God in all things and within itself. It is true that God is in all created things, but not in the way that a kernel is hidden within the shell of a nut, or as a small object is contained within a greater. He is within all things, maintaining and preserving them in being, but He is present in a spiritual way, exercising the power of His Own blessed nature and invisible purity. For just as an object that is very precious and pure is laid in a secure place, so by the same analogy the nature of God, which is supremely precious, pure, and spiritual, utterly unlike any physical nature, is hidden within all things. Anyone who desires to seek God within must therefore forget all material things, for these are exterior; he must cease to consider his own body or even his own soul, and consider the uncreated nature of God who made him, endowed him with life, upholds him, and gives him reason, memory, and love. All these gifts come to him through the power and sovereign grace of God. This must be the soul's course of action when it is touched by grace; otherwise it will be of little use to seek God within itself or in His creation.

In Holy Scripture God is described as Light. Saint John says:

Deus lux est (1 John i, 5). God is Light. This Light is not to be understood as physical light, but in this way. God is Light; that is, God is Truth itself, since Truth is spiritual light. Therefore the soul that by grace possesses the fullest knowledge of truth has the clearest vision of God. But it may be compared with physical light in this sense: for as the sun reveals itself and all material things to the eye by its own light, so God, who is also Truth, reveals Himself first to the understanding of the soul, and by this means bestows all the spiritual knowledge that the soul requires. For the prophet says: *Domine, in lumine tuo videbimus lumen* (Ps. xxxvi, 9). Lord, in Your light we shall see all light. That is: we shall see that You are Truth by the light of Yourself.

In the same way, God is described as Fire: *Deus noster ignis consumens est.* Our God is a consuming fire. This does not mean that God is the element of fire which heats and consumes physical objects, but that God is Love and Charity. For just as fire consumes all material objects that can be destroyed by it, so the love of God burns and consumes all sin out of the soul and makes it clean, as fire purifies all kinds of metal. These descriptions and all other material comparisons applied to God in Holy Scripture must be understood in a spiritual sense, for otherwise they are meaningless. But the reason why such words are employed to describe God is that we are so worldly in our outlook that we cannot speak of God without at first using such expressions. However, when the eyes of the soul are opened by grace, and we are enabled to catch a glimpse of God, then our souls can quite easily interpret these material descriptions in a spiritual sense.

This opening of the eyes of the soul to the knowledge of the Godhead I call reform in faith and feeling. For the soul then has some experience of what it once knew by faith alone. This is the beginning of contemplation, of which Saint Paul said: *Non contemplantibus nobis quae videntur, sed quae non videntur; quae enim videntur, temporalia sunt, quae autem non videntur, aeterna sunt* (II Cor. iv, 18). We do not contemplate the things that are seen, but those that are not seen; for the things that are seen are temporal, but those that are not seen are eternal. It is these things that the soul should aspire to gain, partially indeed in this present life, but fully in the bliss of heaven. For the full bliss and eternal life of the rational soul consist in this vision and knowledge of God. *Haec est autem vita aeterna: ut cognoscant te unum Deum, et quem misisti, Jesum Christum* (S. John xvii, 3). Father, this is eternal life, that Your chosen souls should know You, and Jesus Christ Your Son whom You have sent, to be the one true God.

CHAPTER 34: *How we are to realize that it is not created love which brings the soul to the spiritual vision of God, but Love uncreated, that is, God Himself, who bestows this knowledge*

BUT since the ultimate joy and end of the soul depends upon this knowledge of God, you may perhaps wonder why I said earlier that the soul should desire nothing but the love of God, yet said nothing about the nature of the soul's desire for this knowledge. My answer is that the knowledge of God brings perfect happiness to the soul, and that this happiness derives not only from the knowledge, but from the blessed love which springs from it. Nevertheless, love derives from knowledge, and not knowledge from love; consequently the happiness of the soul is said to derive chiefly from this knowledge and experience of God, to which is conjoined the love of God. And the better God is known the more He is loved. But inasmuch as the soul cannot attain this knowledge, or the love that derives from it, without God who is Love, I said that you should desire Love alone. For God's love alone guides the soul to this vision and knowledge; and that Love is not the soul's own love for God, but the Love of God for a sinful soul incapable of loving Him rightly by itself. God Himself is both the means by which the soul attains this knowledge, and the love that derives from it. And I will now tell you more explicitly how this comes about.

In their writings the saints say, and with truth, that there are two kinds of spiritual love. One is termed uncreated Love and the other created. Uncreated Love is God Himself, the third Person of the Trinity, that is, the Holy Spirit. He is Love uncreated, as Saint John says: *Deus dilectio est* (1 John iv, 8). God is Love; that is, the Holy Spirit. Created love is the love implanted and aroused in a soul by the Holy Spirit when it sees and knows Truth, that is, God. This love is called created because it is brought into being by the Holy Spirit. It is not God Himself, since it is created, but it is the love felt by the soul when it beholds God and is moved to love Him alone. So you can see that created love is not the cause of a soul coming to the contemplation of God, for there are people who think that they can love God of their own accord with such ardour that they can merit the gift of contemplation; but this is not so. Love uncreated, that is God Himself, alone can infuse this knowledge. For because of its sinfulness and human weakness a poor unhappy soul is so far from this clear knowledge of God and the blessed experience of His love that it could never attain them were it not for the infinite greatness of God's love. But because He loves us so greatly, He gives up His Love, that is, the Holy Spirit. He is both the Giver and the Gift, and by that Gift He makes us know and love Him. This is the Divine Love which I said should be the sole object of your desire, the uncreated Love that is the Holy Spirit. Indeed, a lesser gift than that of Himself will not suffice to bring us to the blessed knowledge of God. We should therefore earnestly desire this gift of Love, and ask God for this alone, that in His infinite love He would flood our hearts with His ineffable light, so that we may know

Him, and bestow His blessed Love upon us, so that as He loves us, we may return His love. For as Saint John says: *Nos diligamus Deum, quoniam ipse prior dilexit nos* (1 John vi, 19). We now love God, because He has first loved us. He loved us greatly when He created us in His likeness, but He loved us yet more when He redeemed us from the power of the devil and the pains of hell by His Precious Blood when as Man He willingly endured death for us. But He loves us most when He gives us the gift of the Holy Spirit, that is, Divine Love, by which we know and love Him, and are assured that we are His sons, chosen for salvation. We are more indebted to Him for this Love than for any other love that He has ever shown us, either in our creation or our preservation. For although He had made us and redeemed us, what advantage would this have been to us had He not also saved us? Surely, none.

It appears to me that the greatest pledge of God's love given to us is this; that He gives Himself to our souls in His Divinity. He gave Himself first in His humanity as a ransom for us when He offered Himself to the Heavenly Father on the altar of the Cross. This was a splendid gift, and a great pledge of love. But when He gives Himself to our souls in His Divinity for our salvation, and makes us know and love Him, then He loves us completely, for then He gives Himself to us, and He could not give us more: yet less could not satisfy us. For this reason it is said that the justification of a sinful soul through the forgiveness of its sins is ascribed and appropriated chiefly to the work of the Holy Spirit. For the Holy Spirit is Love, and in the justification of a soul God shows it His Love most clearly, for He takes away its sin and unites it to Himself. This is the highest thing that God can do for a soul, and it is therefore appropriated to the Holy Spirit.

The creation of the soul is appropriated to the Father, because of the sovereign might and power that He displays in creating it. Its preservation is ascribed and appropriated to the Son, because of the sovereign will and wisdom that He displayed in His human nature, for He overcame the devil chiefly through wisdom and not through strength. But the justification and full salvation of the soul through the forgiveness of sins is appropriated to the third Person, that is, to the Holy Spirit. For in this God most clearly displays His love for the souls of men, and it is for this that we should most love Him in return. All irrational creatures, in common with ourselves, are created by God, for He made them out of nothing as He did us. This, then, is the work of His greatest power, but not of His greatest love. In the same way, salvation is offered to all rational souls, both to Jews, Moslems, and bad Christians. For Christ died for all souls, and ransomed them if they are willing to profit by His sacrifice; His death was sufficient for the salvation of all men, even though they do not avail themselves of it. And this was the work of wisdom rather than of love. But the justification and sanctification of our souls comes through the gift of the Holy Spirit, and is the work of Love alone. It is not common to all men, but is a special gift to chosen souls alone. Indeed, it is the supreme work of love for us who are His chosen children.

This is the Love of God that I said you should long for and desire, for this Love is God the Holy Spirit Himself. When we are given this uncreated Love it produces all that is good in our souls, and all that makes for goodness. This Love of God is ours before we love Him, for it first of all cleanses us from our sins, makes us love Him, strengthens our wills to resist sin, and inspires us to obtain all virtues by means of various bodily and spiritual practices. It inspires us also to forsake all love of the world, while it destroys within us all sinful impulses, carnal desires and worldly preoccupations. It protects us from the malicious temptations of the devil, and causes us to avoid useless worldly occupations and the company of worldly-minded people. The uncreated Love of God does all these things when

He gives Himself to us. We ourselves do nothing more than allow Him to act as He wills, for the most that we can do is to yield ourselves readily to the working of His grace. Yet even this readiness does not originate in us, but in Him, so that all good that we do is due to Him, although we do not realize this. Not only does He do this, but in His love He does even more. He opens the eyes of the soul in a wonderful way, shows it the vision of God, and reveals to it the knowledge of Himself little by little as the soul is capable of bearing it. By this means He draws all the love of the soul towards Himself.

The soul then begins to know Him in a spiritual way, and to love Him ardently. It then perceives something of the divine nature, how God is All and does all things, and how all good deeds and holy thoughts proceed from Him alone. For He is sovereign Power, Truth, and Goodness: every good deed, therefore, is done through Him and by Him, and to Him alone are due the glory and thanks for all. For although sinful men usurp His glory here for a little while, nevertheless at the Last Day truth will show clearly that God did all, and that man achieved nothing by himself. Then those who have tried to usurp God's rightful place, and have not made their peace with Him for their evil-doing, will be condemned to eternal death, and God will be adored and thanked for the workings of His grace by all the creatures that He has saved.

As I have already said, and will enlarge upon later, this Love is nothing else but God Himself, who in His Love works all this in the soul of man, and reforms it in feeling to His own likeness. This Love produces the fullness of all virtues in the soul, making them pure and true, tranquil and congenial, and renders them desirable and pleasant to the soul. And I will presently tell you in what way God does this. This Love raises the soul from a worldly to a spiritual plane, from earthly interests to heavenly joys, and from vain concern with earthly matters to the contemplation of spiritual realities and the secrets of God.

CHAPTER 35: *How some souls, moved by grace and reason, love Jesus with fervent emotion and natural affection. And how some, inspired by the special grace of the Holy Spirit, love Him more quietly with a spiritual love alone*

ONE may say that the soul that attains the greatest love for God in this life is most pleasing to Him, and because of this will enjoy the clearest vision of Him in the bliss of heaven.

Love of this kind, however, cannot be attained simply by a man's own efforts, as some imagine. It is the free gift of God's grace, and is received only after great bodily and spiritual struggles. For there are lovers of God who try to compel themselves to love Him, as it were by very force of will. They strain themselves by the violence of their efforts, and desire it so intensely that they break into bodily fervour as though they would draw God down from heaven to them, saying in their hearts and with their mouth, 'Ah, Lord, I love Thee and I will love Thee. For Thy love I would suffer death.' As a result they feel great fervour and great grace. Indeed, this behaviour would appear to be good and praiseworthy, provided that it is well tempered with humility and discretion. Nevertheless, these souls do not possess the gift of love that I described, nor are they trying to obtain it. For anyone who possesses this gift as a result of grace and a personal experience of God – or one who does not possess it, but desires it – does not overstrain himself almost by physical violence in order to enjoy sensible fervour and feel love for God in this way. He realizes that he is nothing and can do nothing of himself, but is as it were inanimate and entirely dependent on the support and mercy of God. He sees that God is All and does all things, and therefore asks for nothing but the gift of His love. And since the soul realizes that his own love is nothing, he desires to have God's love, which is all-sufficient. So he prays and desires that God would touch him with His blessed light, so that he may experience something of His gracious presence, for then he would love Him indeed. This is the way that the gift of Love, that is, God, enters the soul.

The more fully that grace enables the soul to recognize its own nothingness in the light of God's truth – sometimes without any outward signs of fervour – and the less it is conscious of loving and knowing God, the nearer it approaches to perceiving the gift of God's Love. For it is then under the control of Love, which directs the soul, causing it to forget itself and be conscious only that God's Love is working within it. The soul is then more passive than active, and this is the work of pure Love. This is what Saint Paul meant when he said: *Quicumque Spiritu Dei aguntur, ii filii Dei sunt* (Rom. viii, 14). All who are moulded by the Spirit of God are the sons of God. In other words, souls that are so humble and obedient to God that they do nothing of themselves, but allow the Holy Spirit to guide them and to kindle feelings of love in them by His own working, are God's children in a special sense because they are most like Him.

Other souls cannot love in this way, but try to stimulate their affections and stir their imagination by meditation on God and by external discipline, so as to produce the feeling of love accompanied by bodily fervour and other outward phenomena; but these do not love God in a spiritual way. They mean well and deserve commendation, however, only in so far as they humbly recognize that their fervour is not Divine Love experienced by grace, but only the product of the soul's obedience to reason. Nevertheless, because the soul does all it can, the goodness of God transforms this natural aspiration to God into spiritual affection, and this is rewarded as though it had been spiritual from the beginning. Such is the great generosity of God to humble souls that He transforms these affections of human origin into the meritorious spiritual affections of His own Love, as though they had come from Him alone. Affections so transformed may be called aspirations of spiritual love, but they are rendered so only by the generosity of God, and are not due to the direct action of the Holy Spirit within the soul. I do not say that a soul can produce even such natural affections by itself without grace, for I am well aware that Saint Paul says that we cannot do or think anything good of ourselves without grace. *Non enim quod sufficientes simus cogitare aliquid nobis, quasi ex nobis; sed sufficientia nostra ex Deo est* (II Cor. iii, 5). That is: We who love God do not think that we are sufficient to love or to think anything good of ourselves alone, but our sufficiency is of God. For God works in us all, both to will and to do good. As Saint Paul says: *Deus est qui operatur in nobis et velle et perficere pro bona voluntate* (Phil. ii, 13). That is: It is God who brings about in us both the will to good and its fulfilment. But such aspirations, formed by the soul as a result of the general grace that God gives to all chosen souls, are all good. But they are not due to the special grace bestowed by the touch of God's presence in a soul that loves Him perfectly. For in those whose love of God is imperfect His love works indirectly through the natural affections; but in those whose love is perfect God works directly, implanting His own spiritual affections, and destroying all worldly and natural affections. This is how God's Love works directly in a soul. This divine Love may be possessed incompletely in this life by a pure soul through the contemplation of God, but it is perfected in the bliss of heaven by a clear vision of the Godhead, for then all the aspirations of the soul will be entirely Godward and spiritual.

CHAPTER 36: *How the gift of His Love is the most valuable and desirable of all God's gifts: how God, out of love alone, is the source of all good in those who love Him: and how divine Love makes the practice of all virtues and good works light and easy*

Ask nothing of God, then, but this gift of divine Love, that is, the Holy Spirit. For among all the gifts of God there is none so good and valuable, so noble or so excellent as this. For in no other gift of God save this gift of Love is the Giver Himself the Gift, so that it is the noblest and best of all. The gifts of prophecy, of working miracles, of knowledge and counsel, of enduring severe fasting and penance, and all other such are great gifts of the Holy Spirit: but they are not the Holy Spirit Himself, for a reprobate soul might possess all these gifts as readily as a chosen soul.

Therefore gifts of this kind are not greatly to be desired, and they should not be over-estimated. But the gift of divine Love is the Holy Spirit, God Himself, and no soul can possess Him and be lost, for this gift saves it from damnation; He makes it His own, and endows it with the heritage of heaven. And this Love, as I said earlier, is not the natural love that is created in a soul; it is the Holy Spirit Himself, Love uncreated, who saves a soul. For He first gives Himself to a soul before it loves Him, and He creates love in the soul, and makes the soul love Him for Himself alone. And not only this, for by this gift the soul loves itself and all its fellow-Christians as itself for the sake of God alone. It is this gift of divine Love which distinguishes the chosen souls from the reprobate. It makes true peace between God and the soul, and unites all the blessed in God. It is the bond of divine Love which unites God to us, and us to God, and causes us to love one another in Him.

Seek this gift of divine Love above all else, as I have said, for if God of His grace will give it you, it will open and enlighten your spiritual understanding to see truth, that is, God, and spiritual things. It will kindle your affection to love Him wholly and truly, and He will work within your soul entirely as He wills, so that you will contemplate Him with worship and love, and understand what He is doing within you. God tells us through His prophet what we must do, saying: *Vacate, et videte quoniam ego sum Deus* (Ps. xlvi, 10). Be still, and see that I am God. That is: you who are reformed in feeling and whose inward vision is clear to see the things of the spirit, cease from outward activity for a while and see that I am God. In other words, 'Look only at what I, Jesus, God and man, am doing; look at Me, for it is I who do everything. I am Love, and all that I do is done out of love. I will show you how this is true, for you can neither do nor think anything good except through Me, that is, through My power, wisdom, and love, for otherwise it is not wholly good. The truth is that I, Jesus, am both Might, Wisdom, and holy Love: you are nothing, and I am God. Recognize, therefore, that it is I who am responsible for all your good deeds, good thoughts, and holy desires, and that you do nothing of yourself. Notwithstanding, all these good deeds are called yours, not because you are primarily responsible for them, but because I make them over to you out of the love that I bear you. Therefore, since I am God and do all this for love, cease to think about yourself: look at Me, and see that I am God, for I do all this.' This is something of David's meaning in the verse that I have quoted.

See, then, what divine Love does within a chosen soul which He reforms in feeling to His likeness, when the understanding is partially enlightened to know Jesus and to experience His love. Love brings all the virtues into a soul, and renders them pleasing and congenial without any action by the soul itself. For the soul does not struggle painfully to acquire them as it

did formerly, but obtains them easily and enjoys them peacefully through the gift of divine Love alone, that is the Holy
Spirit. This is supreme consolation and unspeakable joy when
it suddenly discovers, without understanding how, that humility and patience, temperance and restraint, chastity and purity,
brotherly love and all the other virtues that were formerly so
burdensome, painful, and difficult to practise have now become
attractive, pleasant, and wonderfully easy. So great is the change
that the soul no longer finds any virtue exacting or difficult,
but very pleasant. And all this is the work of divine Love.

Others, who have the common amount of charity and have
not yet grown in grace to this extent, but are guided by their
own reason, struggle and strive all day against their sins in
order to acquire virtues. Like wrestlers, they are sometimes on
top, and sometimes underneath. Such people are doing well.
They acquire virtues through their own reason and will, but not
because they love and delight in virtue, for they have to exert
all their energy to overcome their natural instincts in order to
possess them. Consequently they can never enjoy true peace or
final victory. They will receive a great reward, but they are
not yet sufficiently humble. They have not put themselves
wholly into God's hands, because they do not yet see Him.

But a soul that has this inward vision of God is not greatly
concerned with the struggle for virtue, and does not devote itself chiefly to this. Its whole purpose is to maintain such vision
of God as it has. It desires to keep its mind on this, to ensure
that its love never wavers, and as far as possible to set aside all
else. When it does this, God subdues all sins in the soul, over-
shadows it with His blessed presence, and gives it all virtues.
And the soul is so comforted and sustained by the wonderful
feeling of love that derives from the vision of God that no
outward tribulation can disturb it. In this way divine Love
destroys all sin in the soul, and reforms it with a new awareness
of virtues.

CHAPTER 37: *How, when the soul is granted the grace of contemplation, Divine Love overcomes all inclinations to pride, and renders the soul perfectly humble by removing all desire for worldly honours.*

I WILL now describe more fully how Divine Love overcomes sin and establishes virtues in the soul. First I will speak of pride, and of its opposite virtue humility. You should understand that there are two kinds of humility, one of which is acquired by reason, while the other is the especial gift of Divine Love. Both spring ultimately from Divine Love, but the former is due to Divine Love acting upon the soul through reason, while the latter comes from the direct action of Divine Love. The first is imperfect, but the second is perfect.

The first kind of humility is born in a man when he considers his own sin and wretched condition. The consciousness of this makes him realize his own unworthiness to receive any grace or reward from God. He thinks it more than enough that God in His mercy should grant him forgiveness for his sins. He thinks himself the worst sinner alive, and that everyone is better than himself. These considerations cause him to regard himself as the least of all men, and he struggles with all his might to resist all inclinations to pride, both worldly and spiritual. And since he despises himself, he does not assent to feelings of pride. And if he is sometimes overtaken by pride – by taking pleasure in his honours or knowledge, in praise or in any other things – directly he realizes it he despises himself and is truly sorry. So he asks God's forgiveness, humbly reveals his fault to his confessor, and accepts penance. This humility is good, but it is not perfect, for it is the degree of humility found in beginners and those who are growing in grace, and it springs from a realization of their sins. Divine Love fosters this humility through reason.

A soul comes to perfect humility through the contemplation and knowledge of God. For when the Holy Spirit illumines the soul's understanding to perceive the truth, how God is All in all and does all, the soul feels such love and joy at this experience that it forgets itself and devotes itself entirely to the contemplation of God with all the love that it possesses. It is no longer concerned with its own unworthiness or its former sins. It forgets itself, together with all its own sins and good works, as though nothing existed except God. David possessed this humility when he said : *Et substantia mea tanquam nihilum ante te* (Ps. xxxix, 5). That is, Lord, the contemplation of Your blessed uncreated substance and eternal Being shows me clearly that my own substance and being are nothing in comparison to You. Similarly in relation to his neighbour, he does not judge him or consider whether he is better or worse than himself, for he regards both himself and other men as equal, all alike as nothing in comparison to God. And this is the truth, for all goodness, whether in himself or others, comes from God alone, whom he acknowledges as All. He therefore regards all creatures, together with himself, as nothing. The prophet possessed this humility when he said : *Omnes gentes quasi non sint, sic sunt coram eo, et quasi nihilum et inane reputatae sunt ei* (Isa. xl, 17). All nations are as nothing, as mere vanity before God, and are accounted as nothing to Him. That is, compared to the eternal and changeless Being of God, mankind is as nothing. For it was created out of nothing, and would return to nothing unless He who made it out of nothing maintained it in existence. This is the truth, and if grace enables the soul to see this truth, it should make it humble. Therefore when Divine Love opens the inward eyes of the soul to see this truth and all its implications, the soul begins to be truly humble. As a result of this vision of God it feels and sees itself as it is, so that it gives up considering or relying on itself, and devotes itself wholly to the contemplation of God. Once it does this, the soul thinks nothing of all the pleasures and honours of the world; for worldly honour is so insignificant in comparison to the joy and love that it feels in the contemplation of God and in the knowledge of truth, that even if it were able to possess it without sin, it would have no desire to do so. Were men to honour him, praise him, favour him, or grant him high rank, it would not give him any pleasure. Neither would it please him to be a master of all the arts, of theology, or of all the crafts, or to have power to perform all kinds of miracles. He would find no more enjoyment or satisfaction in these things than in gnawing a dry stick. He would much rather forget all these things and be alone out of sight of the world, than to think of them and be honoured by all men. For the heart of the true lover of God is made so great by even a glimpse of Him and a little experience of His love, that all the pleasures and joys on earth would not be sufficient to fill a corner of it. He comes to realize that these unhappy lovers of the world who are so obsessed by a craving for personal honour, and who pursue it by every means in their power, have no desire for this humility, and are in fact very far from possessing it. But one who loves God retains this humility at all times, not with weariness and struggle, but with pleasure and gladness. And this gladness is his not because he has rejected worldly honours – for that would be the false type of humility possessed by a hypocrite – but because he has received a vision and knowledge of the truth and the splendour of God through the gift of the Holy Spirit.

This worshipful contemplation and love of God fills the soul with wonderful comfort and upholds it so strongly and tenderly that it cannot find true pleasure and satisfaction in any earthly joys, and has no desire to do so. He is not concerned as to whether men blame or praise him, honour him or despise him. He is not even sufficiently moved to be glad if the scorn of men humiliates him still further, or to feel regret if they honour and praise him. He would prefer to forget both the one and the other, to think of God alone, and to gain humility in that way; for this is the surest way for any who can follow it. This was David's way, when he said: *Oculi mei semper ad Dominum, quoniam ipse evellet de laqueo pedes meos* (Ps. xxv, 15). My eyes are always looking to the Lord, for He will keep my feet from the snares of sin. When a man does this, he completely forsakes himself, and entrusts himself wholly to God. He is then secure, for the shield of truth which he holds protects him so well that no stirrings of pride will hurt him so long as he remains behind it. As the prophet says: *Scuto circumdabit te veritas ejus; non timebis a timore nocturno* (Ps. xci, 5). Truth shall surround you as with a shield, if you set aside all else and look to God alone. For then you will not fear the terror of the night – that is, you will not fear the spirit of pride – whether it comes by night or by day. As the next verse says: *A sagitta volante in die.* Pride approaches by night to attack the soul when a person is despised and criticized by others, and is liable to fall into depression and sorrow. It comes as 'an arrow flying by day' when a person is honoured and praised by all, whether for worldly or spiritual achievements, and is liable to rest content is such transitory things. This arrow is sharp and dangerous; it flies swiftly, strikes suddenly, and deals a mortal wound. But one who loves God, seeking Him constantly in devout prayer and regular meditation, is so protected by the sure shield of truth that he has no fear, for this arrow cannot penetrate his soul. If it comes at him it cannot hurt him, but glances off and passes onward. And this, I think, is the way in which a soul is made humble by the action of the Holy Spirit, that is, the gift of Divine Love. He opens the eyes of the soul to see and love God, and keeps them quietly and securely fastened on Himself. He destroys all stirrings of pride imperceptibly and quietly, the soul knows not how, and along with truth and love He infuses the virtue of humility. Divine Love does all this, but not to the same extent in all His lovers alike. For some possess this grace for short periods and to a limited extent; they possess, as it were, the beginnings of it and a little experience of it, for their consciences are not yet fully cleansed by grace. And some possess it in greater fullness, for they have a clearer vision of God, and feel more of His love. And some possess it fully, for they have the full gift of contemplation. But as I have said, one who has it even in the smallest degree has the gift of perfect humility since he possesses the gift of perfect love.

CHAPTER 38: *How Divine Love quietly destroys all stirrings of anger and envy in the soul, and restores the virtues of peace, patience, and perfect charity to its fellow-men, as it did in the Apostles*

DIVINE LOVE works within the soul as He wills, wisely and quietly. He destroys anger, envy, despair, and all such passions, and brings the virtues of patience, gentleness, peace, and kindness into the soul. For one whose behaviour is governed solely by his own reason, it is very hard to be patient, peaceable, gentle, and charitable to his neighbours when they vex him unreasonably or do him wrong, for he is inclined to retaliate with anger or resentment, either in word, or act, or both. Nevertheless, if although he is upset and troubled, he does not overstep the bounds of reason and restrains his hands and tongue, and is ready to forgive an offence when pardon is asked, he possesses the virtue of patience. It is as yet weak and unstable, but in so far as he desires to have it, and makes a real effort to control his irrational passions in order to acquire it, and is sorry that he does not possess it as fully as he should, his patience is genuine. But to one who truly loves God it requires no great effort to endure all this, because Divine Love fights for him and imperceptibly destroys these feelings of anger and resentment. His spiritual union with God and the experience of

His blessed love renders his soul so quiet and peaceful, so patient and devoted, that he is unaffected by the contempt and criticism, disgrace or villainy inflicted upon him by men. He is not greatly provoked by them, and refuses to be angered by them, for were he greatly provoked he would lose his peace of soul, and he does not wish to do this. It is easier for him to forget all the wrongs done to him than for another man to forgive even when pardon is asked. He would rather forget it than forgive it, for he finds this easier.

Divine Love does all these things, for Love opens the eyes of the soul to the vision of God, and strengthens it with the joys of love that it experiences in that vision. It brings such comfort to a man's soul that he has no cares, and is unaffected by anything that people may do or say against him. The greatest harm that he could suffer would be the loss of that spiritual vision of God, and he would suffer any harm rather than that. When a person's troubles are all external and do not affect the body – such as gossip, contempt, or material loss – he may do all this quite easily and without detriment to his spiritual life. These can be ignored. But when the body is affected and he feels pain, it affects him more deeply and becomes harder. Yet although it is difficult or impossible for the frail nature of man to endure physical suffering gladly and patiently, without bitterness, anger, or depression, it is not impossible for Divine Love, that is the Holy Spirit, to bring this about in a soul when He grants it the precious gift of Himself. To one in distress He grants the mighty experience of His love, and unites it to Himself in a wonderful manner. By His great power He withdraws it from the influence of the outward senses, and bestows such sweet comfort on the soul by His sacred presence that it is aware of little or no bodily pain. This is an especial grace granted to the holy Martyrs and Apostles, of whom Holy Scripture says: *Ibant Apostoli gaudentes a conspectu concilii, quoniam digni habiti sunt pro nomine Christi contumeliam pati* (Acts v, 41). The Apostles came joyfully from the Council of the Jews when they were beaten with scourges, and they were glad to be held worthy to suffer bodily distress for the love of Jesus. They were not moved to anger and resentment, and had no wish to be revenged on the Jews who beat them, as a worldly man would be when he suffers even a small wrong from his neighbours. Nor were they stirred to pride and self-conceit so as to despise and condemn the Jews, as happens with hypocrites and heretics who will endure great bodily pain and are sometimes ready to suffer death with great joy and strength of purpose, as though in the name of Jesus and for love of Him. In fact this love and joy that they feel in bodily suffering is not to be identified with that implanted by the Holy Spirit; it does not come from the fire that burns on the high altar of heaven, but is simulated by the devil in the fires of hell. It is utterly corrupted by pride and presumption, contempt, censure, and hatred of those who punish them. They imagine that they are inspired by charity, and that they suffer everything for the love of God, but they are deluded by the devil that walks at noonday. But when one who loves God suffers hurt from his neighbours, he is so strengthened by the grace of the Holy Spirit, and made so humble, patient, and peaceable, that he always maintains his humility whatever wrong he may suffer. He does not despise or denounce one who injures him, but prays for him in his heart, and has a deeper pity and compassion for him than for others who have never harmed him. Indeed, he loves him more, and desires his salvation more fervently because he knows that he himself will reap a great spiritual reward from the other's unkindness, although this was not his intention. But love and humility of this degree are beyond unaided human attainment; they become possible only by the working of the Holy Spirit in those whom He makes true lovers of God.

CHAPTER 39: *How Divine Love destroys covetousness, impurity, and gluttony, together with all enjoyment of sensual pleasures, doing so quietly and easily through the grace of contemplation*

COVETOUSNESS is destroyed in the soul by the working of Divine Love, for it stirs the soul to such an ardent desire for good and heavenly riches that it holds all earthly riches as worthless. It sets no greater value on a precious stone than on a lump of chalk, and is no more attracted by a hundred pounds of gold than by a pound of lead. It knows that all perishable things are of equal value, and does not esteem one more highly than another, since it is fully aware that all these earthly things that worldly men regard so highly and love so greatly will pass away and come to nothing, both the things themselves and the love which they inspire. Therefore in his mind such a person already sees these things as they will be hereafter, and accounts them as nothing. And while those who love this world struggle and intrigue for earthly goods, one against the other, the man who loves God strives against nobody. He possesses his soul in peace, and remains content with what he has, refusing to seek anything more. He wants no greater share of all the world's riches than will provide for his bare bodily needs for as long as God wills him to live. This he can easily obtain, and desires no more. He is well content when his bare needs are satisfied for the time being, so that he is spared the necessity of maintaining and administering property, and can devote his whole heart and energy to seeking God and finding Him in purity of spirit. And since only the 'pure in heart shall see God,' this is his sole desire. Consequently the love of father, mother, and friends does not influence him unduly, for the sword of spiritual love severs all earthly love from his heart, so that he feels no deeper affection towards his father, mother, and friends than towards other people unless he sees greater virtue or grace in them than in others. On the other hand, he would prefer to see the same grace in his own father and mother than he sees in certain others; but if this is not so, then he loves others who possess more. And this is true charity.* Thus Divine Love destroys worldly covetousness, and brings poverty of spirit into the soul.

Divine Love effects this transformation not only in those who have no worldly possessions, but also in some who enjoy high rank and have great riches at their disposal. Love overcomes covetousness in some of these to such a degree that they value their riches no more than a straw. And if those who are entrusted with their care lose them by negligence, they take no account of it. The reason for this is that the heart of one who loves God is by the gift of the Holy Spirit so fully occupied with the consideration and love of that which is supremely precious and valuable that it finds no satisfaction in any other love that conflicts with this.

Divine Love also destroys inclinations to lust and bodily impurity, introduces true chastity into the soul, and causes it to love it. For the soul feels such joy at the vision of God that it takes pleasure in being chaste, and finds no difficulty in preserving chastity, for by so doing it is most at ease and most at peace.

In the same manner Divine Love uproots gluttony, and makes a man sober and temperate. It gives him such support that he has no craving for food and drink, but takes whatever best meets his needs if it is readily available. He does so not out of love for self, but love of God. One who loves God is well aware that he must sustain his bodily life with food and drink for as long as God wills. Therefore one in whom the love of God dwells must, I think, exercise discretion and take such bodily sustenance as will best enable him to preserve this grace and present fewest obstacles to its working within him. If possible, he will choose the kind of food that is least troublesome and maintains his bodily strength, whether meat and fish, or only bread and ale. For the whole purpose of such a man is to keep his mind fixed constantly on God, and, if possible, to do this without interruption. But since this is bound to suffer interruption at times, the less that food and drink intervene, the better it is. He would rather make use of the best and most costly of food if this interfered less with the custody of his heart, than to take only bread and water if it involved more disturbance, for he is not concerned to acquire great merit by fasting if this causes him to lose his peace of heart. His whole purpose is to keep his heart as steadfastly as possible in the sight of God and in the experience of His love. In fact, I think he might eat the richest fare with less pleasure than another man who, guided solely by reason and without this special gift of love, might eat the poorest fare. Rich dishes prepared solely to tempt the palate are not proper food for such a man; on the other hand, if simple food, such as bread and ale, help him best and keep his heart at peace, it will be best for him to use them, especially if his physical strength is sustained by the gift of Divine Love.

Yet Divine Love does even more than this. It cures spiritual inertia and bodily idleness, and makes the soul zealous and eager for the service of God. Indeed, it desires to be constantly occupied in godly activity, that is, in the contemplation of God. Through this the soul finds joy and delight in prayer and meditation, and, in the doing of all else that requires to be done without reluctance and bitterness, whether the person be a religious or a layman.

Divine Love also checks any foolish tendency to pamper the bodily senses. It controls the sense of sight, so that a person takes no pleasure in seeing worldly things; on the contrary, they disturb him, however beautiful, precious, or wonderful they may be. Those who love the world rush off to see new things, to wonder at them, and to satisfy their hearts with unprofitable gazing at them. But one who loves God tries to withdraw and avoid the sight of such things, so that his spiritual vision may not be impaired. For in the spirit he sees what is far more beautiful, and he has no desire to lose this.

The same applies to speech and hearing. It is painful to the soul of one who loves God to discuss or listen to anything that might lessen his freedom to think of God alone. Any song or music that impairs his ability to pray or meditate upon God freely and peacefully is repugnant to him, and the more delightful it is to other people, the more distasteful it is to him. Similarly, to hear others speaking, unless it furthers the progress of his soul in the love of God, is of no pleasure to him. Indeed, it soon becomes irksome to him. He would rather be at peace, hearing nothing and saying nothing, than listen to the greatest scholar on earth advancing all the arguments known to the mind of man unless he were able to speak with sincerity and fervour of the love of God. For this is his own principal occupation, and he has no wish to discuss, hear, or see anything but what may help him and lead him to a deeper knowledge and closer experience of God. So he certainly has no desire to discuss or listen to worldly matters, nor has he any interest in worldly stories, news, or empty gossip of any kind.

It is the same with the senses of smell, taste, and touch; the more that his thoughts are distracted and his peace of soul disturbed by the sense of smell, taste, or any other physical sense, the more he avoids it. The less he is aware of them the better he is pleased, and were it possible to live in the body without being aware of any of them, he would gladly do so. For they often trouble the heart and disturb its peace, and they cannot be entirely avoided. Nevertheless, the love of God is sometimes so powerful in a soul that it overcomes and uproots all that obstructs it.

CHAPTER 40: *On the virtues and graces which a soul receives when its spiritual eyes are opened and it is given the grace of contemplation. How these cannot be won by its own unaided efforts, but only with the assistance of especial grace*

THESE are the ways through which Divine Love works in a soul, opening its spiritual eyes to see God by the infusion of an especial grace, and rendering it pure, refined, and capable of contemplation. Even the greatest theologian on earth could not conceive of or define the real nature of this opening of the spiritual eyes. For it cannot be attained by study, or by a person's own unaided efforts. It is made possible principally by the grace of the Holy Spirit; a person's own efforts are only secondary. I am reluctant to speak of it at all, for I do not think that I am capable of doing so. It is beyond my capacity, and my lips are not pure. However, since Divine Love seems to ask and demand it of me, I will attempt to say a little more on the matter, trusting in its guidance. This opening of the spiritual eyes is that glowing darkness and rich nothingness of which I spoke earlier. It may be called: *Purity of soul and spiritual rest, inward stillness and peace of conscience, refinement of thought and integrity of soul, a lively consciousness of grace and solitude of heart, the wakeful sleep of the spouse and the tasting of heavenly joys, the ardour of love and brightness of light, the entry into contemplation and reformation in feeling.* All these terms are employed by various writers in spiritual literature, for each of them spoke from his own experience of grace; and although they use different expressions, they are all speaking of the same truth.

If a soul through grace has any one of these experiences, it has all, for when a soul longs to see the face of God, and is touched by the especial grace of the Holy Spirit, it is suddenly changed and uplifted from its former condition to a different level of experience. First of all, it is detached in a wonderful way from the love and desire for all earthly things and withdrawn into itself. And so great is this change that it has lost all desire for worldly things, and for everything save God alone. Then it is *cleansed from all the foulness of sin*. This cleansing is so complete that the memory of sin and all inordinate affection for any created thing is suddenly washed away and expunged, and nothing remains to separate the soul from God but the limitations of bodily existence. Then it is *in spiritual rest,* for all painful doubts and fears, and all other temptations of its spiritual enemies, are driven from the heart, so that they cease to trouble or vex it during this time. It is at rest from the pressure of worldly affairs and the troublesome assaults of sinful inclinations, but is free to engage in the activity of love. And the greater its activity in love, the more complete its rest.

This restful activity is very different to physical idleness and blind security. It is a state of intense spiritual activity, but it is called restful because grace removes the heavy burden of worldly love from the soul, and makes it strong and free through the gift of the Holy Spirit of love, so that it can undertake everything to which grace inspires it, with joy, ease, and delight. It is called a holy inactivity and a most active rest – and so it is – because the soul is *in stillness* from the horrid din of carnal desires and impure thoughts.

This stillness is brought about by the Holy Spirit in the contemplation of God, for His voice is so sweet and so powerful that it silences the clamour of all other voices in the soul. It is a mighty voice, sounding gently in a pure soul, of which the prophet says: *Vox Domini in virtute* (Ps. xxix, 4). The voice of the Lord is a mighty voice. The word of this voice is living and powerful, as the Apostle says: *Vivus est sermo Domini et efficax, penetrabilior omni gladio* (Heb. iv, 12). The word of God is living and powerful, and sharper than any sword. Fleshly love is slain at the sound of His word, and the soul is guarded in silence from all sinful inclinations. The Apocalypse says of this silence: *Factum est silentium in caelo, quasi media hora* (Rev. viii, 1). There was silence in heaven about the space of half an hour. Heaven represents a pure soul raised by grace from earthly love to converse with heaven; such a soul is in silence. But since that silence cannot remain unbroken for ever because of the corruption of human nature, it is compared to an interval of half an hour. However long this interval may be, it appears short to the soul, and is therefore represented by half an hour. The soul meanwhile enjoys *peace of conscience*, for grace banishes the pain and remorse, the restlessness and strain caused by sin, and brings peace and reconciliation, uniting God and the soul in a single will. There is no harsh reproof of the soul for its sins and failures, for God and the soul have kissed and are friends. All its misdoings have been forgiven.

The soul now feels humble security and great joy, and this reconciliation gives it full assurance of salvation, for the Holy Spirit witnesses to its inmost conscience that it is a son chosen to receive his heritage in heaven. As Saint Paul says: *Ipse Spiritus testimonium perhibet spiritui nostro, quod filii Dei sumus* (Rom. viii, 16). The Holy Spirit bears witness to our spirit that we are the sons of God. This testimony which grace affords to our conscience is the true joy of the soul, as the Apostle says: *Gloria mea est testimonium conscientiae meae* (2 Cor. i, 12). My joy is witness to my conscience; that is, the joy that I feel bears witness to the peace and reconciliation, the true love and friendship between God and my soul. And when the soul is in this state of peace, it is also *refined in thought*.

When the soul is enslaved by love of the world, it falls lower than all other creatures, for all things hold it in their power and overmaster it, so that it cannot see or love God. For just as the love of the world is unprofitable and materialistic, so also the love and reliance on creatures is materialistic, and reduces the soul to slavery. But when the eyes of the soul are opened to see

God, this love is transfigured and the soul exalted to its own proper nature above all material things. It then considers and employs them in a spiritual way, for its love is spiritual. The soul will therefore utterly refuse to make itself the slave of material loves, for grace has raised it high above them. It sets no value on the world, because it will soon pass away and perish. While the soul is maintained in this exaltation of heart, no error or trick of the devil can influence it, for its gaze is fixed so closely on God that all things are beneath it. The prophet speaks of this state, saying: *Accedat homo ad cor altum; et exaltabitur Deus* (Ps. lxiv, 6). Let man come to exaltation of heart, and God Himself shall be glorified. That is, a man who by grace comes to be exalted in thought shall see that God alone is exalted above all creatures, and that the soul itself is exalted in Him.

The soul is then alone, for it is entirely estranged from the society of those who love the world, although it still remains among them bodily. It has entirely renounced all worldly love of creatures, and is not concerned if it never sees or speaks to a man, or receives comfort from one, so long as it may always continue in the same spiritual state. For it is so deeply conscious of the intimate and blessed presence of God, and so delights in Him, that for His love it can easily forgo all love of worldly creatures and even abandon the memory of them. I do not say that it will no longer love or think of other creatures, but rather that it will think of them at the right times, and will regard them and love them with a free and spiritual love, not with an anxious and carnal love as heretofore. The prophet speaks of this spiritual solitude, saying: *Ducam eam in solitudinem, et loquar ad cor ejus* (Hosea ii, 14). I will lead her into the wilderness, and speak to her heart. That is, the grace of God leads a soul from the distasteful company of carnal desires into solitude of mind, causes it to forget the pleasures of the world, and by its sweet influence breathes words of love into its heart. A soul is truly solitary when it loves God and devotes itself wholly to Him, and has lost all taste for the consolations of the world. And the better to maintain this solitude, it retires from the company of men if it can, and seeks physical solitude, since this greatly promotes solitude of soul and the free working of Divine Love. And the less interference it suffers from empty chatter without or unprofitable thoughts within, the freer it is to contemplate God. In this way it attains *solitude of heart*.

While a soul is obsessed and blinded by love of the world, it is entirely earth-bound, and like a highway, is common ground for everything, because every impulse of the flesh or the devil enters and passes through it. Then grace draws it into an inner chamber and into the presence of God, where it hears His secret counsels and is wonderfully comforted by them. Of this the prophet says: *Secretum meum mihi; secretum meum mihi* (Isa. xxiv, 16). My secret is my own, my secret is my own. That is, one who loves God, whom grace has raised from the outward feelings of worldly love and caught up into the secrets of spiritual love, gives thanks to Him, saying: My secret is my own. Meaning, O Lord my God, Your secret is revealed to me and hidden from all lovers of the world, for it is called hidden manna, whose nature can be more easily enquired about than defined. And God makes this promise to one who loves Him: *Dabo ei manna absconditum, quod nemo novit, nisi qui accipit* (Rev. ii, 17). This manna is heavenly food and the bread of angels, as Holy Scripture says. For angels are fed and filled by the clear sight and burning love of God; and that is manna. For we may ask what it is, but we cannot fully understand. One who loves God is not filled with manna here, but while he remains in the body he receives a small taste of it.

This tasting of manna is a lively consciousness of grace, which is due to the quickening of the soul's spiritual vision. This grace is no different from that experienced by a chosen soul at the beginning of its conversion; it is the self-same grace experienced and revealed in a different way, for grace increases with the soul, and the soul with grace. And the purer the soul and the more withdrawn from love of the world, the more powerful is grace, and the more inward and spiritual is the soul's experience of the presence of God. So the same grace which first turns a man from sin and enables him to begin and make progress by the exercise of virtues and good works, also makes him perfect. And this form of grace is called a *lively consciousness of grace,* for one who possesses it feels it strongly, and is fully conscious by experience that he is in grace. To him it is lively indeed, for it wonderfully refreshes the soul, and infuses such health into it that it does not feel the pain of bodily disease, although the body may be feeble and sickly. For the power of grace is such that both body and soul are brought to their fullest health and ease.

When this grace is withdrawn, the soul is plunged into sorrow, for it thinks that it will be able to retain it always, and that nothing can take it away. But this is not so, for it passes away very easily. Nevertheless, although the consciousness of grace in all its fullness passes away, its influence remains; it preserves the soul in tranquillity, and makes it desire the return of grace. This is also what is known as the *wakeful sleep of the spouse* of which Holy Scripture says: *Ego dormio, et cor meum vigilat* (Song of Solomon v, 2). I sleep, and my heart keeps watch. That is: I am spiritually at rest, when the love of the world is destroyed within me by grace, and the sinful impulses of bodily desires are so deadened that I hardly feel them and they do not trouble me. My heart is set free, and then it keeps watch, for it is vigilant and ready to love and see God. The more deeply I am at rest from outward things, the more awake I am to the knowledge of God and of inward things. I cannot be awake to Jesus unless I am asleep to the world. So while the grace of God closes the bodily eyes, the soul is asleep to the vanities of the world: the eyes of the spirit are opened, and it wakes to the sight of God's majesty hidden within the clouds of His precious humanity. As the Gospel says of the Apostles when they were with the Lord Jesus at His transfiguration, they first slept, and then *vigilantes viderunt majestatem* (S. Luke ix, 32); they woke to see His majesty. This sleep of the Apostles represents the soul's death to worldly love through the inspiration of the Holy Spirit, and their awakening represents its contemplation of God. Through this sleep the soul is brought from the turmoil of worldly desires into peace, and through this awakening it is raised up to the sight of God and spiritual things. The closer that the eyes of the soul are shut to earthly things in this kind of sleep, the keener is its inward vision, which is enabled to see the beauty of heaven in loving contemplation. This sleep and this awakening are wrought by the light of grace in the soul of one who loves God.

CHAPTER 41: *How the special grace of the contemplation of God is sometimes withdrawn from a soul; how a soul should act in the absence or presence of God; and how a soul should constantly desire the gracious presence of God*

SHOW me a soul whose eyes have been opened by the action of grace to the contemplation of God, a soul so entirely detached and withdrawn from love of the world that it possesses *purity and poverty of spirit, spiritual rest, inward stillness and peace of conscience, refinement of thought, solitude and retirement of heart, and the wakeful sleep of the spouse.* Show me a soul that has lost all desire and love for the world, that is enraptured by the joys of heaven, and continually athirst for and quietly seeking the blessed presence of God. Then I can say with full conviction that this soul is burning with love and radiant with spiritual light. It is worthy to be called the spouse of Christ, for it is reformed in feeling, and ready to receive the grace of contemplation. These are the signs of the inspiration which comes to it when the eyes of the soul are opened, for when its eyes are opened the soul has for the time being the full exercise of all these gifts that I have mentioned.

Nevertheless, it often happens that grace is partly withdrawn because of the weakness and corruption of human nature, and the soul relapses into its former subjection to the body. This causes it great sorrow and pain, for it is blind, insensate, and incapable of good. It is weak and powerless, burdened with the body and the bodily senses. And when the soul seeks and desires the grace of God again, it cannot find it. For Holy Scripture says of God: *Postquam vultum suum absconderit, non est qui contempletur eum* (Job xxxiv, 29). When God has hidden His face, none may behold Him. When God reveals Himself, the soul cannot help but see Him, for He is Light; and when He hides Himself, it cannot see Him because it is in darkness. God's hiding of Himself is only a subtle testing of the soul, and His revealing of Himself is to comfort the soul by His wondrous goodness and mercy.

Do not be surprised when all consciousness of grace is sometimes withdrawn from one who loves God. For Holy Scripture says that the spouse shares the same lot: *Quaesivi et non inveni illum: vocavi et non respondit mihi* (Song of Solomon iii, 1). I sought Him, and did not find Him; I called, but He did not answer. That is; when I relapse into my natural weakness, grace is withdrawn, and the cause of this is my own failure, and not His departure from me. But when God is absent from me I am miserable, so I seek Him with great and heartfelt desire; but He gives me no answer that I can hear. Then I cry with all my soul: *Revertere, dilecte, mihi!* (Song of Solomon ii, 17). Return to me, my Beloved! But even then He does not seem to have heard me. The painful consciousness of myself, the assaults of worldly loves and fears, together with my own lack of spiritual strength, unite in a continual cry from my soul to God. Even so, God remains withdrawn for a while and does not come, however constant my cry. He acts thus because He is sure of one who loves Him, and knows that he will not entirely relapse into love of the world, because he no longer has any desire for it. So God remains withdrawn from the soul the longer.

But at last, when He wills, God returns, full of grace and truth, and visits the soul which is fainting with desire and seeking his presence with so much love. He gently touches it, anoints it with the oil of gladness, and relieves all its pain. Then the soul cries out to God with heartfelt gladness: *Oleum effusum nomen tuum* (Song of Solomon i, 2). Your Name, O God, is like oil poured out. For as long as my soul is sick and sore with sin, burdened by the body, saddened and disquieted by the perils and miseries of this life so long, O Lord God, your Name to me is not oil poured out, but sealed up. But when my soul is suddenly flooded with the light of grace, soothed and healed from all the filth of sin, and when divine light and love brings spiritual strength and unspeakable joy, then I can say with hearty praise and gladness of spirit: 'Your Name, O Lord, is oil poured out to me.' For by Your gracious visitation the true significance of Your Name is revealed to me, that You are JESUS, Healing. For Your gracious presence alone can raise me from sorrow and from sin.

Blessed is the soul that is constantly fed by the experience of God's love when He is present, and supported by the desire for Him when He is absent. Wise and well grounded is the lover of God who behaves himself humbly and reverently in His presence, who contemplates Him with love but without familiarity, and who remains patient and calm, without despair and bitterness, when He is absent.

This variable feeling of the absence and presence of God does not mean that the soul has attained perfection, nor does it prevent the soul receiving the grace of perfection or of contemplation; but in so far as it persists, the soul remains less than

perfect. For the more a soul hinders itself from reaching a continual awareness of grace, the less grace it enjoys. However, the
grace that it already possesses is the grace of contemplation. For
this variable feeling of the absence and presence of God occurs
in the state of perfection, as well as in the beginning of the
spiritual life, but in a different way. And just as the presence of
grace is experienced in different ways in these two states, so is
the absence of grace. As a result, one who does not realize when
grace is absent is liable to be deceived, and one who does not
recognize the presence of grace will not be grateful when it
comes to him, whether he is a beginner or has entered the state
of perfection. Nevertheless, the more stable, unimpaired, and
constant grace is, the more beautiful is the soul, and the more
like to Him in whom, as the Apostle says, 'There is no instability.' And it is right that the soul should resemble Jesus its
spouse in behaviour and in virtues, wholly conformed to Him
in the stability of perfect love. But this happens seldom, and
nowhere except in the true spouse of Christ.

For one who recognizes no variation in his experience of
grace, but thinks that it is always at full tide, stable and constant, is either wholly perfect or wholly blind. When a soul is
perfect, it is isolated from all carnal affections and from contact
with created things. All barriers of corruption and sin between
God and the soul are broken down, and he is perfectly united
to Him in peace and love. But this is an unique grace, transcending human nature. And a man is very blind if he imagines
himself to be in a state of grace without feeling God's inspiration, and thinks himself to be established in grace, as though
all his feelings and actions were the fruit of special grace; for
such a person imagines that everything that he does, feels, and
says is inspired by grace, and that this favour will never be
withdrawn. If there is such a person – and I hope there is not –
he is entirely ignorant of the ways in which grace is experienced.

But you might say that we should love by faith alone, and

have no desire for spiritual experiences nor overestimate them if they occur, since the Apostle says: *Justus ex fide vivit* (Heb. x, 38). The righteous man lives by faith. I reply that we should not desire physical experiences, however pleasant, nor over-estimate them should they occur. But we should always desire spiritual experiences such as I am speaking of now, if they come about in the way that I mentioned earlier. These experiences include the uprooting of all love of the world, the opening of the eyes of the spirit, purity of spirit, peace of conscience, and others similar. We should desire always to be conscious – so far as we may – of the lively inspiration of grace brought about by the spiritual presence of God within our souls. We should de-sire to contemplate Him constantly with reverence, and always to feel the sweetness of His love in the wondrous nearness of His presence. This should be our life, and this our experience of grace, for God is the Source of all grace, and grants this gift as He wills, to some in greater measure and to others less. For He grants this experience of His presence in various ways, as He sees best. And this experience is the goal towards which we should direct our lives and exertions, for without it we cannot live the life of the spirit. For just as the soul is the life of the body, God is the life of the soul by His gracious presence. But however real this experience may be, it is as yet only in faith, and cannot be compared to the experience of God Himself which we shall enjoy in the bliss of heaven.

We should have a deep desire for this experience, for every rational soul should desire with all its strength to draw close to God, and to be united to Him by its awareness of His unseen presence. It is easier to attain knowledge of this presence by personal experience than by reading books, for it is life and love, strength and light, joy and peace to a chosen soul. A soul that has once experienced it cannot therefore lose it without pain; it cannot cease to desire it, because it is so good in itself, and brings such comfort. And what can bring greater comfort to a soul than to be withdrawn by grace from the clamour of worldly affairs, from the corruption of its own desires, and from unprofitable love of creatures into the peace and joy of spiritual love? Nothing can exceed this joy. Nothing can bring greater joy to one who loves God than His own gracious presence revealed to a pure soul. He is never depressed or sad except when he feels imprisoned by the body, and he is never completely glad or happy except when he is utterly unconscious of self, as he is when he contemplates God in the spirit. However, perfect joy is not possible in this life, because the heavy burden of bodily corruption oppresses his soul, bearing it down and greatly lessening his spiritual joy: and this must always be so as long as he remains in this life.

Nevertheless, when I speak of these variations of grace, how it comes and goes, do not fall into the error of thinking that I am referring to the ordinary grace possessed and experienced by a man through faith and goodwill towards God. Unless he possesses and perseveres in this grace, he cannot be saved, for it exists in the least of chosen souls. I am speaking of the special grace that is inspired by the Holy Spirit, as I mentioned earlier. Ordinary grace, that is, charity, remains undiminished whatever a man may do, as long as his will is directed towards God, so that he would not commit mortal sin or do anything that is forbidden as a mortal sin, for this grace is only lost through sin. Sin is mortal when a man's conscience warns him that it is mortal, and yet he deliberately does it. The same applies if a man's conscience is so blinded that he deliberately does something that is forbidden under pain of mortal sin by God and His Church.

The awareness of special grace that accompanies the invisible presence of God and makes the soul perfect in love, does not always continue at its highest intensity, but comes and goes unpredictably as I have said. For our Lord says: *Spiritus ubi vult spirat: et vocem ejus audis, et nescis unde veniat, aut quo vadat* (John iii, 8). The Holy Spirit breathes where He wills, and you hear His voice; but you do not know whence He comes or whither He goes. Sometimes He comes secretly when you are least aware of Him, but you will recognize Him unmistakably before He goes, for He stirs your heart in a wonderful way, and moves it strongly to contemplate His goodness. Then your heart melts with delight at the tenderness of His love like wax before the fire, and this is the sound of His voice. Then before you realize it, He departs. He withdraws a little, but not entirely, and the soul passes from ecstasy into tranquillity. The intense awareness of His presence passes away, but the effects of grace remain as long as the soul keeps itself pure, and does not wilfully lapse into carelessness and worldliness, or take refuge in outward things. For sometimes it will do so out of natural weakness, and not because it has any pleasure in them. It is this variability in grace that I have just been discussing.

CHAPTER 42: *A commendation of the prayer offered to God by a contemplative soul: how stability in prayer is a sure foundation; how every experience of grace in a chosen soul may be said to be of God; and the purer the soul the higher the grace received*

W HEN man's soul is untouched by special grace, it is sluggish and incapable of spiritual activity, unable to make progress. This is due to its own weakness, because by nature it is cold and dry, lacking devotion or delight in spiritual things. Then it is touched by grace, and becomes quick and refined, ready for and capable of spiritual activity. This liberates it, and makes it eager to respond to and cooperate with every stirring of grace. Sometimes this grace will move the soul to pray, and I will now tell you about this form of prayer.

The prayers that people use most frequently and find most helpful are probably the Our Father and the Psalms; the Our Father for the simple, and psalms, hymns, and other devotions of the Church for the educated. Having received this grace, a person will not use these prayers as he did before, nor in the usual way that people pray, using a loud voice or a normal tone. His prayer will be uttered in a very low voice and with deep feeling, because his mind is not troubled or distracted by outward things, but wholly withdrawn from them, and his soul is as it were in the presence of God. Therefore every word and syllable is uttered with understanding, sweetness, and delight, and his lips and heart are in complete harmony. This is because the soul has been set on fire with love, and all its interior prayer is like a flame leaping from a firebrand, kindling every power of the soul and transforming them into love. It fires them with such consolation that the soul desires to 'pray without ceasing', and to do nothing else. The more the soul prays in this way, the better it is able to pray, and the stronger it becomes. For grace brings great help to the soul, and renders everything light and easy, so that it takes delight in reciting the psalms and sings the praises of God with heavenly joy and sweetness.

This spiritual activity is the food of the soul, and this form of prayer is of great power, for it reduces and defeats all the temptations of the devil, both subtle and open. It removes all memory and love of the world, and of carnal sins. It protects both body and soul from being overwhelmed by the sorrows of this life. It keeps the soul alive to the workings of grace and divine Love within it, and constantly feeds the flame of love as sticks feed a fire. It dispels all weariness and dejection, and fills the soul with joy and gladness. Of this prayer David says: *Dirigatur oratio mea sicut incensum in conspectu tuo* (Ps. cxli, 2). Let my prayer ascend in Your sight, O Lord, as the incense. For as incense cast on to the fire causes a fragrant odour as the smoke rises into the air, so a psalm sung or said with love understanding in a fervent heart rises as a fragrant odour in the sight of God and the whole company of heaven.

No fly tries to rest on the rim of a pot boiling over a fire; similarly, no worldly desire can survive in a pure soul that is enveloped and warmed in the fire of love, boiling over with psalms and praises to God. This is true prayer. It is always heard by God, gives glory to Him, and is rewarded by His grace. It makes the soul the friend of God and of all the angels of heaven. Therefore let anyone who can pray in this way do so, for it is good and brings great grace.

Although this form of prayer is not full contemplation, and is not due to the direct action of Divine Love itself, it is nevertheless a measure of contemplation, for it cannot be practised without abundant grace through the opening of the eyes of the spirit. Therefore one who has attained this freedom and state of grace, and has tasted its heavenly joy, has reached a certain degree of contemplation.

This kind of prayer is a rich offering of devotion, which is taken by the angels and presented before the face of God. The prayer of those who are engaged in active works has a double nature, for while their preoccupation with worldly matters often causes them to have one thing in their minds while the words of the psalm they are reciting expresses another. However, provided that their intention is right, their prayer is good and commendable, although it lacks savour and devotion. But the prayer offered by a contemplative has a single nature, for heart and lips are in complete harmony. The soul is so integrated by grace, and so detached from worldly things, that it is master of the body. The body then becomes no more than an instrument and trumpet of the soul, on which it sweetly sounds the spiritual praises of God.

This is the trumpet of which David speaks: *Buccinate in neomenia tuba, in insigni [die] solemnitatis vestrae* (Ps. lxxxi, 3).

Sound the trumpet at new moon. Meaning: You souls who have been reformed in the spiritual life by the opening of your spiritual eyes, sing psalms with devotion, and blow on the trumpet of your bodily tongues. This prayer is so pleasing to God and so profitable to the soul, that anyone who is newly turned to God, who wishes to please Him, and to receive His special grace, should have a strong desire for it. He should strive by grace to attain this freedom of spirit, so that he may offer his prayers and praises to God constantly, stably, and devoutly, fixing his whole mind and ardent love on Him alone, and be ready to pray in this way whenever grace moves him to it.

This is a sure and true form of prayer. If you can practise it and remain steadfast in it, you have no need to go around here and there asking every spiritual man what you should do, how you should love God, how you should serve Him, and discussing spiritual matters that are beyond your understanding, as some may do. This is not at all profitable unless it is really necessary. Hold fast to your prayer even if it is difficult at first, so that you may in time reach this peaceful state of spiritual prayer. This will bring you all the knowledge you need, and guard you from all deception and illusion. If you already possess this grace, try to preserve it and do not give it up; but if it is withdrawn from you for a time, and you are moved to pray in another way, then leave it and resume it later. Whoever has the grace of this kind of prayer has no need to ask what he should fix his thought upon during prayer, whether upon the words of a prayer, or upon God, or the Name of Jesus, for his experience of this grace is a sure guide. For the eyes of the soul turn to God and contemplate Him clearly, and it knows with certainty that it knows and sees Him. I do not mean that it sees Him as He is in the fullness of His Godhead, but that it sees Him to whatever extent He wills to reveal Himself to a pure soul in this mortal life, according to the measure of its purity. For you can be sure that every experience of grace is an experience of

God Himself, and may be called God; and the soul's experience of God is greater or less in proportion to its own degree of grace. Indeed, the soul's first experience of special grace at the beginning of the spiritual life – the grace of compunction and contrition for its sins – is an experience of God Himself, since it is He who infuses contrition into a soul by His presence. At that time the soul has only a crude and elementary knowledge of God, and has no experience of the nature of His Godhead, for its own impurity prevents it seeing Him clearly. But later, if it grows in virtue and purity, grace will bring it to a fuller vision and experience of God. This experience will be of a more spiritual nature, and correspond more nearly to the nature of God Himself.

What is most pleasing to God is to have a soul become by grace what He is by nature, and this is achieved through spiritual contemplation and love of Him. And this must be the aim of all who love God. So whenever you feel your soul moved by grace, especially in the way I have described, by the opening of your spiritual eyes, you may be sure that you are seeing and experiencing God. Hold fast to Him, try to retain this grace, and do not easily let Him go. Seek God alone for Himself, and cooperate with His grace with increased devotion, so that it may grow within you more and more. And although your experience of God is not of Him as He is in the fullness of His Godhead, have no fear that you may be deceived if you surrender to your feeling. If you truly love God, be sure that your experience is real, and that by His grace you may have as True an experience and vision of Him as is possible in this life. Therefore surrender yourself to this experience when grace draws you, and maintain it with love and delight, in order that you may gradually reach a fuller and better knowledge of God. For grace itself will always direct you if you yield to its guidance until you reach your end.

You may possibly wonder why I say at one time that grace

does all this, and at another that it is Divine Love, or Jesus, or God. My reply is that when I say that grace does it I mean both Divine Love, Jesus, and God; for all are one and inseparable. Jesus is Divine Love, Jesus is grace, and Jesus is God, for He does everything within us by grace through His divine Love as God. So when writing of this matter I may use whichever of these names I please.

CHAPTER 43 : *How a soul, by the opening of its spiritual eyes, receives the grace of love, which enables it to understand Holy Scripture; and how God, hidden in the Scriptures, reveals Himself to those who love Him*

WHEN one who loves God has this experience of God in prayer as I have described, he thinks that he will always retain it. But it sometimes happens that grace puts an end to vocal prayer, and calls on the soul to see and experience God in a different way. At first it moves the soul to see God in Holy Scripture, where God, who is Truth, is hidden under the precious cloak of beautiful language, for He wills to be seen and known only by the pure in heart. For Truth will not reveal itself to those who hate it, but only to friends who love and seek it with a humble heart. For truth and humility are true sisters, united in love and charity, and there is no disharmony between them. Humility depends on truth, and not on itself, while truth depends on humility, so that they are in complete accord. In so far, therefore, as the soul of one who loves God is made humble by the opening of its spiritual eyes through grace, recognizing its own nothingness, trusting entirely in the mercy and goodness of God, and depending solely on His help and favour, it has a true desire for Him, and so sees Him. For it sees the truths of Holy Scripture clearly and marvellously revealed in a manner far beyond the reach of arduous study or natural intelligence. And this may well be termed an experience or perception of God, since God is the well of wisdom, and by infusing a small portion of His wisdom into a pure soul, He enables it to understand all Holy Scripture. This wisdom is not bestowed on a soul all at once in a single revelation, but through grace it receives a new and lasting ability to understand anything that comes to its notice.

This clear understanding is brought about by the presence of God within the soul. For in the Gospel we are told how two disciples were going to Emmaus, burning with love for Jesus and speaking of Him, when He appeared to them in the guise of a pilgrim, and taught them how the prophecies of Scripture applied to Himself. *Aperuit illis sensum, ut intelligerent Scripturas.* (Luke xxiv, 45). He opened their minds to understand the meaning of the Scriptures. In the same way the spiritual presence of Jesus opens the minds of those who love Him and burn with desire for Him. Through the ministry of the angels it brings the words and teachings of Holy Scripture to their minds without effort and study, and reveals their meaning, however difficult or obscure. Indeed, the more difficult and remote from human understanding they are, the greater the joy of the soul when their true meaning is revealed to it by God Himself. And if the words permit it, they are interpreted both in a literal, moral, mystical, and heavenly sense. By the literal interpretation, which is the simplest and most direct, man's natural intelligence is satisfied. By the moral interpretation of Scripture the soul is taught about virtues and vices, and enabled to distinguish between them. By the mystical interpretation the soul is illumined to recognize God's workings within His Church, and to apply the words of Scripture to Christ our Head, and to His mystical body, the Church. The fourth, or heavenly, interpretation refers solely to the activity of love, and attributes all the truths of Scripture to the workings of love. And since this corresponds most closely to the experience of heaven, I call it heavenly.

One who loves God is His friend, not because he has deserved this privilege, but because God in His merciful goodness takes him as His friend with a solemn pledge. He reveals His secrets to him, and treats him as a true friend who pleases and loves Him, and does not merely serve Him with fear like a slave. Thus Jesus Himself says to His Apostles: *Iam vos dixi amicos, quia quaecumque audivi a Patre meo, nota feci vobis* (John xv, 15). I now call you My friends, for I make known to you all that I have heard from My Father. To a pure soul, whose palate is cleansed from the corruption of worldly love, Holy Scripture is nourishing food and delicious sustenance. Its taste is wonderfully sweet when fully assimilated by the understanding, for within it is concealed the life-giving spirit which quickens all the powers of the soul, and fills them with heavenly sweetness and spiritual delight. But anyone who wishes to eat this spiritual bread must have good teeth, white and clean, for heretics and those who love the world cannot pierce its inmost substance. Their teeth are dirty, so that they cannot taste its true savour. By teeth we mean the interior powers of the soul, which in lovers of the world and heretics are rotten with sin and vanity. They would like to reach the true knowledge of Holy Scripture by the exercise of their own reason, but they cannot do so, for their reason is corrupted both by original and actual sin, and is not yet healed by grace. As a result they can only gnaw on the outer bark, and whatever they may say to the contrary, they are incapable of reaching the inner savour. They are not humble and pure enough to find it, nor are they the friends of God, so that He does not reveal His secrets to them.

The secrets of Holy Scripture are locked away and sealed with the signet of God's finger, which is the Holy Spirit, so that none may learn them without His love and grace. God alone holds the key of knowledge, as Scripture says, and He

Himself is the key. He admits whom He will by the inspiration of His grace, and does not break the seal. And this is how God treats those who love Him. He does not treat all in the same way, but grants special favours to those who are inspired to seek truth in the Scriptures after devout prayer and diligent study. These may learn the truths of God when He chooses to reveal them.

See, then, how grace opens the eyes of the soul and enlightens its understanding in a wonderful manner beyond the capabilities of our weak and fallen nature. As I said earlier, it gives the soul a new ability to understand Holy Scripture and to grasp its truths, whether it is reading it or meditating upon it. It is enabled to understand the spiritual meaning of all the words and teachings that it hears. And this is nothing strange, for the spirit that reveals its meaning for the comfort of a pure soul is the Holy Spirit who first inspired it. This grace is granted to the unlettered as well as to the learned, for these can and do grasp the substance, the truth and the spiritual savour of Holy Scripture. And although they may not understand all its implications, this is not necessary for them. And when grace gives the soul this ability and enlightenment, it sometimes wishes to be alone, away from the distraction of creatures, in order to employ freely the instrument of reason, and consider the truths contained in Holy Scripture. At such times sufficient words, teachings, and phrases will come to mind, and keep the soul regularly and profitably occupied.

A soul can only learn by experience what comfort and spiritual joy, savour, and sweetness this light of grace may bring to it, whether inward perceptions, hidden knowledge, and sudden visitations of the Holy Spirit. And I am sure that such a soul will not go astray provided that its teeth – that is, its spiritual senses – are kept white and clean from pride and intellectual presumption. I think that David was experiencing great joy in this way when he said: *Quam dulcia faucibus meis eloquia tua, super mel ori meo* (Ps. cxix, 103). How sweet are Your words to my lips, O Lord; sweeter than honey to my mouth. That is: O Lord God, Your holy words, recorded in Holy Scripture and brought to my mind by grace, are sweeter to my lips – that is, to the affections of my soul – than honey to my mouth. How wonderful it is to see God in this way without wearisome labour!

As I said earlier, this is one way of seeing God. We do not see Him as He is, but under the forms of works and words, *per speculum etiam in aenigmate:* in a glass and under a symbol, as the Apostle says (1 Cor. xiii, 12). God is infinite power, wisdom and goodness, righteousness, truth, holiness, and mercy. But what God is in Himself none may see or know, but He may be seen in His works by the light of grace. His power is seen in His creation of all things out of nothing, His wisdom in His ordered disposition of them, His holiness in His gifts of grace, His righteousness in the punishment of sin, His truth in His sure reward of good works. All these things are shown in Holy Scripture, where the soul sees them together with all the other attributes of God. Hence you may see how such knowledge, whether bestowed through the Holy Scriptures or through any other writings inspired by grace, is nothing other than an affectionate correspondence between a loving soul and Jesus whom it loves: or more correctly, between Jesus the true Lover and the souls whom He loves. He has a tender love for all His chosen children who are subject to the limitations of this mortal body, and therefore although He dwells apart from them, hidden from their sight in the bosom of the Father and in full enjoyment of the Godhead, yet He bears them in His Heart, and often visits them with His presence and His grace. He comforts them with His words in Holy Scripture, and drives away heaviness and weariness, doubts and fears from their hearts. He gives gladness and joy to all who truly believe His promises, and humbly abide the fulfilment of His will.

Saint Paul said: *Quaecumque scripta sunt, ad nostram doctrinam scripta sunt, ut per consolationem Scripturarum spem habeamus* (Rom. xv, 4). All that is written for our learning is written that through the consolation of the Scriptures we may have hope of salvation. And this is another aspect of contemplation, that once our spiritual eyes are opened, we see God in the Scriptures. The clearer our vision in contemplation, the deeper the love of God that we feel. When a pure soul experiences even a little of this grace given through the Scriptures, it will set little value on the seven sciences or on any worldly knowledge. For the end of this sacred knowledge is the salvation of the soul in eternal life, while unless grace re-directs it to this right end, the end of the other is but vanity and passing satisfaction.

CHAPTER 44: *How the secret voice of God sounds within the soul, and how the illuminations brought to the soul by grace may be called God's voice*

THESE new experiences within a pure soul are wonderful, and could a soul enjoy them continually, it might truthfully be described as partly reformed in feeling, although not as yet fully. For God reveals even more to it, and draws it closer to Himself. He begins to speak to it even more intimately and lovingly, and the soul is eager to respond to the stirrings of grace. For the prophet says: *Quocumque ibat spiritus, illuc gradiebantur et rotae sequentes eum* (Ezek. i, 20). Wherever the spirit goes, there go the wheels following him. The wheels represent the true lovers of God, because they are perfectly round in virtue, without any angle of obstinacy, and they turn freely because their wills conform to the movements of grace. For, as the prophet says, they obey and act as grace moves and directs them. But before they do so, they are able to make a sure test and verification of this voice of grace, so that they are not deceived by their own imagination or by the devil. Our Lord says of those that love Him: *Oves meae vocem mean audiunt, et cognosco eas, et cognoscunt me meae* (John x, 27). My sheep hear My voice, and I know them, and they know Me. The secret voice of God is true, and it makes the soul true. In it there is no deception or illusion, no pride or hypocrisy, but gentleness, humility, peace, love, and charity, and it is full of life and grace. So when this voice sounds within a soul, it is sometimes so powerful that the soul immediately lays aside whatever it is doing – whether prayer, speaking, reading, meditation, or any physical occupation – and listens to it alone. And as it listens to the sweet sound of God's voice, it is filled with peace and love, transported far beyond all thought of earthly things. In this peace God reveals Himself to the soul, sometimes as Lord to be feared, sometimes as a Father to be reverenced, and sometimes as a Spouse to be loved. At such times the soul is absorbed in a wonderful reverence and loving contemplation of God, which brings it a delight far transcending anything it has ever known. It enjoys so great a sense of security and peace in God, and so acute a realization of His goodness, that it wishes always to remain in this state, and never to do anything else. The soul feels that it is touching God Himself, and by virtue of His ineffable touch it is made whole and stable, reverently contemplating God alone, as though nothing existed save God and itself. At these times it is upheld solely by His favour and wonderful goodness, and is profoundly conscious of this truth.

This feeling often comes without any special study of Holy Scripture, and with only a few words in mind. But the soul may employ words to give expression to the feelings in its heart, whether of love or worship. While it enjoys this grace, it is far removed from all love of the world, and from any thought of it: it pays no attention to it, and has no time to spare for it. At these times grace will bring to the soul certain illuminations, which I call the words of God and the perception of spiritual things. For you will realize that the whole purpose of God's action in a soul is to make it His true and perfect spouse in the height and fullness of love. And because this cannot be done suddenly, God who is Love, and wisest of all lovers, employs many wonderful ways to bring this about. And in order that the chosen soul may come to be truly united to Himself, He addresses it in the gracious words of a lover. He shows it His wonders, and gives it rich gifts, promising even more, and showing it great affection and courtesy. I cannot describe the workings of God in detail, nor is it necessary. Nevertheless I will say something as grace inspires me.

Firstly, when the eyes of a pure soul have been opened, it is drawn towards perfect love by the revelation of spiritual matters, not in order that the soul should rest content with these and cease its quest, but that it should seek and love God Himself, who is above all things, having no regard for anything but Him. If you enquire about the nature of these spiritual matters that I am often speaking of, my answer is that they are all the truths revealed in Holy Scripture. Therefore a soul that by the light of grace comprehends the truths of the Scriptures sees these spiritual things to which I have referred.

CHAPTER 45 : *How when grace opens the eyes of a soul, it is given wisdom which enables it humbly and surely to recognize the various degrees in the Church Militant, and the nature of the angels*

NEVERTHELESS, there are other spiritual matters that the light of grace reveals to the soul, and they are these. The nature of rational souls, and how God works in them by grace : the nature and activity of the angels, both blessed and fallen :

and the knowledge of the Blessed Trinity in so far as grace reveals it.

Scripture says of the spouse in the Song of Songs: *Surgam et circuibo civitatem; et quaeram quem diligit anima mea* (Song of Sol. iii, 2). I shall rise and go about the city, and seek Him whom my soul loves. That is, I shall lift up my thoughts and go about the city. This city symbolizes the whole of creation, both material and spiritual, which by God's decree is governed by the laws of nature, of reason, and of grace. I go about this city when I study the nature and origins of material creatures, the gifts of grace, and the joy of spiritual beings. And in all these I seek Him whom my soul loves. It is wonderful for the eyes of the soul to see God in the material universe, and to see His power, His wisdom, and His goodness in the ordering of it. But it is far more wonderful to see Him in spiritual beings. First we see Him in rational souls, both chosen and reprobate; we see how mercifully He calls His chosen; how He turns them away from sin by the light of His grace; how He helps them, teaches them, corrects them, and comforts them; how He sets them right, cleanses and nourishes them; and how He makes them burn with love and light by the richness of His grace. And He does this not to one soul alone, but to all His chosen, according to the measure of His grace. In the case of the reproved, we see how justly He forsakes them and leaves them in their sin, yet does them no wrong thereby; how He allows them their reward in this world, and afterwards punishes them in eternity.

This is a partial vision of the Church Militant as it is in this world. We see how black and foul it appears in souls that are reprobate, and how fair and lovely in chosen souls. And all this spiritual vision is nothing other than a vision of God, not as He is in Himself, but in His secret and merciful operation and in His awful and just judgements, which are daily revealed to and renewed in rational souls. Furthermore, we see with the eyes of the soul the anguish of the reprobate and the joy and bliss of chosen souls brings great consolation, for a pure soul cannot see truth without feeling great delight and ardent love.

This vision also reveals the nature of the angels, both blessed and fallen. The pure soul feels great joy when grace enables it to see the devil as a clumsy ruffian, bound by the power of God, and unable to harm anyone. The soul does not see him in bodily form, but spiritually, with his true nature and malice revealed. It throws him down, strips him, and reduces him to nothing. It scorns and despises him, paying no attention to his malice. In this way it fulfils the scriptural injunction: *Verte eum, et non erit* (Prov. xii, 7). Overturn the wicked, that is, the devil, and he shall be as nothing. The soul is astonished that the devil has such great malice, and so little power. There is no creature so powerless as he, and it is therefore great cowardice when men fear him so greatly. He can do nothing without God's leave, not so much as enter into a swine, as the Gospel says, much less harm a man. And if God gives him leave to trouble us, He does so only with a good and merciful purpose. Therefore welcome God, both in Himself and in all His messengers. The soul need have no more fear of the devil's blusterings than of the movements of a mouse. The devil is full of anger if we refuse to listen to him, but his mouth is stopped by his own malice, and his hands are tied like those of a thief who deserves to be condemned and hanged in hell. So the soul accuses him and condemns him justly according to his deserts. Do not let this surprise you, for this is what Saint Paul meant when he said: *Fratres, nescitis quoniam angelos judicabimus?* (I Cor. vi, 3). My brothers, do you not know that we shall judge angels? Meaning those who through malice have become wicked spirits, but who were created good angels by nature. This judgement takes place before the Last Day in the case of contemplative souls, for in a small measure they already take part in all that God will do openly and perfectly in due time.

It brings great shame and disgrace to the devil when he receives this treatment from a pure soul. He would like to escape, but cannot, for the eye of God is upon him still, and this gives him greater distress than all the fires of hell. The soul then turns humbly to God with heartfelt praise and thanks for having saved a simple soul by His power and great mercy from all the malice of so deadly an enemy.

CHAPTER 46: *How by the same light the soul may perceive the nature of the blessed angels, and recognize how Jesus is both God and man, transcending all things*

AND after this by the same light the soul may see the beauty of the angels, the nobility of their nature, the refinement of their being, and how they are confirmed in grace and in the fulness of eternal bliss. It can also recognize the various orders of angels, distinguish between them, and see how they all dwell in the light of eternal truth, each in his own order aflame with the love of the Holy Spirit, constantly seeing, loving, and praising God in perfect peace. This perception of the angels is neither physical nor figurative, but wholly spiritual.

The soul then begins to have a real affinity and fellowship with these blessed spirits. They give it loving and active help, they become its instructors, and often dispel its fears by their presence and by the light that they bring. They bring the light of grace to the soul, and sometimes they speak sweet words of comfort to the heart. And if the soul is afflicted by any spiritual malady, they serve it and minister to all its needs. So Saint Paul says of them: *Nonne omnes sunt administratorii spiritus, missi propter eos qui hereditatem capient salutis?* (Heb. i, 14). Do you not know that all these holy spirits are ministers sent by God to those who are to be heirs of salvation? That is, to chosen souls.

In other words: Understand that all this spiritual activity by which words and teachings are brought to the mind, and other wonderful things as well, are due to the ministry of the angels when the light of grace shines brightly in a pure soul. It is not possible for mortal men fully to describe their experiences, this spiritual light, the graces and consolations which pure souls receive through the favour and fellowship of the blessed angels. The soul is so happy to watch their activity that it would like to attend to nothing else.

But with the help of the angels the soul sees even more. For a pure soul rises above all these things to contemplate the blessed nature of Jesus Himself. First it sees His glorious manhood, and that it is rightly exalted above the nature of all angels. Then it begins to contemplate His divinity, for knowledge of creatures leads a soul to knowledge of the Creator. The soul then begins to perceive a little of the mysteries of the Blessed Trinity. And it may well do this, for the light of grace is its guide, and it will not err so long as it walks in this light.

Then, so far as it is possible in this life, the soul clearly perceives the unity of substance and the distinction of Persons in the Blessed Trinity, and it understands many other truths concerning the Trinity which are set forth and interpreted by the doctors of the Church in their writings. And these selfsame truths concerning the Blessed Trinity which the holy doctors are inspired to set forth in their books for our instruction may be perceived by a pure soul by the light of grace. But I will not enlarge on this matter, for it is not necessary.

When enabled to do so by special grace, the soul feels wonderful love and heavenly joy in the contemplation of this truth, for light and love are inseparable in a pure soul. For no love that springs from contemplation brings the soul so close to God as this does; it is the highest and most perfect knowledge of Jesus, God and man, that the light of grace can bring to a soul. Therefore the burning love kindled by this is greater than that kindled by any knowledge of created things, whether material or spiritual.

All this knowledge of God's creation and of God Himself, the Creator and Sustainer of the entire universe, which is infused into a soul by grace as I have mentioned, I call the fair words and communications of God to the soul chosen as His true spouse. He reveals mysteries and often offers rich gifts to it out of His treasury, and adorns the soul with them with great honour. She has no need to be ashamed when she appears before the face of God her Spouse in the company of her fellows. All this loving and intimate conversation between God and the soul may be called a secret word, of which Holy Scripture says: *Porro ad me dictum est verbum absconditum, et venas susurr i ejus percepit auris mea* (Job iv, 12). A secret word is spoken to me, and my ear has caught the low murmur of His voice. The inspiration of God is a secret word, for it is hidden from all who love the world, and revealed to those who love Him. It is by this means that a pure soul readily catches the sound of His murmured words, by which He reveals His truth. For each truth revealed by grace, and received with inward delight and joy, is a secret murmur of God in the ear of a pure soul.

One who wishes to hear these sweet spiritual murmurs of God must possess great purity of soul, meekness, and all other virtues, and be partly deaf to the clamour of the world. This is the voice of God, of which David said: *Vox Domini praeparantis cervos, et revelabit condensa* (Ps. xxix, 9). The voice of God prepares the harts, and He will show them the thickets. That is: the inspiration of God makes souls as light as harts, that spring up from the ground and leap over the bushes and briars of worldly vanity. And He shows them the thickets, that is, His secrets, which can be discerned only by sharp eyes. This contemplation, surely founded in grace and humility, makes a soul wise, and fires it with a longing to see the face of God. These are the spiritual matters that I spoke of earlier, and they may be called new experiences of grace. I only touch on them briefly, for the guidance of your soul. For a soul that is pure, and moved by grace to engage in this spiritual activity of contemplation, may learn more in an hour than could be written in a long book.

LAUS DEO

NOTES

BOOK 1. CHAP. 1 (page 1). Enclosure. *The Ladder of Perfection* was originally written for the guidance of an enclosed anchoress – that is, a woman who, like her contemporary Dame Julian of Norwich, lived the enclosed contemplative life as a solitary.

CHAP. 2 (page 2). The seven corporal works of mercy are: To feed the hungry; to give drink to the thirsty; to clothe the naked; to visit the prisoner; to shelter the stranger; to visit the sick; and to bury the dead. The seven spiritual works of mercy are: To correct the sinner; to teach the ignorant; to counsel the doubtful; to comfort the sorrowful; to bear wrongs patiently; to forgive all injuries; and to pray for the living and the departed.

CHAP. 11 (page 12). A medieval legend – long since discounted – told that Mary Magdalene, with Martha and Lazarus, came by sea to the south of France, and spent thirty years in a cave near Marseilles.

CHAP. 56 (page 68). This statement is not in accordance with the teachings of the principal Doctors of the Church.

CHAP. 58 (page 70). Hilton's severity towards heretics was doubtless sharpened by the controversies and disorders of his time. He tends to assume that all heretics wantonly and presumptuously reject the teachings of the Church, and proclaim the superiority of their own personal opinions. Were this true, every heretic would doubtless 'sin mortally through pride'; but a more common cause for making 'shipwreck of the Faith' to-day is ignorance or inherited prejudice.

BOOK 2. CHAP. 6 (page 122). Hilton would not intend to imply that an unbaptized child is doomed to eternal punishment. He means that it remains in its unregenerate state, deprived of grace and of the merits of Christ's Passion, so that it is incapable of attaining the redeemed state intended for man by God; that is, the perfect enjoyment of Himself in heaven.

CHAP. 7 (page 124). Hilton's simile, intended to explain the sacrament of penance, is not altogether satisfactory. For were absolution by the Church merely formal and confirmatory, this would overthrow the nature of a sacrament, which is an outward and visible sign of an inward and spiritual grace conveyed to the soul. Where there is perfect contrition, God grants pardon for the guilt of sin, but there remains the duty of confession and amendment. In the case of imperfect contrition, which is more usual, the obligation of confession and the receiving of absolution is even more essential.

CHAP. 39 (page 220). Hilton is emphasizing that true charity is not a matter of natural sentiment, but of will. Our Lord Himself gives a vivid illustration of this in the parable of the Good Samaritan, who was clearly not moved by any feelings of natural affection towards the wounded Jew, who if conscious might have refused the help of a despised Samaritan. But he was moved by true compassion and charity for his neighbours, regardless of relationship or race. The Christian should have a higher regard for those who love and serve God than for those who do not, whether related to him or otherwise, although he will rightly have a deep concern for the spiritual welfare of his own family and people.

FOR THE BEST IN PAPERBACKS, LOOK FOR THE

In every corner of the world, on every subject under the sun, Penguin represents quality and variety – the very best in publishing today.

For complete information about books available from Penguin – including Pelicans, Puffins, Peregrines and Penguin Classics – and how to order them, write to us at the appropriate address below. Please note that for copyright reasons the selection of books varies from country to country.

In the United Kingdom: For a complete list of books available from Penguin in the U.K., please write to *Dept E.P., Penguin Books Ltd, Harmondsworth, Middlesex, UB7 0DA*

In the United States: For a complete list of books available from Penguin in the U.S., please write to *Dept BA, Penguin, 299 Murray Hill Parkway, East Rutherford, New Jersey 07073*

In Canada: For a complete list of books available from Penguin in Canada, please write to *Penguin Books Canada Ltd, 2801 John Street, Markham, Ontario L3R 1B4*

In Australia: For a complete list of books available from Penguin in Australia, please write to the *Marketing Department, Penguin Books Australia Ltd, P.O. Box 257, Ringwood, Victoria 3134*

In New Zealand: For a complete list of books available from Penguin in New Zealand, please write to the *Marketing Department, Penguin Books (NZ) Ltd, Private Bag, Takapuna, Auckland 9*

In India: For a complete list of books available from Penguin, please write to *Penguin Overseas Ltd, 706 Eros Apartments, 56 Nehru Place, New Delhi, 110019*

In Holland: For a complete list of books available from Penguin in Holland, please write to *Penguin Books Nederland B.V., Postbus 195, NL–1380AD Weesp, Netherlands*

In Germany: For a complete list of books available from Penguin, please write to *Penguin Books Ltd, Friedrichstrasse 10 – 12, D–6000 Frankfurt Main 1, Federal Republic of Germany*

In Spain: For a complete list of books available from Penguin in Spain, please write to *Longman Penguin España, Calle San Nicolas 15, E–28013 Madrid, Spain*

FOR THE BEST IN PAPERBACKS, LOOK FOR THE

PENGUIN CLASSICS

Saint Anselm	**The Prayers and Meditations**
Saint Augustine	**The Confessions**
Bede	**A History of the English Church and People**
Chaucer	**The Canterbury Tales**
	Love Visions
	Troilus and Criseyde
Froissart	**The Chronicles**
Geoffrey of Monmouth	**The History of the Kings of Britain**
Gerald of Wales	**History and Topography of Ireland**
	The Journey through Wales and The Description of Wales
Gregory of Tours	**The History of the Franks**
Julian of Norwich	**Revelations of Divine Love**
William Langland	**Piers the Ploughman**
Sir John Mandeville	**The Travels of Sir John Mandeville**
Marguerite de Navarre	**The Heptameron**
Christine de Pisan	**The Treasure of the City of Ladies**
Marco Polo	**The Travels**
Richard Rolle	**The Fire of Love**
Thomas à Kempis	**The Imitation of Christ**

ANTHOLOGIES AND ANONYMOUS WORKS

The Age of Bede
Alfred the Great
Beowulf
A Celtic Miscellany
The Cloud of Unknowing and Other Works
The Death of King Arthur
The Earliest English Poems
Early Christian Writings
Early Irish Myths and Sagas
Egil's Saga
The Letters of Abelard and Heloise
Medieval English Verse
Njal's Saga
Seven Viking Romances
Sir Gawain and the Green Knight
The Song of Roland

FOR THE BEST IN PAPERBACKS, LOOK FOR THE

PENGUIN CLASSICS

Netochka Nezvanova   Fyodor Dostoyevsky

Dostoyevsky's first book tells the story of 'Nameless Nobody' and introduces many of the themes and issues which will dominate his great masterpieces.

Selections from the Carmina Burana   A verse translation by David Parlett

The famous songs from the *Carmina Burana* (made into an oratorio by Carl Orff) tell of lecherous monks and corrupt clerics, drinkers and gamblers, and the fleeting pleasures of youth.

Fear and Trembling   Søren Kierkegaard

A profound meditation on the nature of faith and submission to God's will which examines with startling originality the story of Abraham and Isaac.

Selected Prose   Charles Lamb

Lamb's famous essays (under the strange pseudonym of Elia) on anything and everything have long been celebrated for their apparently innocent charm; this major new edition allows readers to discover the darker and more interesting aspects of Lamb.

The Picture of Dorian Gray   Oscar Wilde

Wilde's superb and macabre novella, one of his supreme works, is reprinted here with a masterly Introduction and valuable Notes by Peter Ackroyd.

A Treatise of Human Nature   David Hume

A universally acknowledged masterpiece by 'the greatest of all British Philosophers' – A. J. Ayer

A Passage to India   E. M. Forster

Centred on the unresolved mystery in the Marabar Caves, Forster's great work provides the definitive evocation of the British Raj.

The Republic   Plato

The best-known of Plato's dialogues, *The Republic* is also one of the supreme masterpieces of Western philosophy whose influence cannot be overestimated.

The Life of Johnson   James Boswell

Perhaps the finest 'life' ever written, Boswell's *Johnson* captures for all time one of the most colourful and talented figures in English literary history.

Remembrance of Things Past (3 volumes)   Marcel Proust

This revised version by Terence Kilmartin of C. K. Scott Moncrieff's original translation has been universally acclaimed – available for the first time in paperback.

Metamorphoses   Ovid

A golden treasury of myths and legends which has proved a major influence on Western literature.

A Nietzsche Reader   Friedrich Nietzsche

A superb selection from all the major works of one of the greatest thinkers and writers in world literature, translated into clear, modern English.

FOR THE BEST IN PAPERBACKS, LOOK FOR THE

PENGUIN CLASSICS

John Aubrey	**Brief Lives**
Francis Bacon	**The Essays**
James Boswell	**The Life of Johnson**
Sir Thomas Browne	**The Major Works**
John Bunyan	**The Pilgrim's Progress**
Edmund Burke	**Reflections on the Revolution in France**
Thomas de Quincey	**Confessions of an English Opium Eater**
	Recollections of the Lakes and the Lake Poets
Daniel Defoe	**A Journal of the Plague Year**
	Moll Flanders
	Robinson Crusoe
	Roxana
	A Tour Through the Whole Island of Great Britain
Henry Fielding	**Jonathan Wild**
	Joseph Andrews
	The History of Tom Jones
Oliver Goldsmith	**The Vicar of Wakefield**
William Hazlitt	**Selected Writings**
Thomas Hobbes	**Leviathan**

Samuel Johnson/
    James Boswell
	**A Journey to the Western Islands of
	        Scotland/The Journal of a Tour to the
	        Hebrides**

Charles Lamb	**Selected Prose**
Samuel Richardson	**Clarissa**
	Pamela
Adam Smith	**The Wealth of Nations**
Tobias Smollet	**Humphry Clinker**
Richard Steele and Joseph Addison	Selections from the **Tatler** and the **Spectator**
Laurence Sterne	**The Life and Opinions of Tristram Shandy, Gentleman**
	A Sentimental Journey Through France and Italy
Jonathan Swift	**Gulliver's Travels**
Dorothy and William Wordsworth	**Home at Grasmere**